A Trash Hauler
in Vietnam

A Trash Hauler in Vietnam

Memoir of Four Tactical Airlift Tours, 1965–1968

BILL BARRY

McFarland & Company, Inc., Publishers
Jefferson, North Carolina, and London

Photographs are from the collection of the author unless otherwise credited.

LIBRARY OF CONGRESS ONLINE CATALOG DATA

Barry, Bill, 1939–
 A trash hauler in Vietnam : memoir of four tactical airlift tours, 1965–1968 / Bill Barry.
     p.   cm.
 Includes index.

 ISBN 978-0-7864-3924-9
 softcover : 50# alkaline paper ∞

 1. Barry, Bill, 1939– 2. Vietnam War, 1961–1975—Personal narratives, American. 3. Vietnam War, 1961–1975—Aerial operations, American. 4. Airlift, Military—Vietnam. I. Title.
 DS559.5.B384   2008
 959.704′348092 [B]—dc22   2008034158

British Library cataloguing data are available

©2008 Bill Barry. All rights reserved

No part of this book may be reproduced or transmitted in any form or by any means, electronic or mechanical, including photocopying or recording, or by any information storage and retrieval system, without permission in writing from the publisher.

On the cover: Bill Barry on a C-130 ramp with sleeping co-pilot; *background* Vietnam forest on fire ©2008 Shutterstock

Manufactured in the United States of America

McFarland & Company, Inc., Publishers
  Box 611, Jefferson, North Carolina 28640
    www.mcfarlandpub.com

This book is dedicated to all of the crews who professionally flew the Tactical Airlift, or "trash hauler," missions during the Vietnam War, to their wives and children, and most especially to those whose lives were lost in carrying out such missions.

The following survivors and casualties of the war, not all trash haulers, are particularly important to me in remembering the times, the missions, the base locations, the good times and the bad: Al Storey, Art Steinhauer, Bill Helker, Bill Olson, Bob Boelke, Bobby Doyle, Bruce Ferrier, Cal Roulson, Charlie Mills, Chris Dixon, Dave O'Donnell, Dave Rickel, Dave Weingartner, Dick Callahan, Don Lehtola, Don Lewis, Don Wadsworth, Ed Batten, Ed Kato, Ed Rotz, Gary Bennett, Jerry Sherrill, Hans Ulrich, Irv Lott, J. C. Richards, Jack Ryan, Jim McClure, Jim McKenzie, Joe Lanahan, John Stewart, Jon Greenley, Ken Lawrence, Kent Gibson, Nelson Neil, Norm Sauvage, Paul Gilbert, Phil Collier, Phil Hughes, Reed Mulkey, Robert Whitlatch, Ron Dorcy, Sammy Ionnetta, Scott Fisher, and Tom Dempsey.

I am also most grateful to my daughter, Sara Devine, and my youngest son, Sam Barry, without whose proofreading and mastery of English this work would not be readable.

Table of Contents

Preface	1
Vietnam: The Atmosphere and the Beginning	3
The First Tour	9
Between Tours	21
The Second Tour	23
Between Tours Again	60
The One-Year Tour	62
Between Tours Yet Again	161
Five Months in Japan and Vietnam	164
Aftermath	198
Author's Military History	203
Index	205

Preface

The Vietnam War has been over for more than thirty years now. As it is with many other veterans of it, this war is still alive in my memory. I often have had thoughts of writing about it, or at least of my experience in it.

My thoughts of writing about Vietnam were always centered around how the war changed each time I went back to it, the various unsuccessful attempts to define a winning strategy, the eternal pace and face of war, and the lies and falsehoods told by the U.S. government while the war was ongoing.

I thought I remembered when and how things happened, but twenty years after the war I found my old flight logs in the attic. In them I had recorded the days I flew, where we went, and the landing and takeoff times at each base. By scanning these entries, I soon learned that my memories, like those of most other after-the-fact biographical writers, were warped. Things that I thought happened in a certain sequence did not. Events which I thought may have been linked were not. But now, with the flight logs, I at least had the time lines correct.

I have put my memories into the time line of my flight records and have woven them as best I can into a logical recollection of a bygone period. I apologize for errors in data, dates, descriptions, names and spellings. I cannot assure you that every specific incident truly happened at the place and time that it appears in this writing. I know for sure that on a given date and time I was at a specific place. I have then put my recalled incidents into the places it seems they best fit. If we stopped at a field to on- or offload at a given date and time and it took an hour or less, we probably were flying passengers, did a rapid offload, or had no onload. Stops greater than two hours probably meant a delay because of a lack of loading equipment (forklifts), a broken airplane which needed maintenance, refueling, explosive ordnance loading, or other types of delays.

What follows are four separate sets of remembrances dated between 1965 and 1968, plus comments reflecting on those events, and stories and impressions gathered along the way.

VIETNAM: THE ATMOSPHERE AND THE BEGINNING

It was the spring of 1962. As a junior at the United States Air Force Academy, I sat listening to an army major from the Pentagon brief our squadron on the Kennedy administration's military policy. The world was a troubled place, with the U.S. as the leader of the Free World facing off against the Soviet Union, the champion of Communism. Nuclear warfare was the major threat, but it was a threat so ghastly it left neither side with any hope of winning. The most likely scenario, according to this Washington pitchman, was going to be between the free and communist worlds in the Far East, between the capitalist West and the underdeveloped world. Sides were being taken between India, a would-be champion of democracy, and China, Russia's counterpart in Asia.

All of this, of course, was a change from the previous Eisenhower administration, which had favored a nuclear buildup against the Russians as a way to maintain defense without breaking the back of the United States with regard to massive conventional force levels and defense spending. John Kennedy and company were going to do a back step of sorts and bring conventional warfare forward again.

According to the major, the most likely threat we as young American military men would face was that of unconventional, or guerrilla, warfare, based on the Chinese model as laid down by Mao Tse-tung. It would be a real test, but we were ready for it with our newly created Special Forces, a Kennedy-favored counterinsurgency force built around the army's Green Berets.

The major commented that there was considerable resistance in the military establishment, both in Washington and elsewhere, to some of the ideas he was presenting. He also admitted that there was also considerable military opposition to President Kennedy's defense secretary, Robert Strange McNamara—he of the slicked back hair, thick glasses and zeal for mathematical solutions to all problems and the quantification of results. As the major spoke, I decided he was a McNamara man, and later in the briefing he said as much. At the end of the discourse, Vietnam appeared as the major's choice for the most likely testing ground for the forthcoming conflict between East and West, democracy and communism. Victory in Vietnam was a noble goal that he was sure we could win.

A question and answer period followed the briefing, but few of us lowly cadets felt like matching wits with this experienced and knowledgeable Pentagon insider. Even our senior, and usually all-knowing, first classmen seemed hesitant to disagree too strongly with the major's central theme or points of view.

It had now been some eight years since the U.S. and a smattering of its allies had been fought to a draw by China and the North Koreans in the Korean War, but no mention of that was made in the course of the afternoon's discussion. I remembered how America's actions in that conflict had continually been hampered by concerns for the potential widening of the war, escalation to nuclear weapons and direct Soviet intervention to go along with the surprising Chinese participation. I, therefore, dared to ask the major a question concerning his assumption of a just and certain victory in a counterinsurgency conflict in Vietnam. "What," I asked, "if we enter such a conflict, defeat the North Vietnamese and the Viet Cong? What will we then do if the Chinese or the Russians rush to their aid and intervene militarily?"

The major delayed not a minute nor batted an eye with his nearly instant and possibly memorized reply. "As military men, that's not our problem," he said. "Other people in Washington are paid to handle problems like that and you can be sure it will enter into their deliberations at the appropriate time and place." That day I bought off silently on the response. No one else had anything else to ask and the session quickly broke up. We left the briefing room and headed back to our quarters to do a quick bit of studying before the evening meal formation.

I now realize that the major's response, like a politician's response in a debate, was less an original statement than a prepared answer to a question identified beforehand as one likely to emerge from his briefing. Were we a target audience of guinea pigs to help him practice for a future pitch to a more important audience? I have no way of knowing. But in years to come, and to this day, I am not convinced that the high level people in Washington or the Pentagon that he was speaking of ever properly or directly addressed my question before we were deeply committed in Vietnam. Due to administration changes and the retirement of key personnel, the U.S.'s historical memory was less than a decade, as measured from Korea, and more tuned to internal political maneuvering than to real world events or military risks.

Personal Progression

Following graduation from navigation school in 1964 as a 24-year-old first lieutenant, I was assigned to the 774th Troop Carrier Squadron (the name was soon changed to Tactical Airlift) of the 463rd Troop Carrier Wing. The squadron history dated back to the Second World War and our patch showed a green weasel overlaid on a world globe. Accordingly, our nickname was the Green Rats or the Chicken Thieves. We were stationed at Langley Air Force Base (AFB) in Virginia. The Wing was composed of three squadrons of C-130B aircraft and our crews consisted of many very experienced C-130 veterans. They had been members of the original C-130A units at Seward AFB in Tennessee.

Another sizeable contingent of the Wing was made up of flyers who had been stationed at Langley in a tanker unit that flew KC-97 aircraft. That unit had been disbanded and the crews were incorporated into the C-130 wing. The KC-97 had a mysterious and frustrating habit of blowing up in midair and all the personnel who came from that unit were noted as being especially quick and thorough in their knowledge of aircraft emergency procedures. Since they weren't original members of the "old hand" C-130 Group, they were nicknamed "Brand X." The rest of the wing, like me, were either "New Guys" (also known as Fucking New Guys, or FNG's) or had a varied flying background not based in either the "Old Guy" or "Brand X" groups.

Immediately on arrival at Langley in January of 1965, I was trained in over-water, long distance, high altitude flying. These missions prepared us to deploy or carry cargo to anywhere in the world. Once qualified in this type of flying, the training course then switched to training in low altitude (300–500 feet above the ground at 250 knots) flying which culminated in an airdrop of either personnel or cargo. These missions were a holdover from World War II airborne operations and were usually conducted in formations so as to put a large number of paratroops and their equipment on the ground at the same time. There was an emphasis on preceding the airdrops with low-level routes in an attempt to prevent the formations from being picked up and tracked on radar. A mission was judged successful if it arrived at its delivery point within two minutes of the planned drop time and the drop was within 300 yards of the desired impact point.

Navigation training in the C-130 was the responsibility of the wing and consisted of first qualifying in long range flying and over-water flights. When that was mastered, the new flyer then began training in airdrops and low-level flying. At an early point in my over-water training, a crisis erupted in the Dominican Republic, where a communist regime was suspected of taking over. The U.S. responded by sending in troops.

The 463rd deployed to Pope AFB in North Carolina to support the initial insertion of forces. Pope, located just outside of Fayetteville, was the home of one of the army's airborne divisions and a great deal of the joint airdrop training between the army and the air force took place there. Since there were no planes left to train in at Langley and much of the Santo Domingo resupply effort was over-water from Pope down to the island in the Caribbean, I was sent to Pope to get some over-water training.

I went to Pope as a spare passenger on one of our flights out of Langley and got off the airplane just in front of the Base Operations (Base Ops) building on the airfield. The aircraft I arrived on parked nearby to offload some cargo to support the operation. There were aircraft all over the base, mostly C-130s, and several more were coming and going every minute. The Base Ops building had a large sign on the front door directing all aircrews in the Santo Domingo operation to report next door for assignment. Next door turned out to be a small white wooden shack or storage building that looked like it had been built in the Civil War. Immediately inside was a haggard and weary first lieutenant who took one look at me in my new flight suit, navigation kit and clothes bags (B-4 by air force designation) and said, "What in the hell do you want?"

I informed him that the 463rd, in their wisdom, had sent me down to get some over-water training and would he please schedule me accordingly. At this point he said, "Take a look around." I did. Outside, it was a bright, sunny, clear spring day in North Carolina. As my eyes grew accustomed to the little light that existed in this windowless shack, I noted that every spare inch of space, other than the lieutenant's desk, was crammed from floor to ceiling with B-4 bags, flight helmets and flight kits, while ten or more aircrew members of all ranks were asleep on the floor, in chairs, and under tables. "There ain't an unfilled bed in North Carolina and we're too busy to arrange training missions while there's absolute chaos in the resupply schedule. Get your ass back on that airplane that brought you and tell the 463rd we can't support training right now." I did as I was told. There had been no course in, or mention of, screw-ups like this anywhere in the precise air force academy curriculum; but now I was learning about the real air force.

I returned to Langley on the same airplane I had arrived in and my round-trip drew a few guffaws from those back in Virginia. In future years, due to the C-130 airdrop association, I would see more of Pope AFB than I ever desired; but that first visit stayed with me. It was just like a scene out of numerous World War II movies or stories. Despite its having been 20 years since the end of World War II and the numerous technical advances made since then, the military had changed only minimally. In such ways was progress measured.

The Aircraft

The C-130 Hercules first flew in 1954. It was built by Lockheed Corporation and entered the air force inventory in December 1956. Tactical Air Command (TAC) got the first C-130s for its mission of supporting the army through cargo/passenger hauling and airdrops. Later models of the aircraft also were delivered to the Military Air Transport Service (MATS, subsequently renamed Military Airlift Command, MAC). MATS specialized in long distance, worldwide, multi-service cargo delivery.

One of the stories told of the C-130 in the unit of veterans that I belonged to involved its introduction to the Strategic Air Command (SAC). Soon after it entered the air force inventory, a C-130A model was sent to Biggs Air Force Base in El Paso, Texas. On landing, it delivered a cargo load and then refueled to go elsewhere. The low-slung, ugly, tube-shaped machine must have appeared primitive to the Strategic Air Command personnel who stood by watching its landing and taxi performance.

SAC was the air force's darling of the nuclear age. It was equipped only with the latest U.S. bombers (sleek, new B-52s and KC-135 tankers) and their sole mission was nuclear warfare, dropping atomic bombs, and the strategic reconnaissance associated with them. SAC was an air force within the air force. It even had its own promotion system outside of that run for the rest of the air force.

Biggs AFB had a 10 or 12 thousand foot runway. In the summer, with the high heat of west Texas, SAC's large ungainly atomic and fuel loaded aircraft would need all of that runway to get safely airborne. An empty C-130A flew somewhat like a fighter plane. Once, a crew requested takeoff clearance from the SAC personnel in the Biggs tower for their outbound flight. But, as luck would have it, the wind had just changed on the base and the C-130 was sitting at the wrong end of the 10,000 plus foot runway. Seemingly, it would have to turn around and taxi to the opposite end for takeoff.

"Request permission for an opposite field takeoff," said the C-130 pilot.

"Negative," came the reply. "Taxi to the end of the opposite runway." After all, SAC aircraft could never take off in opposite wind conditions, since they barely struggled into the dry hot air even when the wind was with them.

Not to be outdone, the C-130 aircraft commander returned to the airwaves with another request: "Request clearance for a high-speed taxi to the opposite end of the runway." This was approved. The new, ugly air beast was allowed to taxi down the main runway in the opposite direction to the wind for takeoff, thus avoiding an even lengthier takeoff delay by navigating twisting taxi lanes. Accordingly, the C-130 started down the main runway at high speed, lifted off the ground about 1 to 2 feet and landed at the far end before turning around and then requesting the tower to allow it to officially take off and depart.

The C-130 was very accommodating to the Tactical Airlift role. Today's production models (the J) are giving the plane a life span greater than the previously legendary C-47 of World War II fame. Over 2,300 C-130s have been built, and there are some 70 different models or variants of the Hercules serving in 70 countries around the world.

The C-130 was ugly, slow, and not jet propelled. Mounting four turboprop engines, it was capable of carrying 40,000 pounds of cargo 2,500 miles. It had floor mounted cargo rails which allowed palletized cargo to be quickly slid in and out directly through the rear door and ramp. In an hour, the five man crew could pull up the cargo rails and put down seats or litter bearing straps. The plane could then take 50 paratroops on an airdrop or carry 70 passengers to a distant destination. In similar fashion, it could also carry 50 hospital patients, each in his own litter.

The C-130 was fully pressurized and cruised at 20,000 feet at 300 knots. It could take off in 1,500 feet or in 2,000 with a sizable load. It could land and come to a complete stop in less than 2,000 feet and operated easily from 3,500 and 5,000 foot airstrips. It was an all-weather, 24 hour a day machine with its own airborne radar and navigation equipment. Ugly, but practical and relatively cheap, the 130 was ahead of its time and a wonderful combination of '50s technology suited to the Tactical Airlift mission. Normally it had a crew of five, including a pilot, copilot, navigator, flight engineer and loadmaster.

THE FIRST TOUR

May 1965

U.S. Troops in Vietnam	U.S. War Casualties (KIA)
180,000	1,600

In early May 1965, 16 C-130Bs and 24 of our crews rushed across the Pacific and established ourselves at Clark Air Base. This was in response to the growing insurgency in Vietnam. The guerrilla war in South Vietnam was not going well for our Vietnamese allies and several U.S. airbases and other facilities had been attacked by the Viet Cong.

The day after the entire deployment squadron flew into Clark, we were given an intelligence briefing by an officer from 12th Air Force headquarters. He gave us the latest status of the Vietnam insurgency and then covered the situation in other countries around the region since we would most likely be flying into them as well. I no longer remember much of what he said, except that when he got to Bangkok he remarked that they had girls there "who made other little girls look like little boys." At the close of the briefing someone asked what he thought was the worst thing than could happen with regard to the war. In the officer's opinion, the worst thing was that we would continue to respond to each crisis by flying large deployments of aircraft across the Pacific to meet the crisis and then send them home again. Such actions would both wear us out and cause crises to become run of the mill events.

A few days later, we began flying cargo missions into South Vietnam itself. As a navigator not yet fully checked out in the aircraft, I could not fill a line crew member spot. But I could fly as a student trainee with an instructor or flight examiner and that was how I first got a look at South Vietnam and several locations that I would become intimately familiar with in the next three years.

On my first mission we left Clark with a full load of cargo pallets and flew down the center of the island of Luzon into the western edge of Manila

Bay. En route, we flew over the Bataan peninsula and the island of Corregidor, made famous by the U.S. experience in World War II. Just off the southern tip of Corregidor our routing turned 90 degrees due west. We then proceeded at 20,000 feet and 300 knots out into the China Sea. After three hours of flight, we were cleared into the U.S. occupied airbase at Da Nang. I had flown as navigator on the flight from Clark and had no problems. My flight instructor helped translate some of the strange phraseology and directions I heard over the headset from our route control agencies. Otherwise, the route was clear of weather and the winds across the South China Sea were light or almost nonexistent.

We followed air traffic control's directions over the offshore islands around Da Nang and landed to the south over the bay that lay north of the city of Da Nang. The circular bay contained hundreds of small and large ships and was surrounded by steep cliffs. There was a large contingent of South Vietnamese military on the base at this time due to demonstrations and unrest among the Buddhist population in Da Nang. The Buddhists were exerting pressure on the central government and disrupting the military effort against the Communists, which to us was our sole rationale for being in the country. The instability of the Vietnamese government and the lack of a fully supportive population in opposition to the Viet Cong would continue to be a weak point in the U.S. attempt to maintain democratic ideology in the country.

Aside from the large numbers of armed Vietnamese military loitering around all of the buildings on base, Da Nang appeared to be just another hot and dusty tropical stopover point. Its sole distinguishing features were the whitewashed stone buildings and outdated metal hangars and support facilities, indicating it was not a U.S. built or maintained base. It was different, not necessarily French but certainly not American, and not too up-to-date or well maintained either.

Inside the small, whitewashed, single story building which served as base operations we found an eight foot by eight foot office with no door. It was occupied the by the U.S. Air Force Airlift Control Element (ALCE). In the Tactical Airlift force, the ALCE controlled the routing of planes and distribution of cargo. We reported our offload and they told us what cargo we would pick up and carry on our next flight, which was to go to Saigon. Once finished with this procedure, we rechecked the weather for Saigon and returned to the airplane to complete the on-load and offload of the cargo.

After an hour and a half delay for off- and on-loading, we took off from Da Nang and headed south. I again sat in the navigator's seat, but the flight required no navigation, just radar monitoring of the coastline. The land immediately south of the base was flat and filled with yellowish-orange rice paddies. As we climbed to altitude, the countryside turned to low rolling hills, scrub forest and vegetation. Then we were over the beach and out over the ocean. Not far to the west were heavily forested dark green mountains rising to several hundred feet.

For an hour we flew due south, passing two-thirds of the South Vietnamese coastline. Off to the right passed soon-to-be familiar base names including Qui Nhon, Nha Trang and Cam Ranh Bay. To me, at the time, they were only spots on the map where settlements or small towns sat along the coast and stood out against the forest and hills. Just south of Cam Ranh Bay the coast turned to the right and, after another 15 minutes of flight time, turned due east. We stayed off the coast the whole time. An hour and a half after we left Da Nang, we turned due north and came over land. We were south of Saigon, just to the right of the Saigon River as it proceeded southward to the sea. The Saigon airport, Tan Son Nhut, had a radio beacon which we tuned in, and the radio compass arrow pointed nearly due north as our straight-line route in.

As we came overland, a small marking on the map indicated we were about to fly through a premarked artillery area that extended above our flight altitude. I pointed this out to the instructor navigator, who indicated it was no big deal; but he did ask the copilot to confirm with our air traffic control whether or not this was an active area. The English-speaking air traffic control confirmed that no artillery was active and we were cleared direct to Tan Son Nhut. The map was evidently outdated relative to the rapidly changing insurgency situation. The pre-insurgency artillery training area was no longer in existence. Artillery fire was random throughout the country. When and where they knew about it, the air traffic authorities would broadcast warning and avoidance areas. The problem was they knew in advance about only a limited number of the firings there were; but at this time, we didn't know that. Nor were there as many firings as there later would be when the U.S. military buildup escalated.

As we flew along the Saigon River, I got a good look at the ground beneath us. What had been described as a "Green Hell" in much of the literature that I had read was in fact more of a brown or mottled color. The forests in the delta were tall but not impenetrable, and the ground beneath them stood out as a deep red-clay color. The jungle canopy was frequently broken by large areas of swamp, and then again by cultivated and clearly zoned and identified rice fields. So it continued all the way to Saigon: A constantly broken expanse or forest, swamp and habitation. Through it flowed numerous streams on their way into the Saigon River, which appeared to be a half mile wide current of dark and swift flowing brown mud and water. It was certainly no Blue Danube.

Ten miles south of Tan Son Nhut, we were directed to swing out to the right and get on the approach path into the airport runway, which ran almost perfectly east and west. In doing so, we flew right over a large bend in the Saigon River when on our final approach. The area below was swamp and brush forest and, as our preflight directions indicated, held the possibility of ground fire; we stayed at higher than normal altitudes in the landing pattern. The mass of the city of Saigon sat south of the airport, though a rich concentration of paddies and villages surrounded Tan Son Nhut.

Once on the ground, the Saigon ALCE answered our cargo call-in report and gave us parking and on- and offloading instructions. Like Da Nang, Tan Son Nhut was not a very busy place and the buildings and hangars around the field were all single story and dusky white or of outdated corrugated metal construction. One hangar adjoining the cargo loading area belonged to South Vietnamese Airlines. In front of the hangar sat a French design jet transport. It always sat there and never seemed to fly or to be capable of flight. Perhaps there was no traffic because of the war, or perhaps the aircraft was always out of commission for parts or maintenance.

We parked the C-130 and went to recheck the weather for our flight home and confirm the load with ALCE. ALCE was set up in a 5 foot square wooden booth which sat in the open in the parking area near the airport's operations building. It was of the same design and construction as a hot dog stand at a church picnic or country fair. Two lieutenants, each about a year older than I was, were manning the ALCE and confirmed our load and route for heading home. In an hour and a half, we had completed our on/off load and weather check and were on our way out of Tan Son Nhut and back to the Philippines. The return flight was uneventful, though we did retrace our route of the way in and exited Saigon to the south, staying 5 to 10 miles off the Vietnamese coast once we hit the sea. The flight back took four and a half hours and our cargo hold was virtually empty. Large amounts of cargo were flowing into Vietnam. Not much was coming out.

This became our daily or every other day routine. We would load up with cargo at Clark and fly for three hours across the South China Sea to Vietnam. Our first Vietnam stop would be somewhere on the coast, either Da Nang in the north, Qui Nhon on the Central Coast about 40 minutes south of Da Nang, or Nha Trang, which was another 20 minutes south of Qui Nhon. If there was no coastal stop, we would fly along the coast and follow it where it turned east to the Mekong Delta and fly up to Tan Son Nhut. These were the only bases we used. We shuttled between these sites, alternately dropping off and picking up cargo. Then at the end of an eight or ten hour day in-country, we would fly back to Clark.

We had brought enough crews from the States to allow us to rotate crews between missions and aircraft so that we were flying 2 to 3 round-trips per week. All missions were daylight as long as we were in Vietnam and we saw little, if any, evidence of combat or enemy activity. Our loads were primarily palletized cargo for U.S. support forces. If we had some spare space or seats once we got the main load on, we might haul some U.S. personnel who were traveling to another location or going on leave. Occasionally we'd carry a small load of beer cases and food from the base exchange for a U.S. Army courier who'd come down to Saigon for the day to shop and take his supply back to a small camp or outpost somewhere near one of the other bases.

Nha Trang was a relatively large base that sat in a long east-west valley. It had elements of army, air force and Australians operating from it. Nha Trang's single runway sat close to a mountain ridge on its southern side. A village adjoined the base, so that when you took off or landed over the eastern approach you were looking at huts and ox carts. Adjoining the village and running for five or ten miles on either side of its seaside was a wide, white beach. It was one of the places forecasters and political commentators said could become a great seaside resort once peace was established. There was a sizable U.S. Army force on the base and they ran the flight operations out of a large house-like structure near the flight line.

Qui Nhon, on the other hand, was small, used almost exclusively for airlift supply to army units in the area. The single runway ran north-south on a small peninsula. As you approached the base for landing to the north, if the weather and time of day were right, you could look down in the water about a mile and a half from the end of the runway; there, deep enough in the water to cover tail and all, sat a C-130. In making a landing attempt in bad weather or at night with minimum communications, the crew had probably flown too low due to a bad altimeter setting. Thinking they were several hundred feet above sea level, they probably quickly found out they were in error and were about to go below it. The aircraft was right on centerline for the field and looked to be intact; so it may have been a smooth water landing even though the crash killed four people. The Vietnamese military ran the base with assistance from the U.S. Army, which had an air operations and weather/flight plan station in Base Operation (a very small, very dark shack), which adjoined the small cargo and passenger loading area.

Da Nang had only a single, 10,000 foot runway but was quite a large base. The airstrip ran north-south, with a large bay off its north end and a large flat valley to the south. To the east and west, there were high and steeply rising mountains. The town was quite a distance from the base, so there was little civilian interaction. A Vietnamese garrison inhabited the north end of the base itself. It had been a French air base and operations center in the war against the Viet Minh in the 1950s. Then it was known as Cap (or Cape) Tourraine.

Our home for this Temporary Duty (TDY) was Clark AFB. Clark was 60 miles northwest of Manila on the Philippine island of Luzon. It had been General MacArthur's headquarters in the years prior to World War II. The air force base was built around the infrastructure of the previous army base. MacArthur's parade ground was in the center of the living area of the base. It was surrounded by the homes of the higher officers, the library, the officers' club and several other imposing structures.

The base was also the home of the 12th Air Force, whose area of responsibility included Vietnam and most of the rest of Southeast Asia. Some ten miles from Clark, and plainly visible across the runway and aircraft parking area, was a perfectly formed cone volcano called Mount Ararat. Clark had a large American air force community, including the 12th Air Force headquarters, a hospital, permanent fighter and airlift squadrons, large transient airlift maintenance and support operations, a jungle survival school and several communications and radar units which were deployed out of there to sites around the region.

Our airlift operation's arrival was unplanned for by the headquarters. We ended up living in abandoned family houses which had been scheduled to be torn down. One, two or three air crews split a large tropical bungalow for the duration of our stay. The houses had fans in some rooms, but no air conditioning. The furniture in them had come from the base's family furniture storage warehouse and was sturdy if not ornamental. The beds were all typical foldouts: metal frames with thin cotton mattresses. Stoves and kitchenware were made available, but we did little or no cooking. If something went wrong with the house's plumbing or its roof leaked, we called the base repair facility and they sent out a Filipino who was supposed to fix or repair the problem.

Each house had a maid or housekeeper from the local population. The housekeeper, male or female, kept the place clean, made the beds, did everyone's laundry (for an additional fee) and occasionally took the liberty of stealing anything valuable which was left out. There were frequent arguments between the residents and the housekeepers as to whether something was missing and who might have taken it. The housekeepers could be reported to the housing authority who hired them; but, somewhat like stateside labor unions, it took a wealth of overwhelming evidence to get them fired. A different housekeeper was usually the best you could hope for.

There were also several confrontations and fisticuffs among members of our unit who dwelled together. Personal dislikes, bad or conflicting habits, noise making, card playing, debts and overindulgence in alcohol all led to minor and major conflicts.

Clark had a movie theater, a separate officer's club annex which, like a country club, was away from the main base on a higher elevation, and a large base exchange (BX) and commissary. Transport around the base came from a fleet of buses or relatively cheap taxicabs driven by Filipinos. In the '60s, the Yankee dollar was stable and well valued as international currency. Also, the U.S. military was a far-flung enterprise supporting our position in the Cold War. The BX and other parts of the base infrastructure sold things at what would be considered bargain prices in stateside markets, and they did so with no tax applied. An example might be a wristwatch, which could be purchased in the BX for 50 percent to 60 percent of what it would cost at home. Foreign goods such as tape recorders, cameras and motorbikes might be purchased at cheaper rates. Thus, an overseas tour or TDY was an opportunity for buying presents either to take home or to ship by mail. Since the BXs were situated at foreign, often exotic, locales, they featured local arts and crafts, which also were cheaply priced and tax free. The Philippines specialized in carved wood and teak products, as well as jewelry.

The center of our existence, as it was for many of the people stationed there, was the Clark Officers' Club and its adjoining swimming pool. The club was very large, as you would expect for an overseas base with multiple large and varied units. On the main floor was a dining room that could probably seat 100 or more. The meals were good and very cheap. Next to the dining room was the bar. A large, S-shaped teakwood bar with a brass rail curved around to the right as we entered. To the left of the bar was a large open area with tables. The bar could hold 150 or more customers at a time. Drinks were 10 to 25 cents. Behind the officers' club, in a separate building, was the barber shop. A shave and a haircut were something like 50 cents, although the barbers did very well on tips.

On the far side of the large bar room were patio doors which opened onto a sun porch. Probably 30 or 40 people at a time could enjoy the sun porch, sitting on chairs around tables or lounging on sofas. The far side of the porch had a 2 foot white fence, and beyond it was a single lane sidewalk that wound from the front of the club to the barber shop. A three foot open metal fence separated the walkway from the pool. The pool was Olympic size, with a large, paved seating area around it and plenty of chairs, tables and adjustable pool lounge chairs. A 30 or 40 foot high, two level diving platform was at the deep end of the pool. Populated all day long and into the early evening, the pool was heavily used by all manner of men, women and children. Most interesting to us unattached but semi-permanent residents of the base were the schoolteachers, female dependents and airline stewardesses, who were as attracted to the pool for swimming or sunbathing as we were for ogling and daydreaming.

In the basement of the club was the always casual Stag Bar, which featured drinks, gambling, and quick hamburger and sandwich meals. At this time, slot machines were a regular feature of American military clubs, and the revenues they generated, most especially from TDY travelers, were very large. You had to pay dues to be a member of a military club, and you had to be a member of some club in order to enjoy the privileges of any of the others when you were away from your home station. Depending on how much money a club made, it dispensed benefits and freebies to its own members. Members of the Clark Club during this period were truly fortunate in that regard. In return for a $10 a month membership fee, they got monthly rewards of free haircuts, or permanent waves for the ladies, a couple of free meals, several free drinks and several dollars in chits for use in the club's slot machines. All in all, members were making money from being members, as the benefits were in excess of the membership fees.

The club and swimming pool stayed crowded and busy from breakfast to closing. We transients nestled there most of each day when we weren't flying. Breakfast, lunch and dinner were, of course, busy periods, but the daily highlight was the happy hour period from 4:00 to 6:00. Drinks fell from a quarter to 10 cents then and we joined other visitors and the base's residents for a cheap couple hours of drinking, gossip and big-time tale-telling. At those times the bar would be packed. With the crowd and the drinking, there were constant squabbles and name calling but surprisingly few fights. There were no strippers or prostitution on Clark. The distance between the base and the nearest town (Angeles City) that did have such activities kept the atmospheres of the two places pretty well distinct and separated.

The officers' club manager was a uniformed air force officer. Aside from a few dependents who worked there in conjunction with their spouse's tour at the base, almost all of the employees were Filipino. They all spoke excellent English and traded slang with us. The girls who served as waitresses in the bar were all young and comely. They came in a variety of sizes, shades and facial features, much as do the Filipinos from the various islands which make up the Philippine archipelago.

One day we had been flying and landed late in the afternoon. After finishing our flight reports and leaving our equipment at the squadron's flight line building, we caught a bus that wound around the base and stopped at the officers' club. In the course of the 20 or 30 minute ride, the bus halted at a stop sign just on the southern edge of MacArthur's parade ground. It was 5 o'clock and it was pouring rain as hard as it can only in the tropics. The rain was coming down in sheets, pounding on the tin roof of the bus. One of the passengers on the bus who wasn't as familiar with the base and the officers' club routine as we were commented in a loud voice, "It's five o'clock, I wonder if happy hour has started yet"? I was sitting by a window on the right-hand side of the bus and at just that moment something in the very heavy rain caught my eye. I gazed down through the window at the stop sign, which was only some 5 feet away from me. There, at the base of the sign, on his knees and soaked by the rain, was a totally drunk individual. He was hanging onto the base of the sign as if it was the only thing keeping him from being washed away by the deluge. His hair was soaked and the water was running out of it down his red, alcoholic face. The bus lurched as it began to turn the corner. Still looking at the inebriated figure outside, I answered the questioner by saying, "I'm pretty sure happy hour has already started." Such can frequently be the price for an afternoon of killing time in a place where the drinks are terribly cheap and the climate is smoldering. Or, as Kipling said, "Send me somewheres East of Suez where the best is like the worst."

Once, in the happiest part of happy hour (when the crowd was at the fullest, drinks were already at cut rate prices, and everyone was talking up a storm), into the assemblage came one of my fellow lieutenant navigators in training. He more or less raced to the far side of the bar to join us, pushing aside a number of senior officers engaged in vital conversation. The only problem was that, in his rush to get to us and relate something that had happened in that day's flight, he neglected to take off his flight cap.

Not only in the air force, but in its sister services as well, there is an old tradition that one does not wear a hat or cap into the bar in a club. The price of doing so is that the offender is required to buy everyone present a drink of their choice. The only catch is that someone of the assembled multitude must point out the hat wearer to everyone else before he gets it off his head. In the Clark Club, as in most other service clubs around the world, there was a bell hung on one of the barroom walls for the express purpose of alerting all present that the rule had been violated and a sucker was going to pay the price for the enjoyment of all. The price included not only paying for all drinks, but also being grossly called a nerd and a dumbass by all in the gathering.

There were easily 150 or more thirsty inhabitants of the bar at the time of the offense. As we watched the poor slob approach us, several members of our group tried through hand signals and head rolls to call his attention to his crime. This was necessary, because any vocal call to unhat himself could result in someone else pointing him out to the crowd or ringing the cursed bell. At any rate, as he drew into our circle he was instantly told to get the damn thing off. He immediately did. A split second later the bell gonged, but we all testified to the fact that he had beaten the gong, whereat the offender refused to buy any drinks. He was still informed that he was a nerd and a ninny, however. At 10 cents a drink, the 150 potential freeloaders would only have cost $15, but there were sure to be champagne guzzlers and special order charlatans in the group. No telling what the final tally would have been. At any rate, a disaster had been avoided as far as a lieutenant's pay was concerned.

Several miles outside of Clark Air Base was the town of Angeles, or Angeles City. Angeles had a little bit of everything: tourist shops, motels, bars, souvenir stands, and a good stock of girlie bars, whorehouses and bath houses. In the Philippines, as a site of congested sin and illegality, it was probably second only to Olongapo and Subic City, which were just outside of the U.S. Navy bases of Subic Bay and Cubi Point on Luzon's western shore. Angeles' location close to Clark gave the base a feeling of some insecurity, since the town was known for its non-adherence to sobriety, legality and family life.

As previously noted, thievery was a part of the climate at Clark in a number of forms. You always had to remember where you left your watch or wallet, even in your own quarters. The maids and cleanup help were mostly hired from Angeles and had a pass to get on base and work. If you weren't careful, they could leave for the day with some of your valuables, which would never be seen again.

We had a very large and muscular loadmaster who went to Angeles one afternoon with another airman. The two jumped in a small open-backed vehicle, called a jitney, for a cheap ride from the Clark gate to town. The rest of the passengers were two or three Filipinos. Once the jitney got a good distance away from the gate, one of the Filipinos stuck a large knife at the loadmaster's stomach and asked for his wallet, watch, rings and any other valuables. The two airmen surrendered what they had and then were left standing in the road. Just getting to Angeles could be trouble if you did not carefully pick your mode of transport and watch who else was a passenger.

Nor was the base itself safe from some of the forms of crime which inhabited Angeles. One day there was a fire alert and one of Clark's large, brand-new, U.S. fire trucks started up with all sirens and lights on. It went off through the main gate on its way to Angeles, driven by unknown Filipinos, and was never seen again at Clark. The truck had been stolen from the fire station. Sometime later, so the story went, the same truck was seen; its engine number and other identification means were checked while it was serving at the main airport in Manila. Supposedly the U.S. did not, or would not, diplomatically ask for its return.

On another occasion, two vehicles, one a jeep mounting a .50 caliber machine gun in the rear, pulled up in front of the Clark Officers' Club just as the club was counting its profits for the day. In short order, everyone in the front lobby of the club adjoining the management offices was forced at pistol point to hit the floor while the manager and his staff were relieved of all the money they had just been counting. Now, since the club was in the center of this very large base and since the base itself was completely fenced in with guards at every gate, one might assume that the robbers would be swiftly apprehended and the cash returned. Unfortunately, that didn't happen. The robbers escaped, the cash was never seen again, and no one was ever jailed for any part in the crime.

Crimes like those of the fire truck theft and the officers' club robbery, and the escape of the perpetrators, could not have occurred without in-depth knowledge of the base, its functions and the manning and duties of its security force. There was always a bit of a feeling on Clark that everything was not quite as nice and settled as it seemed, and that at any moment anything could happen.

Clark was my home base during my first two tours. Mactan Island and Tachikawa, Japan, were the sites of the second two tours and they will be described in turn. Even when we were flying out of Mactan and Japan, however, Clark was a frequent stopping and Remain Overnight (RON) point for us. A great deal of the air cargo and personnel who were transiting the war zone went in and out from Clark. As for the base, its hectic activity level and crowded nature changed little during the four years that I spent flying in and out of it. With the war going on a scant three hours away, and Clark serving as one of the main resupply and maintenance points for that war, the base was a major air force hub.

This first time, I was at Clark for less than a month. Our TDY squadron had a regular schedule of cargo flights in and out of Vietnam every day and I had gone on a couple. They were pretty much the same as the first one: From Clark to Da Nang, from Da Nang to Saigon and then back to Clark. Each was a full day of activity with the on- and offload of cargo. However, I was still not airdrop qualified and there was no airdrop training available at Clark.

One day, after lunch in the Clark Officers' Club, we sat on the veranda at the back of the club watching the U.S. dependents and schoolteachers swimming. I was told by a passing acquaintance that several other personnel in training and I were going home. The squadron operations officer was having lunch in the main dining room and he confirmed the rumor. A few days later, ten of us rode in the back of a C-130 going east and returning to Langley. My first tour in Vietnam was over.

The rest of the squadron stayed at Clark, and a regular rotation of crews and aircraft was established. There was now a commitment to keep a C-130 squadron at Clark to perform airlift operations in support of the buildup in Southeast Asia. Every two months, new crews and several new airplanes from our Wing at Langley would rotate in and an equivalent number would head back to the States.

Between Tours

Upon returning to Langley, I went through a crash course of getting qualified in airdrop procedures through an intensive round of local training flights. In one operation, we deployed several aircraft to Byrd Field, just outside of Richmond, Virginia, and dropped a large contingent of army troops on the Fort Lee drop zone. On one drop, a heavy equipment load had a parachute malfunction and some 10,000 pounds of palletized equipment went right through the roof of a farmer's barn that sat just off the edge of the Drop Zone (DZ). The farmer, who had been a big fan of the air force for renting his property, began to have second thoughts about its use.

In early August, with most of the personnel we had deployed to the Philippines back at home, our entire Wing deployed to Pope AFB for a week. This was our Operational Readiness Inspection, or ORI. The air force used ORI's to test how well a unit met its combat mission. ORI's were an annual or biannual requirement to deploy to a non-home location and operate from it for a week or so. The Wing was scored on how well the aircraft were maintained and how good the drops were. The crews were also given oral and written tests involving procedures and safety items. I had done quite well in my airdrop and low level flight training and, in the course of the ORI, I was picked to fly in one of the large ORI airdrops.

The Wing did very well in the ORI despite my one drop, which landed just on the margin of successful at 300 yards from the desired impact point. We returned to Langley, and within a week the entire Wing was called to a briefing on the results of our ORI. Many TAC senior officers, including the commander, four-star general Dissosway, appeared at the briefing and congratulated us on a superior performance. We had passed with flying colors.

Normally, only the inspected Wing and the ORI inspectors came to the ORI debriefing. The number of senior commanders who showed up at this one started the rumor mill going. There was something more to our ORI than we knew, the rumormongers said. Supposedly, the 463d had done such a good job that its reward was going to be a permanent change of station from Langley to Clark AFB in the Philippines or somewhere else in the South Pacific, where the Wing would permanently replace the temporary Southeast Asia rotation squadron we had established at Clark in May.

The rumors persisted through the summer. Having successfully completed all my training, I was now a full fledged airlift qualified crew member; a "TAC trained killer," as the line went. My weekly routine consisted of several local airdrop training flights or maybe a trip carrying cargo or doing a drop somewhere else in the U.S. The rumors said we were surely going to Southeast Asia shortly, but the site was uncertain and constantly changing. Saigon, Bangkok, Japan, Okinawa, Guam and Clark were all mentioned at one time or other. There was, however, no confirmation of where it was going to be or even the fact that the Wing was going for sure. We waited with baited breath for the authorities to give us the straight word.

One day, after a local airdrop mission, four crews boarded the Flightline bus that would take us to the debriefing point. When we were all aboard, the teenage-looking bus driver turned and said, "I hear you're all going PCS [Permanent Change of Station] ... to Mactan Island."

Boy, this was a new rumor. Everyone laughed. No one had ever heard of Mactan Island, and besides, we all chose to believe the rumor that said we were going to Bangkok. The remainder of the bus ride and the debriefing went as scheduled. As I was putting my flight helmet bag into my personal bin in the squadron navigation room, two crew members who had been on the bus sat there poring over a large map of the South Pacific. Finally one said, "My God, there is a Mactan airbase. Here it is on an island about five hundred miles south of Clark."

It turned out that Mactan was a 10,000 foot runway with no base or operations facilities. It was a U.S.-built and Philippine-authorized Cold War development. The U.S. had built the runway clandestinely as an emergency landing field for strategic bombers which might need a place to land after bombing Russia or China should a nuclear war occur. The island of Mactan just happened to be across a small bay from Cebu City, the second largest city in the Philippines after Manila. In later years, the Mactan runway became the civil International Airfield for Cebu and the southern Philippines.

Since then, I have always listened closely whenever bus drivers speak. Experience has taught me that they know more than might be imagined.

The Second Tour

It was now October 1965. I had become a full fledged Tactical Airlift Navigator and part of a regular crew in the squadron structure. That meant I was no longer navigating on local training missions with mixtures of one-day-at-a-time trainees and instructors/examiners. Every once in a while, I'd draw one of those missions because no one else was available to fill the navigator's seat in a formation, but usually I flew with the same four people both locally and on short trips around the U.S. Once a year I got an over-water navigation check ride with an examiner looking over my shoulder. Six months after that, our crew got a check ride on a tactical low-level airdrop to ensure that our procedures were correct and that we successfully met all mission time and drop accuracy requirements.

The crew consisted of five men. Captain John Dunn was the pilot. He was an ex-fighter pilot (F-100s), new to airlift and having to look after a crew rather than just himself for the first time; but he was a good pilot and a nice guy. Married, he was in his thirties and had a wife and two boys. Hal Thorson, an ex-farm boy and college wrestler, was the copilot. Like me, he was a totally new trainee. Quiet and good natured, Hal was married and had a son. Hal was my age, mid-twenties. John, Hal and I were commissioned officers.

Then there were the enlisted men (also known comically as the enlisted swine). Ed Frame was our flight engineer. A sergeant with several years of experience as an aircraft mechanic, he was new to flying and being a crew member. His job was to monitor the cockpit instruments and watch for and correct, when possible, any mechanical problems, instrument errors, or engine fluxes which took place in flight. Finally, our loadmaster was a young airman, Carl Gross. He was about 20, big and lively, and a novice like Hal, Ed and me. His job was to move the cargo, tie it down so it wouldn't move in flight, or roll on takeoff or landing. He also monitored the rear of the airplane in the air and threw the switches and locks that held the palletized cargo in place during airdrops.

Fall 1965 — The author leaning on a chock block at Tan Son Nhut.

Most crews were a mix of new guys and veterans. Ours was less experienced than most of the others. Dunn's hands were going to be fuller than most. Though he was a good, experienced pilot, he had no experience in TAC airlift and that was a big factor. The other four of us on the crew were all inexperienced in numerous ways, as we were soon to find out.

There were a lot of young aviators mixed in with veteran flyers to make up the 24 crews the squadron had. Usually, all 24 were never present at any one time, someone always being TDY. The crews, together with a small number of personnel from Wing, flew all our assigned missions in the 12 aircraft the squadron had. The crews also performed all the planning, alert and administrative functions of the squadron. Everyone had one or more other tasks in addition to flying the line. Initially, my additional duty was as squadron historian. Once a year, I wrote a report on the "great" things the squadron had accomplished.

By October of 1965, the squadron-level presence we had established at Clark in the Philippines had become a normalized Tactical Airlift rotation. One unit of 16 aircraft was maintained at Clark, with a primary mission of providing airlift support between there and South Vietnam. In addition to the one day, in-and-out cargo hauling missions which I had gone on in May, the planes now deployed in-country in Vietnam for a week or more, flying cargo from one internal site to another. In late September, we were told that our squadron would take up this mission in October and stay TDY doing it for two months.

In early October, we left Langley and headed west on a four day trip to McClellan Air Force Base in California, through Hickham in Honolulu and then on to Wake Island. We flew from Wake on to Guam and finally into Clark. Once at Clark, our accommodations were somewhat different than before. Instead of multiple crews residing in abandoned houses, now we lived in single crew trailers. Each officer crew of three people had an air conditioned trailer for its home during the rotation. Like most trailers of the time, it had a small kitchen area, three small separate bedrooms and a shower/bath. The trailers were cleaned and bedding changed weekly by Filipino maids. Other than that, Clark was pretty much the same as it had been in the spring, only more crowded with both airplanes and people.

12 October 1965: After two days at Clark recovering from the trip over, we pulled our first mission into Vietnam. We went from Clark to a base on Taiwan that the U.S. shared with the Nationalist Chinese, picked up a load and took it to Bien Hoa Air Base. We went to Taiwan carrying parts for a C-130B. We were flying the B model and so was another unit that was based in Taiwan at the time.

Bien Hoa was a fighter/tactical airlift base about 20 miles northeast of Tan Son Nhut. U.S. F-100 tactical fighters were based there as well as C-123 airlifters. The C-123 was a leftover or holdover transport from World War II. It began as an unpowered, towed glider in World War II and then someone added engines to it. It was roughly half the size of a C-130, with a crew of two pilots and a loadmaster. It could carry 10,000 pounds into short strips and was vital in resupplying small Special Forces and native Vietnamese resistance camps. The C-123 was the airplane used to spray Agent Orange defoliant into suspected Viet Cong deployment areas. That unit also operated out of Bien Hoa. Bien Hoa was just slightly north of Tan Son Nhut, although it was 20 miles further to the east. The runways of both bases were less than ten degrees different in their orientation. One of my old roommates from Langley landed at Bien Hoa one foggy morning when the plane should have been landing at Tan Son Nhut. The crew quickly realized their mistake and took off again before anyone else detected their blunder.

From Bien Hoa, after a one hour download, we went on to Tan Son Nhut. At Tan Son Nhut there was now a large part of the parking area on the side of the runway near the airport terminal which was reserved for C-130 loading and unloading. Adjoining it, instead of the two-lieutenant hot dog stand, ALCE, that we had grown used to seeing just five months ago, there was now an air conditioned double-wide trailer where we filed flight plans and picked up our load and offload orders. After a ten hour day (6 hours and 15 minutes of flying time, 3 hours on the ground in Taiwan and another 55 minutes offloading at Bien Hoa), we were finished and went into crew rest.

Our lodgings for the night were at a U.S. rented villa in downtown Saigon. Some ten or so crews stayed in the same place. We each had a small room to ourselves for the night and left our bags for the duration of the stay since we knew we'd be coming back each night. The villa was maintained by a Vietnamese staff which did the housework and made the beds each day. A young Vietnamese girl ran the front counter and checked us in and out just like a stateside motel. For several hundred piastres, which amounted to less than ten dollars, you could get your laundry done on one day service.

The villa didn't serve meals, unless you wanted to trust your luck to the local variety of Vietnamese takeout, which few people did and I certainly did not. Usually we ate on base at the Tan Son Nhut Officers' Club. Going into the base, we would stop there, eat and then catch the base bus to C-130 Ops. Coming from a mission and going back into town, we would reverse the procedure.

There were congressional limits on the number of Americans who could be based in Vietnam, fighting the war. The limits were placed so as to contain the cost of the war and also the number of troops which the various administrations could commit to the war. Everyone who was sent to a base in Vietnam as their home for a period of time fit into the authorized limit. They generally had quarters assigned to them and could eat in a mess hall or have rations provided on a daily basis. It didn't matter if they were sleeping in provided quarters in Saigon, or out in the field sleeping in a tent, or just in the field period. Because they had things provided on a regular basis, they got $1 a day in extra pay for being separated from their families.

There was also a congressionally mandated monthly payment of $35 just for being in the combat zone of Vietnam itself. Everyone who spent at least one day in Vietnam, Thailand or Laos or a certain designated distance off their shores (for the navy) got an extra $35 a month. We airlifters got the same $35 for flying in, spending at least one day out of a month on a shuttle, and coming back out. Sometimes, at the end of a month, units of all services would gather up personnel supporting the war from out of country (paper-workers, mechanics, communicators, headquarters types, etc.) and fly or boat them just inside the declared theater limits so as to qualify for the extra $35.

Because we were based in the Philippines, we were not counted against the congressional limits of how many people could be stationed in Vietnam, even though our primary job was flying shuttle missions in Vietnam. The limits of being stationed there did not apply to us. When we flew out of the Philippines and stayed for at least half a day, we were entitled to Temporary Duty (TDY) pay. TDY pay was a daily stipend to cover the cost of living for spending a day in a city or base other than a designated home station. TDY pay was intended to cover the costs of hotels and meals for each day that you were assigned away from your base, where otherwise meals and quarters were provided. If we stayed on a base and quarters were provided, then we were reimbursed for the official cost of meals at that stop.

People assigned in Vietnam or Laos or Thailand might be exposed daily to being shot at or shelled, but they collected only $1 a day and $35 a month extra per month in addition to their basic pay. During all my tours in Southeast Asia, I got $1 a day for being permanently based in a remote site (Clark, Mactan) rather than a U.S. base or a U.S.-European base, $35 a month for every month that I spent at least one day in the combat zone, and daily stipends of $10 to $15 a day for every day spent away from my permanent base. Through my four tours in support of the Vietnam War, I was making good extra money in addition to my basic salary and flight pay. I had saved several thousand dollars by the time I finished my last tour in 1968. Such money mongering seemed unfair to those people who were fighting the war from Vietnam, but it was all legal and appropriate, according to the rules of the services at the time.

Saigon was bustling. Plenty of pedicabs (half bicycle/half passenger seat) filled the streets, together with minibikes, motorcycles and a few cars. Many of the minibikes were driven by "Saigon cowboys," young Vietnamese who sped around the streets and hung out in Saigon bars and sidewalk cafes. Since we were there defending the young Republic of Vietnam, we often wondered who the cowboys were and why they weren't in the Army; but we didn't ask.

Saigon was also dirty, with a musty smell and lots of dust in the air and on the streets. Red clay dust. Years later I had a discussion with another veteran and he said he was in Saigon in the early sixties and he liked it "when it was clean." Well, I was there in the mid-sixties and it was never clean.

The Vietnamese women were very thin and wore their native *aio dai* costume, which consisted of very thin pants and a very thin blouse above the pants. Most often a large conical sunhat went with the costume to shield the face and keep the sun off of it. Now, when I say thin, I mean thin, as far as some of the pants and blouses went. Most of the blouses were transparent white. Some of the pants were near transparent, especially on the young Vietnamese, or very tight so that not many body features were hidden. I first discovered multicolored brassieres and thong or bikini underwear on the Saigon streets. But, as one visiting Japanese newsman said, "the Vietnamese women were a lot like little boys." They sure weren't corn-fed American girls.

At the time, and dating since after World War II by an agreement within the Department of Defense, support operations for U.S. military operations in Vietnam and Tan Son Nhut were the responsibility of the navy. When we finished a day's labor and sought transport to downtown or our assigned villa, we would pick up the phone that connected us into the U.S. network for Saigon and ask for the transportation desk. We would then order a cab or pickup truck to pick us up and take us from the airbase to downtown. The war was in its infancy and the rapid buildup of all U.S. services in Saigon was putting the established organization to a severe test. The navy has always been known for its different military vocabulary from the rest of the services. For example, in the army, air force and marines, captain is a lowly rank held by one who is just senior to a lieutenant. In the navy, however, a captain is a high and meritorious rank indicating the capability to command a ship, boat or independent unit. Thus, if someone called the navy transport office and said a crew needed transport, they might wait an hour or two before a small bus or shared pickup truck appeared. If, however, the caller said a captain and a crew needed transport, within 15 minutes a large, well maintained sedan would appear to take only that crew directly and courteously to its exact destination. Naturally, we always had air force captain Dunn make the call for our transport. It took the navy establishment in Saigon several months to realize that the expanding war effort had overtaken their service rank prioritized transport service. Soon, any captain, regardless of service, got the same priority when calling in for a ride to or from base. We all started riding in the shared vans after indeterminate periods of waiting. So much for rank and privilege.

The day after our Bien Hoa stop, 13 October, we got to go to another new location. We left Tan Son Nhut just before noon and flew for an hour

Late 1965 — French bread delivery in Saigon.

out to the east coast of Vietnam to a new base which was just under construction. Its name was Cam Ranh Bay. Cam Ranh Bay was a historical naval anchorage on the South China Sea because it provided a large sheltered harbor for ships. At the turn of the century, the Russian fleet had stopped there en route to Tsushima, where they were destroyed by the Japanese in a famous naval engagement.

The airbase at Cam Ranh was being constructed, and aside from resupply flights in and out, there was no other air traffic there. The base was built on a large sandy area directly adjacent to the bay from which it got its name. It was five or ten feet above sea level and several miles from any hills, vegetation or villages. The initial runway, which was going to be 10,000 feet or more to accommodate fighters, was less than half that when we landed on it.

We were bringing in the materials to increase its length or to assist in the construction of numerous buildings which were going up to support future operations. The runway was made of preformed, interlocking aluminum panels, which seemed an interesting and novel way to go about its construction. In time, the first runway that they built at Cam Ranh proved to be unstable because the preformed panels and the sand underlay didn't go together very well. Two long, concrete runways were eventually installed at Cam Ranh to support its role as both a fighter base and a major logistic site later in the war. It also became a site we would grow very familiar with in the future

From Cam Ranh, we flew back to Saigon and called it a day after only two hours of flying time. We ran into maintenance problems when we got back to Tan Son Nhut and ran out of our 12 hour crew day before they could get the aircraft repaired for another sortie.

The following day we carried cargo to Pleiku and Cam Ranh again. Both sorties started and ended at Tan Son Nhut. Tan Son Nhut had a lot of cargo waiting for movement, but a lack of forklifts to move the pallets and load them on aircraft was resulting in long aircraft ground delays.

The next morning we flew from Tan Son Nhut to Pleiku in the Central Highlands. The one-way trip to Pleiku took an hour and 15 minutes. From Saigon we would fly for 45 minutes on a northeast heading of 45 degrees or so. We'd fly by Bien Hoa, and the next major point of habitation would be the town of Ban Me Thout. There was a radio beacon at Ban Me Thout which could be used for identification and tracking purposes. Between Bien Hoa and Ban Me Thout, the land below was dense jungle and rolling hills. On clear days, as we flew toward Ban Me Thout, we could look below and see C-123s from Bien Hoa flying in and out of small runways and sites which usually sat on the top of some of the highest cleared terrain in the hills. These were Special Forces and infiltration watching posts. The runways were 2,000 feet long or less and many of them were surfaced only with dirt or the red laterite soil which abounded in South Vietnam.

When we swung the radio beacon at Ban Me Thout, the next heading was due north to Pleiku. That leg of the trip was 35 or 40 minutes long. The land below was also changed from that on the earlier leg. The highlands were several thousand feet higher than Tan Son Nhut and Bien Hoa, which are near sea level. The highlands were low rolling hills, not heavily treed or covered with foliage, and with many open grassland fields.

Pleiku had a six thousand foot concrete runway. It was the center of U.S. operations in the highlands. At this time, the major American activity in this

Late 1965 — Fruit market in Saigon.

region consisted of building a rapport with the local Montagnard hill people who lived in the highlands. Basically, Pleiku was a runway, a small parking apron on which to load and unload cargo and a Base Operations tower from which flights were controlled. There was a U.S. Army logistic base a short distance from the airbase, but it was not within walking distance and our ground times at Pleiku were kept as short as possible.

We would unload, check the weather and the cargo, then load and move on to our next destination as quickly as possible. On this day, our next stop was back to Saigon, where we landed 4½ hours after we left. We had spent three hours on the ground at Pleiku due to loading delays. We then spent another four hours on the ground at Tan Son Nhut getting offloaded and then reloaded. We flew from there to Nha Trang, on the east coast. At Nha Trang we spent an hour and a half on the ground offloading.

Just at dusk, we took off from Nha Trang to return to Tan Son Nhut. We had flown for half an hour towards Saigon when air traffic control made an area-wide broadcast that Tan Son Nhut was closed due to artillery firing in all quadrants around it. Our fuel load on leaving Nha Trang had been in the neighborhood of ten thousand pounds for what we had thought would be a one hour flight. The C-130B burned four thousand pounds of fuel an hour. We went into an orbit halfway between Nha Trang and Tan Son Nhut and remained there for half an hour in the expectation that Tan Son Nhut would soon reopen. That proved not to be the case, so we decided to return to Nha Trang.

Hal called Nha Trang to tell them that we were returning. The approach control at Nha Trang replied, "Negative on your request for landing at Nha Trang. We have a damaged aircraft on the runway with live ammunition aboard. The field is closed and we anticipate it will remain so for an hour or more." Now we had no place to go within the limits of our rapidly dwindling fuel supply. With just over 6,000 pounds remaining, and recognizing that not all of the 6,000 might be useable, we considered our options. Qui Nhon, 15 minutes beyond Nha Trang, had no lights. Pleiku had lights and operated at night, but it was probably too far.

Feeling a bit pinched, we next called Cam Ranh Bay, where we had landed in daylight just days ago. Luckily, we caught someone on the radio who said that in light of our predicament they would let us make the first night landing on the half of the runway which was now constructed. But, said the speaker, they would have to clear the runway of construction materials and vehicles first. He estimated that would take another half hour. "Roger that," snapped Thorson.

At least we had a place to go, but getting there and then holding indefinitely could turn out to be risky business. Luckily we were almost empty in the cargo hold and could shut two engines down to conserve fuel if necessary. Just as Capt. Dunn was about to start the engine shutdown procedures, another call came over the radio from Saigon. Tan Son Nhut was declared open again. Hallelujah! We immediately turned and proceeded direct to Saigon while simultaneously calling Cam Ranh to thank them for their help and explaining that we would not be landing there after all.

When we got back to Saigon at nine in the evening, our one hour trip from Nha Trang had turned into two hours and our crew day was done. We'd been up for 14 hours, flown two complete round-trips out of Saigon and had logged four hours and five minutes of flying time all day. We got on the base bus, rode to the officers' club, got a quick meal of the daily special for dinner, had a drink or two at the overheated bar and then called for a taxi to take us to our villa in town for a night's sleep.

John Dunn and I had stayed at the officers' club a bit longer than usual that night (maybe more than two drinks worth) since we knew we weren't flying early the next morning. Hal, who rarely imbibed, took an early cab and went back to the villa ahead of us. When we finally decided to depart, we called the base taxi and told them stop at the club for us. A little later, a small pickup truck arrived in front of the club. This was our taxi to town. The back of the pickup had been converted with two long benches along the long sides. A chicken wire cage sat above the sides of the rear and was covered with a tarpaulin so that you couldn't see into the rear passenger compartment from the sides. The rear of the truck bed had a mesh screen that hung from the tarpaulin roof and could be rolled up to let people in and out. The tarpaulin and the mesh screen served as protection from shots being fired into the cab from the side, or from grenades or firebombs being thrown into it from the rear. The tarpaulin also screened us, unintentionally, from seeing into the driver's compartment and the front windshield.

The truck left Tan Son Nhut and proceeded downtown, taking us to our villa. Inside the rear with us was a major who worked at a desk job on base. Everything was going fine as we rolled through the streets. We could look through the mesh in the rear and see all the bikes and cycles and cars traveling behind us through the streets, but we could not see anything in the front. After some ten minutes the van suddenly came to a screeching halt. When it stopped, we heard very loud crowd noises coming from in front of the van. Traffic wasn't moving at all and we could see it building up to our rear. Pretty soon we were in a full size traffic jam with trucks, busses and the usual cycles and bikes, all in a tight gridlock. Horns blew, lights flashed, the crowd noise grew louder by the minute. Occasionally the crowd sounds rose into chants, shouts, and applause.

For twenty minutes the traffic didn't move and by this time the major and Dunn and I were wondering just what was going on. We knew that, in addition to the Viet Cong, the Buddhists had a large following in Saigon and might act against both the Vietnamese government and Americans who supported it. The major was sober and unarmed. Dunn and I were carrying our shoulder holstered .38 pistols. John and I vowed that if we were rushed or attacked we'd defend ourselves and go out fighting. We assured the unarmed major that we'd protect him as well. He gave us a strange look and laughingly said, "Thanks a lot."

Slowly the traffic began to creep forward in the darkened street. Finally we stopped at the corner of a broad street crossing which we saw out of the sides of the van. All the while, the crowd noise and cheering kept growing louder and louder. As the vehicle finally made its way to the intersection, we could see large crowds of Vietnamese standing in a park on the left side of the street corner. Strung up in the trees of the park were four or five television sets, evidently part of a public support campaign and no doubt American funded. The Vietnamese were watching *The Lone Ranger* in Vietnamese on TV and cheering and discussing the show with greatly animated gestures and shouts.

Once the van cleared the intersection at the next red light, we continued on our way to the villa at our original speedy pace. Dunn and I laughed both at the cause of the delay and at our own plans to fight off an imaginary assault. We asked the major if he was glad we were along for protection under such circumstances. "No," he answered, "the only thing that frightened me about all that was you two planning gunplay."

16 October: We didn't fly again until the next evening. After sleeping late and sitting around the villa reading or drinking Cokes, we caught a taxi to Tan Son Nhut, ate the dinner special at the club and then reported to C-130 Ops. At nine in the evening, we flew out of Tan Son Nhut on another cargo haul to Nha Trang. After an hour on the ground there, we returned to Saigon and spent two hours loading for a trip to Tahkli in Thailand. We were now flying nights and had 24 hour, seven day a week airlift operations out of Tan Son Nhut.

Since early in 1964, Thailand had been a site for U.S. Air Force bases being used in the war. There was a cargo operation which ran out of Bangkok International Airport. About 30 minutes' flying time from Bangkok was Tahkli, which was an emerging F-105 tactical fighter base. A wing of F-105s and support aircraft was based there with the mission of flying bombing sorties against North Vietnam. There was also another F-105 wing not too far from Tahkli at a base called Korat. An hour north of these two bases were two F-4 fighter escort and interceptor bases called Ubon and Udorn. They would each house F-4 wings whose mission was to escort the F-105's on missions over North Vietnam as well as flying attack missions themselves.

Further north and just on the Laotian border, but still within Thailand, was a reconnaissance and intelligence gathering base at Nhakom Phenom (NKP). Much of the activity at Nhakom Phenom, which was also known as Naked Fanny, centered on monitoring enemy activity in Laos and on the Ho Chi Minh Trail, which was used by the North Vietnamese as a logistics highway between North and South Vietnam.

Our cargo was aircraft parts and construction related materials, as Tahkli was still under construction. We only spent an hour on the ground and then flew three hours back to Tan Son Nhut. Our second straight 14 hour day netted us seven hours and 45 minutes of flying time, since we had lesser ground times than the day before and each leg of the trip to Thailand was three hours long.

On 18 October, our activity started at four in the morning but ended at noon after only one round-trip to Pleiku. We left Tan Son Nhut at 6:05 and landed in Pleiku an hour later at 7:05. Pleiku was often the first base we carried loads to in the morning and that was unfortunate. Being in the Highlands, Pleiku got a lot of morning and evening fog. The fog was often very thick and did not burn off until late or mid-morning. There were a total of 60 C-130s lost in Vietnam during the course of the war. I know of at least three which were lost attempting landings at Pleiku. Later, the early morning runs into Pleiku were shifted to later arrival times.

There was lots of cargo to be hauled to the myriad of U.S. operations that were picking up all over South Vietnam and the airbases that were being installed in Thailand. However, not all elements of the buildup were in synchronization. There was a real shortage of forklifts at the airlift bases, and without forklifts there was no way of getting the palletized cargo onboard the aircraft. Since there were only so many forklifts to go around among a larger number of aircraft, we frequently had to spend a lot of ground time waiting for our loads to be up- and downloaded. The more time spent on the ground between flights, the fewer flights and flying hours we had per day. The overall buildup of U.S. forces in Vietnam was only as efficient as the sum of its parts. Forklifts and their drivers were one cog in the wheel.

Another problem had to do with maintenance on the aircraft themselves. The plan for deployed operations like ours was to keep the aircraft we had in country flying. They would have many small maintenance problems in their logbooks, but as long as none of them prevented flight operations, major fixes were delayed until the planes were flown out to Clark. That worked as long as no major discrepancies occurred. When one did come up, such as an engine change, a maintenance crew and parts might be flown in to fix the plane where it was. Every nonflying plane, however, lowered the number of sorties we were able to get off on that day. When there weren't enough planes, a crew might get a surprise day off, or they might be called in to fly and then spend the day sitting around the flight line in 90 plus degree heat waiting for the plane to come out of maintenance.

There are always certain rules regarding aircraft and maintenance. I thought at first that they only applied to air force operations, but now I know that civilian airliner operations also have the same problems, although their facilities are better when it comes to putting up with the distractions. One is that every time a problem arises which will delay a flight, you are told that maintenance will have the problem fixed by such and such a time. It never is. It always takes longer than you are first told. Second, when a part needs to be repaired or replaced as part of the maintenance, you are always told that it has been ordered and is on the way from the parts center. Wrong. The needed part is never ordered or delivered very quickly and, more often than not, the wrong part is put on order and delivered and then the process has to repeat itself.

We were to spend long hours in the loading area, or waiting in or near the grounded aircraft. The ALCE, or Base Operations, were other waiting areas for cargo up- and download problems and aircraft maintenance problems. The constant daytime heat of 90 degrees plus (and the lack of diversionary facilities while waiting) just made the time that much harder to pass. The standard mode of operation was to keep the crew standing by while the load or plane was being worked on. We were kept in the waiting posture until the problem was fixed or the delay and estimated in-commission time exceeded the remainder of our crew day. Then and only then were we released and told what time to appear the next day. If the temperature in the outside waiting areas was over 90 degrees, it was closer to 110 or 120 in the cockpit without the aircraft power and air conditioning on. Heat, delays, frustration and back to back long work days tend to wear your down physically, which I guess is one reason that military air crews have age limits. The following day, we made two round-trips to Pleiku and back. A short ten hour day with 4 hours of flying time. Then we had an off day.

21 October: We appeared about noon at 130 Ops with our clothing bags. We were going back to Clark. From Tan Son Nhut we stopped to off- and upload cargo and passengers at Qui Nhon and from there flew back to Clark. We got four hours' flying time out of a ten hour day. We had also completed our first 10 day in-country shuttle.

Five days after we got back to Clark, we flew a one day in and out mission to Da Nang carrying cargo and people. From Da Nang we flew a short 15 minute flight up the coast to Hue. Hue was the old capital of the united Viet Nam. In the old city was a French designed, star shaped, concrete fortress and near it was an airstrip, but it was too small for C-130 operations. We landed in a newer, larger strip on the outskirts of the city called Hue, Phu Bai. After a short 20 minute offload (indicating we flew only passengers) we flew back to Clark. We landed at 8:00 P.M.

The next day at 1:30 in the afternoon we were off on another one day round-trip to Cam Rahn Bay. These missions were evidence of the pace of the U.S. buildup and the logistic network then in place. We were carrying people and cargo out of Clark to the main bases on the coast of Vietnam and then turning around and coming back. We were clearing Clark of the cargo which was coming in on strategic airlift and depositing it into the new U.S. bases in Vietnam on an individual base basis. Each trip took three hours to cross the South China Sea carrying five pallets of cargo which, at best, was 30,000 to 40,000 pounds of total cargo. These were less than the maximum cargo weights which the aircraft could carry, but it was necessary to keep the cargo moving, even if doing so was not maximally efficient, as the U.S. buildup had not yet created a cargo network within Vietnam itself.

We had a rest day at Clark after getting back from the second mission. The following day, 30 October, we left for Bangkok. It took us four hours to fly to Bangkok using a route around the southern coast of Vietnam and then straight up the Gulf of Thailand into the city itself. We landed at Bangkok International Airport, which was known as Don Muang, where a portion of the field had been taken over for U.S. military cargo operations. Our load into Don Muang was palletized cargo that Thai civilian crews offloaded.

A Volkswagen van took us from the airport to our rooms in a hotel the U.S. military had rented nearby. The hotel was a three story, air conditioned building with its own restaurant and bar. It was clean and the staff spoke English or, at least, pidgin English. Each room had its own bath. The hotel also had its own hot and cold running maid service, which amounted to in-house prostitution. There was an Indian snake charmer, complete with a defanged cobra, at the front door. The rooms were clean. John Dunn, as the aircraft commander, got his own room. Hal and I shared a room and the loadmaster and flight engineer shared a second.

After we cleaned up, we called a taxi and went downtown to a few places that earlier crews had recommended. We hit a jewelry store that also sold all types, colors, lengths and patterns of silk. The silk was very cheap by U.S. prices and probably better than anything we could buy anywhere else. The jewelry was of any and all types, from pure stones to bracelets, rings and wristbands. Some of it was falsely advertised and was not what it was said to be. If you knew what you were buying, you could save a lot of money compared to U.S. prices for the same objects. Some was man-made, but sold as nature's own (such as cat's eyes). But it was all gaudy and it was all cheap. If you didn't want finished products, you could even buy 10 or 20 pound bags of unrefined soil from the gem mines which you could water down and process on your own at home or in the hotel bathtub. God only knows how many real gems were supposed to be concealed in these purchases.

Late 1965 — A Bangkok cobra charmer outside our hotel.

    The gem stores were usually Caucasian owned or named enterprises such as "Johnnie's Gems" or "Fitzgerald's Jewelry." They had a sort of casino or Asian explorer-like atmosphere. While you wandered through and looked at their wares there were pretty Thai girls in silk sarongs offering free whiskey, beer and sodas. All the clerks spoke good English and if you were just looking and not really buying, they didn't seem to care. The drinks were still free and you could stay as long as you liked.

    From the gem shop, where we all bought something, we proceeded by cab to a restaurant which had also been recommended. The restaurant was Oriental/American, with a thatched roof, individual tables or booths, a bar, lots of neon and its own band. The food was water buffalo-level beef, much like we got everywhere else in Asia (including the officers' clubs), but better than anything seen in Vietnam. The vegetables and other items were also good. The native Thai food was hot, but with a spice very different from the chili we were all used to. In some ways, it was hotter, but the heat mellowed quickly.

The band in this place was comprised of five or six musicians. You named the tune and they seemed to know it. They then played without recourse to notes or sheet music. The restaurant was full and stayed that way as long as we were there. Everyone, a seemingly even mix of Thais and Caucasians, was having a good time as well as a good meal. I asked the band to play the old Frankie Lane tune "Rose, Rose, I Love You," which had been popular in the States years earlier and referred to the love affair of an English sailor and a local oriental beauty. The band struck it right up. Later in the meal I asked them play it again, but they wouldn't. There seemed to be a polite but firm resistance to referring too much to past colonialist associations and failed Eurasian romances.

We ended the night relatively early after a full meal and by 8:00 the next morning we piled into the van for our trip back to the airport. At 11:30, we were soaring into the stratosphere, delivering an airplane-full of newly arrived U.S. personnel to the upcountry air bases. In a half hour, we were in Tahkli dropping people off and picking up some air force personnel who were traveling between our next stops. I'm not sure if it was Takhli or the particular day we were there, but it was hotter than Hades. By now we had acclimated ourselves to Asia; but it must have been 120 degrees, with no wind and a very high humidity.

Dunn knew the sergeant major of the fighter wing, who told us that they had uncovered hundreds of cobras in building the base over the course of a year. He also commented that the Wing had a low rate of mission aborts daily, considering that they were flying against the heavy air defenses that had been built up in North Vietnam. After an hour on the ground, we took off for Udorn. We spent an hour on the ground there and then flew back to Clark. Our route home was to fly north from Udorn and then head due east just south of the Thai, Laotian, Vietnamese border. That route led directly to Da Nang, which we overflew on our route home to the Philippines.

3 November: We left Clark for our second in-country stay. We carried cargo from Clark to Cam Rahn Bay where the new airfield was still under construction. We landed on the first 5,000 feet or so of what was to be a 10,000 foot runway. The remainder of the base was sand, tents and construction equipment. From there, we flew 20 minutes straight up the coast to Nha

Fall 1965 — U.S. Army Special Forces headquarters in Nha Trang Vietnam (from the collection of Fred W. Straub).

Trang, which was to be our overnight home base for this series of missions. It took an hour and a half for us to get cargo onboard. We then flew overland to Ban Me Thout in the center of the country. There was only a small U.S. operation at Ban Me Thout, only a few people to run U.S. operations at the otherwise Vietnamese airport. There were one or two forklifts and then trucks ran back and forth with the cargo from the airbase to the nearby but unseen army compound. We offloaded our cargo and then flew to Da Nang, off-loaded cargo and flew back to Nha Trang for the night. We'd had a 12 and a half hour crew day with six hours of flying time. We didn't know it at the time, but the in-country portion of this day was to become the pattern for the future: several short flights to varied U.S. occupied fields from one central base in the course of a day.

Nha Trang was now a major U.S. Army operation on the east coast of Vietnam. The army ran the base and the air force was more or less tenants on it and the airfield. We stayed downtown, which was a ten minute van ride from the runway, in a rented chalet with one or two beds (read cots) to a room and one shared bathroom. The chalet had a small in-house bar and tables for playing cards. You could walk from the chalet into town and then down to the beach in about 10 minutes. Having been something of an old French beach resort, bolstered by the U.S. Army presence, the town featured several restaurants where you could get a hamburger or a water buffalo-like steak or roast in addition to Vietnamese fare. The beef throughout the Orient was good; but it tasted different from similar American food, probably due to the feed the animals ate and the oil the food was cooked in. We usually ate on base in the officers' club which adjoined the runway. The club also had a well stocked bar, which we repaired to after flights before going on to bed downtown.

Nha Trang also featured some Spartan night time entertainment. The base was overlooked on the south by hills that went up several hundred feet and were seemingly inhabited by a number of Viet Cong. At night, the Cong became active, or the base intelligence people thought they did. We could sit outside the villa or outside the officers' club and watch A-1s bomb, strafe and drop napalm on the hills. I don't remember any enemy firing on the base, but the evening air display was entertaining. It was also rumored, that although the beautiful beach in town was used daily by large numbers of the U.S. and Australian community, at night it belonged to the Viet Cong, who did their swimming and clothes washing nocturnally.

We got up the next morning about 7:00, reported for duty at 8:00, after having breakfast in the club, and were in the air carrying mixed loads of cargo and people to Qui Nhon, then to Pleiku, then back to Qui Nhon and then two more round-trips between Qui Nhon and Pleiku before returning to Nha Trang at 6:30 in the evening. The army at this time was building up its presence in Pleiku, as well as expanding its new base for the 1st Airmobile Division at An Khe. An Khe was halfway between Qui Nhon and Pleiku along an old colonial road (Highway 19). We took cargo from the port at Qui Nhon and then carried it to Pleiku for use in the buildup of both inland army camps. When we got back to Nha Trang that night, John Dunn got his ass chewed for landing later than 5 o'clock. Harry Barner, the full colonel from our unit who was in command of our six-aircraft operation at Nha Trang, ran a daylight-only flying operation which was supposed to end at 5:00. When you landed after that, you had compromised his maintenance and loading operation that got the planes ready for the next day. We were firmly told not to be late again.

The following day we began about 6:00 A.M. and were off the ground by 7:45. We then flew two round-trips between Nha Trang and Pleiku by noon. Shortly after noon, we left Nha Trang and flew to Catecka. Catecka was a small, short, laterite airstrip some 30 or 40 miles south of Pleiku. There was nothing there but the airstrip — no base operations, no offloading area or equipment, no U.S. camp.

Before landing, we flew over the strip and made sure there was no other activity there, such as a Viet Cong field unit, for example. Someone in the cockpit remarked, "Well, if there is someone there they know we're coming now." When we saw nothing on the fly over we landed and offloaded some personnel. Then we turned around on the runway and flew off to Pleiku and offloaded the rest of our cargo, which was all passengers. We were on the ground at Catecka for 15 minutes and at Pleiku for 10. Another round-trip between Nha Trang and Pleiku completed our day, which ended just 10 minutes prior to the 5 o'clock magic hour that Col. Barner had demanded.

Since we were finished early for a change, we adjourned to the officers' club to eat before taking a base van back to our villa for the night. The club was small; but it had a long, rounded, wooden bar and served the usual round of U.S. style dinners: hamburgers, meat loaf, turkey and dressing, etc. It sure beat eating in downtown Nha Trang. The club also featured two young (late 20s, early 30s), blonde, good looking Australian girls — the Donnally sisters, I believe. They were present every night and surrounded by a large U.S. Army contingent who seemed to know them very well. Rumor had it that they had come to Nha Trang as dancers in an Australian entertainment company, somewhat like our American USO shows. Entertainment apparently hadn't paid quite enough and they were now said to be making much more money and having more fun while plying another career field. As I said, they were in the club every night.

6 November: The day began almost as a repeat of the previous day. We flew empty out of Nha Trang at 8:00 A.M. and flew direct to Catecka. The flight took 30 minutes; and when we got over Catecka, we could see that a thick ground fog covered the highlands, although the airstrip itself was clear. Due to the higher altitude, humidity and great temperature changes, fog was a regular feature of the highlands in the morning. As we came down on final to land, the fog appeared light and wispy, as we were looking through it on the slant. Once on the ground, however, we found that the fog went up to eight or ten feet, and over the grasslands it was very thick when seen laterally.

We landed and did a 180 degree turnaround on the narrow airstrip. Our load out was going to be people, and the loadmaster immediately set to work putting seats down for them. Usually the loadmaster exited the aircraft first on landing and put a pair of chocks under the plane's wheels to prevent it from rolling; but since he was busy with the seats, I climbed out of the rear cargo door and put the chocks in. Having done so, I turned and looked around. It was about 9 o'clock, but the air was still cool and the field was vacant as far as I could see. Everything around the edge of the strip was fog enshrouded and there appeared to be not another living thing in the area.

Just as I stood there wondering where our load was, a single black figure rose out of the grass not ten feet from me. I was startled; it could have been a friendly or one of the Cong. There was a lot of activity in this area, and just 20 or 30 miles from here a daily firefight had been going on around a Special Forces Camp at Plei Mei. As I stood gaping, the figure muttered, "Let's go, everybody up." Some 30 or 40 other similarly dark figures rose from the grass. Like ghosts, they materialized out of nothing. This was our load.

It was a squad of U.S. Army troops. They were all young, big, and, considering that they had been lying in the open for some period of time, pretty clean. It was about the most impressive looking group of military men I'd ever seen. I think now that they must have had a supporting role in the Plei Mei fight; but I never found out for sure.

They came onboard and we then took off and went back to Nha Trang and offloaded them. Within a half hour, we had loaded up with palletized cargo and carried that into Qui Nhon. We were supposed to offload at Qui Nhon and then go back to Nha Trang, but once on the ground the Qui Nhon, ALCE told us to stand by for an emergency air evacuation mission that would soon be coming in. We waited for an hour. We were told to refile our daily flight plan and forget the rest of the missions we had been scheduled for that day. Our next destination was to be Clark.

We waited for a helicopter to bring in a Korean guard who had been burned in a gasoline fire. The Koreans had come into the war as our allies to assist in pacifying South Vietnam. Their area of responsibility was north of Nha Trang and South of Qui Nhon. Just about one o'clock in the afternoon, a small convoy of army vehicles, including an ambulance, pulled into the loading area. We had the cargo compartment empty except for nine or ten canvas seats that Carl had set up in the forward area behind the fire wall and crew compartment. One of the vehicles backed up onto our ramp and a stretcher came out of it.

There were two American military nurses and a doctor with it. In the rear of the plane, together with our loadmaster, they quickly set up a makeshift bed on a canopy of straps and hoists usually used to make up tiers of stretchers in our normal casualty evacuation configuration. Then, from one of the other vehicles, they brought onboard loads and loads of ice and set the stretcher-borne casualty within the bed which sat in the ice.

It turned out that the Korean had been guarding a gasoline depot when he suddenly felt the urge for a cigarette. As they brought him onboard and set him in the ice bed, he was naked except for a small napkin taped over his pubic area. He was without a wound except that he was as red as a steamed lobster all over. He hadn't really been burned; it was more like he had been completely steam boiled. His ears, eyelids and every hair on his head and body were gone. Since he couldn't close his eyes he appeared to be awake, but never made a sound. Probably he was in shock and doped up to ease the terrible pain he must have been in.

The medical crew placed hydration bags around his bed and fastened them to the stanchions and cargo straps that were holding the whole structure together on the rear floor of the cargo compartment. Once they declared they were ready, we started the engines and made ready for takeoff. We were going to Clark because there was, as yet, no military burn facility in South Vietnam to deal with such cases. The closest one was in the Clark hospital back in the Philippines.

It took us three hours and ten minutes to arrive at Clark. The air controllers en route and the Clark tower were all aware of our mission as we progressed across the South China Sea, and we received priority treatment with regard to landing and offload. We landed and taxied to the Clark offload area, the ambulances and medical staff were already there and waiting. They took the Korean and relieved the nurses and doctor who had flown in with us in very short order. What happened to the patient after that, I have no idea.

It was just 5:00 P.M. when we landed, so we checked into our quarters, cleaned up and set off for the officers' club. The nurses who had been with us went off on their own to a separate BOQ or maybe an off-base hotel. The army doctor captain tagged along with us and we found some spare clothes for him back in our trailer.

We knew we would be going back to our shuttle in Nha Trang the next day, but we still had time for a few drinks and dinner. After cleaning ourselves up with a shower and shave, we hit the club at the high point of happy hour. The bar was jammed and we spent much of our time telling some of our squadron mates who were present about the air evacuation flight and how we had gotten a break from shuttle work in order to bring the Korean to Clark.

In the course of some of this drinking and storytelling, the doctor ran into a crew of surly civilian transport flyers who began to question his manhood, but we rescued him from them by buying a round of drinks and engaging them in humorous small talk for five or ten minutes. It seems it was their pilot who had caused the unpleasantness; and the other two members of the crew regarded him as a mean, drunken lout whom they were hoping we would hammer senseless in a barroom brawl. However, being peace-loving and harmonious airlifters, we did no such thing. We left them to handle the pilot for the rest of the night and went off to dinner.

For us, the drinks and dinner in the club were a one day escape from the less relaxing ordeal of the Vietnam shuttle. For the army doctor, however, it was like a one night trip through a near paradise. From the largely male and sterile atmosphere of the Vietnamese Highlands, he had been transported to the luxury of the Clark Club, complete with air conditioning, drinks, good food and even un-uniformed women to gape at.

He had been in Vietnam for several months, mostly in the Pleiku area. He told us of a patient he had recently treated. One evening Pleiku had come under mortar fire and everyone had gone into the sandbagged "bunkers" that were maintained for protection in such events. The shelling went on for a while and some of the people in the bunker fell asleep around the bunker's walls.

One soldier was sleeping in a curled position near the center of the bunker floor when a direct-hit mortar round broke through the roof and landed right on him. The shell fell exactly in the center of his curled up body and in his quickly awakening drowsiness he had wrapped his arms around it on impact. Luckily, the shell was a dud and did not explode. The soldier was treated for a burn on his stomach where the hot shell of the mortar round had burned through his shirt. Miracles do happen.

At 9:30 the next morning, we set off again for Vietnam. We carried cargo, the doctor and nurses, and a few other passengers. Our first stop was Da Nang and from there back to Nha Trang. The doctor and nurses left us there and we flew another load of troops to Catecka. When we got back to Nha Trang, we were told to stand by, as we would be taking another plane back to Clark for maintenance. We left at 8:00 that night and got into Clark at 11:00.

We had gotten eight hours of flying time in a 15 hour crew day. Our passenger on the trip to Clark was none other than Col. Barner, the commander of our Nha Trang operation. He piloted the plane on the way back. When we got to Clark the radar controller put us on a downleg to the runway, which headed us toward the mountains west of the field. Barner had had a close call on this approach once before when the controller had forgotten about him and left him headed for the mountains much longer than he wanted to be. This time, after a few minutes, he called the approach and asked if they still had him in view. Evidently, the colonel was hard on everybody and not just the crews that worked for him. This was the end of our second full in-country shuttle.

We got the next two days off and spent it just lounging around Clark.

Dinner at the officers' club on the first night turned into an experience. It was the monthly free steak dinner for all club members and the place was literally jammed. We ended up eating in the basement in a small dining room set up in what was usually the slot machine section of the club.

We had dinner with some visiting Australians while all around us visitors pulled off the slots. Many drinks and toasts were consumed, and one of the Aussies and I traded Kipling quotes before we called it a night. In the course of the evening, we noticed one of the airline stewardesses who worked for a charter company that flew incoming soldiers to Vietnam on a daily basis. She was a nice girl, although a bit substandard with regards to looks when compared with some of the Pan Am and TWA stewardesses who passed through Clark but were based in the States. Still, she was a female roundeye in a place where such a commodity was few and far between. Since her nose was slightly longer than normal, we decided that her name as far as we were concerned should be Cyranette in memory of the noted French swashbuckling hero Cyrano de Bergerac. As far as I know, she never knew about our nickname for her.

10 November: Three days after we had gotten back from Vietnam, we turned out for another midnight Bangkok run. We left Clark at 1:30 in the morning. First stop was Ubon, where we dropped off air force F-4 personnel and some cargo and then on to Korat, where we did the same with the F-105 people. Korat was the second of two F-105 bases (Tahkli was the other) which the USAF had built in Thailand, and it was filling up with people, planes and equipment.

We left Korat after an hour and a half on the ground. It was 8:30 in the morning when we got into Bangkok. We washed up and ate a little breakfast at the hotel and, about noon, took a taxi into town. We had a stop or two at the gem stores, but really didn't buy all that much. Just enjoyed a free beer or soda. We took a cruise on the canal to the tourist trap, where you could go in and see the Bhudda statues and the old palace, as in the days of Anna and the King of Siam. By mid afternoon, we were in the center of town and walking through the open air market there. That place had a little of everything. It was like a large flea market, and independent sellers came in and set up their stalls every day then took them down at night.

For sale were gems, silks, teak furniture and carvings, live animals and animals to be eaten, including fish, snakes and monkeys. One of the stands was selling what were said to be ocelot kittens, small cats with greenish spots on their yellow skin. They looked sick and the colors didn't look quite natural. I wasn't sure the cats were real ocelots or just painted housecats, although I did see similar sales later in both Bangkok and Saigon.

Late 1965 — Bangkok Buddhist temples.

We journeyed back to the motel, ate a hamburger or their in-house version of a U.S. meal and then embarked via taxi for a recommended tour of the local hotsi bath. None of us really needed another bath or shower, but the place and the tour were recommended by other crews. The taxi took us to the door of this place and the driver assured us he would return to take us back when we called for him.

Inside was a large lobby. The far wall was a large plate glass window behind which sat some 20 or 30 Thai girls dressed in small white kimonos tied with orange sashes. Just like the menu in a drive in restaurant, you picked out the one you wanted by pointing at her and she became your bath partner, masseuse and whatever else you might want or be willing to pay for the remainder of the evening or an hour or two. Since we were flying again the next day, we left after an hour or two.

One of the Wing's crew members became a real cleanliness fanatic from an experience like this. But, as far as we knew, only when he was in Bangkok. On almost all future trips, he seemed to spend more and more time in this place or others like it when his crew hit town. He might have been the cleanest Yank in the Far East, but I doubt it. We didn't get to Bangkok that often and other people were stationed there.

The next day, we reversed course after an 11:30 A.M. takeoff. First was Takhli and then it was on to Udorn. On the outbound mission we usually had air force passengers leaving Bangkok for their upcountry bases. Some of these people were new arrivals who had flown or been shipped into Bangkok. Others were people already stationed at the bases who had been given a pass to the big city for a day or two and used us as their transport in and out. If we had any cargo to haul it was usually broken equipment or an empty stack of pallets to take back to Clark for reuse. We flew into Clark at 7:40 at night and got the next four days off.

16 November: We woke up at six and started our usual routine. We caught the crew pickup van in front of the trailer and rode down to Base Operations, where we ate a quick sausage and egg sandwich breakfast before going into squadron ops and getting our schedule for the day. Then it was on to the weatherman for a briefing on the weather en route and at each base. Then we went into Base Ops itself and checked all the notices which had anything to do with the South China Sea area or the Philippines and the specific bases where we were going to stop for the day. After that, we filled out the flight plan. I worked up the flight times for each leg and we filled out the day's flight form. We were ready to go.

While we had been doing all that, the loadmaster had been securing our load onboard the airplane and the flight engineer had preflighted the aircraft, checked the write-up book to determine what was good or bad with the airplane, given it a walk-around inspection, fueled it and rechecked the fuel load.

When we got to the plane from the crew bus which ran from Base Ops, I preflighted and prepared the navigation instruments while the pilots did their walk-around. We all checked the write-up book with regard to the plane's equipment, and became aware of what was in need of maintenance or not working properly; and then we were ready to go.

We left Clark, flew south toward Manila Bay, then turned right over Corregidor Island and flew out over the China Sea. Almost three hours after we had left Clark, we were on the runway at Cam Ranh Bay offloading a mixed load of passengers and palletized equipment. We then left Cam Ranh, which was still in the building process, and flew 15 minutes north to Nha Trang. We landed there at 12:20. We were back in-country for another 10 days of shuttling.

The squadron operation at Nha Trang was still flying daylight missions only and we had six or eight aircraft deployed there. Our quarters were again downtown in a villa which was an adjunct to the base hospital. We ate and drank in the officers' club on base between missions. For the next two days we flew mainly cargo to all of our previous in-country stops. Using Nha Trang as home base we flew to Qui Nhon, Pleiku, Tan Son Nhut, and Da Nang. The buildup of U.S. Army units in the Central Highlands was continuing and these were all army loads.

On our third day in-country we left Nha Trang at 8:00 in the morning, stopped at Pleiku to offload part of our cargo and then flew 25 minutes due east from Pleiku to the new army base at An Khe. An Khe sat squarely on Route 19, which was the main road between Pleiku in the highlands and Qui Nhon on the coast. During the previous war between the French and the Viet Minh, An Khe had been the site of a Viet Minh ambush which destroyed the French mobile force that had previously fought with distinction alongside Americans in the Korean War.

An Khe was to be the home of the first U.S. Airmobile Division, which was the keystone of the army's plan for combating guerrilla warfare. The Airmobile Division was built around the use of helicopters for logistic and firepower support of ground forces. The division had just had its major introduction to combat in the Ia Drang Valley battle and its home base at An Khe was still in the process of major construction and expansion.

The base at An Khe sat in a large valley. Route 19 ran through it in a due east-west direction. To the south about 10 or 15 miles was a mountain range which rose sharply to 3,000 feet. To the east was An Khe Pass, where Route 19 climbed before beginning a downward spiral to Qui Nhon and the coast. To the north of the base was a 15 or 20 mile flat area before low hills began to rise and form the north wall of the valley. The entire region was covered with forest. The aircraft runway at this time was situated in the center of the base and ran in a north/south direction. The only thing that marred this seemingly quaint picture was that right next to the east side of the runway was a 500-foot-high steep rock formation. This was no problem in good daylight weather; but at night or in bad weather, which was frequent in the valley, An Khe was less than an ideal destination.

We spent over three hours on the ground at An Khe. The base was building up and one of the things they were short of was forklifts. None of the few forklifts that they had was in working condition and we had to wait for a maintenance effort to be completed before we could load up with palletized cargo. We left An Khe and flew an hour due south into the delta, which stretched from Saigon to the sea. Our next landing point was Vung Tau. Vung Tau was an old French seaside resort which sat on the east side of a peninsula extending from the tip of Vietnam into the South China Sea. In the old days, Vung Tau was known to the French as Cap Ste Jacques, and it functioned as the beach community to which the Saigon bureaucrats flocked on weekends and holidays.

Vung Tau was now a U.S. Army base for support of operations in the delta and surrounding area. Forklifts were a problem at Vung Tau also, and it took us two hours to get one load of palletized cargo off and to load another along with some Vietnamese and American troops. When that was completed we left for Can Tho, another new stop for us. Can Tho was 25 minutes further southwest from Vung Tau in the delta. In addition to now being a U.S. Army support base, Vung Tau was also a provincial capital sitting right on one of the main waterways through which the Saigon River and the Mekong flowed to the sea. This part of the delta was composed of large areas of flat rice fields, swamps, marshes and small waterways. The U.S. ground force buildup which we had been supporting in the highlands was also occurring in the delta. Once we got to Can Tho, the offload was done in 10 minutes and we went back to Nha Trang for the night.

The next day it was another series of flights to Pleiku, Da Nang, and then Tan Son Nhut. It was 20 November 1965, and we were making our last airlift stop of the day as we pulled into the cargo area at Da Nang. ALCE told us we'd be going from there to Tan Son Nhut, but there would be a longer than usual delay to reload because some higher priority missions were coming in just behind us.

In October and early November there had been a large siege and combat around a small Special Forces camp called Plei Mei about halfway between Ban Me Thout and Pleiku and just to the west of our flight path. The Viet Cong had laid siege to the camp, and the U.S., South Vietnamese and Montagnard native allies had fought them in daily firefights with air support by helicopters and fighter bombers. On several of our flights in the past weeks, we had flown to the east of Plei Mei on our way to Pleiku or Da Nang and had been on the lookout for any signs of firing, fighter action or flares.

The Plei Mei siege was followed by a larger battle in the Ia Drang valley further to the west near the Cambodian border. We knew much less of that fight. We had never visually detected evidence of it and neither the *Stars and Stripes* (the daily U.S. forces newspaper) nor the radio seemed to have a complete story on it. During the morning, on our way to Da Nang, I'd heard over the radio in the cockpit that it was a U.S. victory but that 35 to 50 U.S. casualties had been reported.

Now we sat in the cockpit of our plane and watched another of our Wing's C-130s pull into the Da Nang cargo area next to us. We recognized the call sign and even the copilot's voice as he asked the ALCE for offload instructions as the plane taxied in after landing. They parked off to our left and slightly behind us. From our cockpit windows we could see the unusual number of fire trucks and ambulances which were following them as they shut down their engines and prepared to offload.

We weren't paying too much attention to their offload until Carl Gross came over our rear interphone system and said, "Look at the crew scatter from that plane!" As soon as their propellers had stopped spinning and they were clear to come out of the cockpit, the entire crew ran from the stopped aircraft as if they were evading a cockpit fire. They then stood away from the plane at a distance of 30 yards. Now our interest was up.

Since our onload was going to be delayed, we had nothing better to do than walk over to see what the problem was with the other aircraft. We knew the entire crew, who were part of our temporary duty unit back at Clark and from another squadron in our Wing at Langley. We walked up to them and asked what the problem was that had caused their rapid and unorthodox departure from the cockpit. No one answered directly. They only told us to go take a look. They all appeared somewhat antagonized and hostile to our approach and questions.

I mounted the steps leading to the cockpit and forward cargo area of the aircraft. The plane had been rigged for Personnel Air Evacuation. In this procedure, the C-130 had a series of metal stanchions which clipped into the floor and ceiling and created a U-shaped aisle formation inside the cargo compartment. Using the stanchions for support, a web of heavy nylon straps clipped into them and intermeshed into triple tiered levels of stretcher supports in the manner of the old Pullman railroad bunks. In the aircraft there were 50 or 60 individual stretchers, three levels high, in four aisles around the cargo compartment.

Slowly and silently, together with the rest of our crew, I walked down the aisle on the right side of the cargo compartment between the two rows of three stretcher tiers. I took a left turn at the end of the aisle and walked forward to the flight station wall down the second aisle on the other side of the plane, also bounded on both sides by three high stretcher tiers. I noted that the plane was almost at the maximum number of stretchers that it could carry in this rigging assembly. Each stretcher contained one green body bag. In some of the bags the outline of a soldier could be trace horizontally from the feet to the head. In others, the occupant appeared contorted. Some were clearly less than a complete body. One, about the size of a basketball, sat alone on its stretcher, taking up little more than a quarter of the stretcher space. It was held in place by a seat strap. Most of the stretchers had a pair of boots and a dog tag fastened to them.

THEY WERE DEAD. THEY WERE ALL DEAD! THIS WAS AN AIRPLANE FULL OF DEAD MEN.

My walk through the darkened aircraft took less than five minutes. During that time I smelled the sickening sweet odor that permeated the entire craft. I noticed it as soon as I entered the cargo hold, but it wasn't initially overwhelming or disturbing. The longer I stayed in the compartment, the stronger a contaminated sweet portion of the overall odor came to the fore. This smell had driven the aircrew from the plane as soon as the doors were opened after their fifty minute flight. The buildup of this nauseous aroma within the sealed aircraft had made them all nearly airsick. In carrying only a very limited number of bodies in the past, such a smell had never before permeated an entire aircraft as this load did. It was a smell never to be forgotten, but one we would become increasingly familiar with.

I exited the aircraft and exchanged words with the flight crew. The bodies were the results of the recent Ia Drang battle in the Central Highlands. All of the dead men were Americans. They had been loaded on the C-130 at Pleiku, the closest main airbase to the battle site, and had been sent to Da Nang since it held the only U.S. mortuary in Vietnam at the time. There were two more similarly configured and loaded C-130s coming in to land behind this one.

We returned to our airplane where a load of palletized cargo bound for Tan Son Nhut was now ready to be put on. At the other C-130, the rear cargo door had been opened and the body laden stretchers were being put into waiting ambulances. As we took off for Saigon, we heard the other two planes from Pleiku call in for landing and parking instructions.

We flew an hour and a half flight to Tan Son Nhut. Normally we would have been involved in a discussion of what had transpired that day, or where we'd eat that night, or what we might expect for the next days' mission. Now there was only silence. We each individually considered what we had seen at Da Nang. After about an hour, when we were at altitude and there was a lull in the copilot's conversation with ground control facilities, John Dunn asked if anyone had any thoughts on what the planeload of U.S. casualties meant for the future. We all agreed that the context of our Vietnam experience had just undergone a major change. But we could not foretell the future impact.

We arrived at Tan Son Nhut at two in the afternoon and were originally supposed to go from there to Nha Trang with cargo. But when we got to Tan Son Nhut, we were told to sit and wait, as our schedule was being changed. We sat for five hours and were then told our mission had been changed and we were to go to Bien Hoa and stay there for the night, as we would be involved in a multi-ship army support mission the next day.

We left Tan Son Nhut at 7:40 in the evening and flew northeast at about 5,000 feet en route to Bien Hoa, which was only 20 miles away. By now it was getting dark and there was a very large lightning-encrusted thunderstorm right over the runway at Bien Hoa. There were also airplanes all over the sky trying to dodge the storm and sneak into the base before the storm closed it. There were several C-130s, like us part of the next day's multi-plane mission. There were also C-123s coming back from their day's cargo deliveries to short fields. And finally there were F-100s, which were based at Bien Hoa, coming back from ground support operations.

Everybody was trying to get on the ground, dodge the storm and also keep from running into each other. The base tower finally established a priority for landing which had the fighters or anyone with trouble landing first, then the C-123s and finally us. The base radar got up and running and vectored people into landing, while the others went into spaced and altitude differentiated orbits several miles away. We and the other C-130s flew off to one side of the base and assumed a holding pattern at 500-foot vertical altitude separations. Then, one at a time, the remaining aircraft came out of orbit and were led in for their landing.

What should have been a 20 minute flight from Tan Son Nhut turned into two hours. Finally we broke out at 1,500 feet on final approach for landing. We were in the rain and just out of the trailing edge of the thunderstorm that was moving on towards Saigon. The tower broke in on the radio: "C-130 on final, be alert to a potential machine gun a mile from the end of the runway on final. This was reported by the aircraft which just landed ahead of you."

We continued on, landed and taxied over to our parking place on the ramp. Tower then broke in again and asked if we had taken any hits or thought we had. Everyone, including the loadmaster, who was the only one with a view of the rear compartment, stated no; but I thought I had heard something hit the right side on our approach and said so. When we got out, we all took a look; but nothing was damaged. We'd taken no hits. It must have been the rain or gusts from the storm — or my imagination.

When we got to Base Operations they asked about our being fired on; while we were talking, you could hear artillery being fired somewhere not too far away. It was evident we were responding to possible guerrilla activity with high explosive, area coverage artillery fire on the basis of vague reports of when and where that fire may have come from. Having read a bit of Sun Tzu and Mao Tse-tung on the subject of guerrilla warfare and some of how the British had defeated guerrillas in Malaya using high manpower but precise use of weapons, I began to wonder if we were fighting the right war, or at least if we were fighting this war correctly.

It was now 10 o'clock at night. We were driven to our quarters for the night in a tin topped, single story bungalow with netted windows. Each cot had a pillow, army blanket and two sheets. The only place still open to eat was the officers' club, which was jammed. We grabbed a quick bite and headed back to grab as many winks as we could. We'd have to be up about 5:00 the next morning, flying in the same clothes we'd worn all day. Our long ground time in Saigon before we were put on this mission and the limited amount of crew rest we had between landing at Bien Hoa and having to be up the next morning all indicated that this army support mission had been put on the schedule in a great hurry.

21 November: The day dawned hot and foggy. There was a blanket fog from ground level to about 500 feet. Above that, it was clear up to about 3,000 feet, where it was completely clouded over up to no one knew where. Our mission for the day was to shuttle an army combat unit from Bien Hoa to a small strip called Vo Dat that was only some 30 or 40 miles away. We were to fly as many sorties as we could until either the sun set or the army was all in place. The mission was to have started at 7:00.

Because of the fog, no flights were allowed to take off under visual flight rules (VFR). Our army support mission was delayed until the weather improved, which was supposed to happen later in the morning as the fog burned off. Instrument flight rules (IFR), which were now being impressed on all departing flights, required a five minute interval between takeoffs to prevent aircraft from running into each other. There was a long backup of planes because of this and it involved all the same types which I had mentioned from the previous evening's stack-up.

One of those waiting was a C-130 from Tan Son Nhut which had flown into Bien Hoa first thing in the morning and now wanted to take the 20 minute flight to Saigon. Rather than wait his turn in the long delayed queue, he asked for a VFR clearance, saying he would fly low level at about 1,000 feet direct from Bien Hoa to Tan Son Nhut since the other runway would be visible just about the time he reached altitude and cleared the top of the fog.

This C-130, which was part of our TDY unit at Clark, was cleared for its low level flight. We found out later that it did indeed go direct to Tan Son Nhut, where it landed after a 10 or 15 minute flight. What was unexpected was that on landing the crew found they had taken over 100 rounds of small arms hits which had to be patched by the aircraft skin maintenance people. Someone had to pay for the number of hits, so the pilot was chastised for going at low level rather than waiting his turn and time in the IFR takeoff queue. What no one ever explained was how that many rounds could have been fired at the plane in daylight when he was flying over an area that supposedly, at least in daylight, was owned and controlled by our allies the South Vietnamese Army. Either that force was not really in control of anything (which may well have been the case considering the firing the night before) or its internal discipline was so poor that even allied aircraft were not safe from their random and uncontrolled fire. Such was the state of the "control" in Vietnam at the time.

The ground fog burned off about 10:00 in the morning. We and the other nine C-130s that were part of this mission began loading up with army personnel and vehicles and then heading for the runway. A 20 minute takeoff separation was established between each plane in the mission so that the aircraft would have time to unload at Vo Dat and take off from there before the next plane came in. We took off at 11:10, landed at Vo Dat at 11:35, and were ready to take off back to Bien Hoa by 11:45.

Vo Dat was a flat, narrow, laterite strip of about 5,000 feet length that sat out in the middle of open country, with a small, 200–300 foot, hill about ¼ of a mile from its eastern end. There was room for one airplane in the offloading area at a time. But, the offload area was at the far end of the runway that we were landing on. When we completed our landing roll, we continued right into the offload area after slowing down to taxi speed. The area was a semicircle-like packed dirt area which was rapidly turning to mud with the continued aircraft presence.

Our cargo was either jeeps, trucks and trailers ready for immediate drive off on landing, or armed and ready soldiers with their rifles and packs on their backs. Offload was accomplished in a matter of minutes. The army charged off in all directions once they got out of the airplane, and there was some pretty hectic activity not far from the offload spot. The little hill to the east was getting fired on heavily, and artillery located within a hundred yards or so of the cargo area was firing fast and furious in that direction.

When we got back to Bien Hoa, we told the air force colonel in charge of the operation that 20 minutes between takeoffs was probably twice what was needed and the whole operation could be sped up by moving that to 10 minutes. He agreed and that became the rule of thumb for the rest of the day. Later in the day there was some palletized cargo of food and ammunition loaded and offloaded. The army had several forklifts in the offload area and there was little delay in the turnaround time. Despite the late start to the operation, we flew 6 round-trip missions before quitting for the day about 4:30 in the afternoon.

The next day we again rose at 5:00 A.M. and were off the ground and headed back to Vo Dat at 7:05. Since our clothes were back in Nha Trang, we were flying a second day in the same flight suits and underwear. There was an old joke that airlifters, or "trash haulers," could get four fresh days out of a pair of underwear by first wearing them back to front and then turning them inside out and doing the same.

Most of the cargo going to Vo Dat now was either all palletized cargo and vehicles, or mixed loads of both, and personnel. Accordingly, the offload time and time between aircraft on the mission was increased slightly to some 15 or 20 minutes rather than 10, but things went very well during the day regardless of that change. All in all, we flew nine round-trip missions between Bien Hoa and Vo Dat that day.

Prior to our last sortie, we were told that we were released from this mission and would leave Vo Dat for Nha Trang after the next offload. We got into Vo Dat at six o'clock P.M. on the dot. After a rapid offload, we took the runway for takeoff just as the plane ahead of us was in the air from the far end. As we sat there waiting for him to clear the area, a very heavy rainstorm which had been threatening all day broke. The day had been the usual boiling hot and muggy Vietnamese afternoon, and the first drops caused steam to rise from the runway surface. Within an instant the rain was so heavy it was hard to see the length of the runway through it.

John Dunn called over the intercom, "Get ready we're going to have to take off as the brakes aren't holding on this wet laterite." We all, including Gross in the rear, called in "Ready," then settled into our seats. As we rolled down the runway, I could see off to the side one of the newly landed army people digging into the red clay soil in the pouring rain as his buddy held the pole and tent which would be their home for the night. Anticipating that we'd be back in our air conditioned trailer at Clark under clean sheets that very same night, I reflected that I was glad I had joined the air force and not the army.

The two-day Bien Hoa/Vo Dat shuttle was the start of the U.S. Army's "Search and Destroy" missions in the Vietnam War. We'd been in at the outset, although we didn't know it at the time. There would be more of them and bigger ones in the future, although it still remains debatable as to what or how much they ever accomplished.

We landed at Nha Trang and switched airplanes so we could take one back to the Philippines that needed maintenance more than what we had flown in on. While the aircraft switch was being accomplished, we collected the clothes that we'd left prior to being surprised by the assignment to the Vo Dat mission. We got a quick meal on base and then flew off to Clark as a deadhead crew in the back of the airplane. We landed at 1:45 in the morning. It had been a 20 hour day, with seven and one half hours of flying time, including the trip back to Clark.

26 November: Two days after getting back to Clark, we flew a one day cargo haul to Cam Ranh Bay and then from there to Ubon in Thailand. Both bases were either equipped or being equipped with F-4 aircraft and personnel. From Ubon we returned to Clark — eight and a half hours of flying time in a 14 hour day. Three days after that, we flew round-trip from Clark to Da Nang and back. Six hours' flying time in a ten hour day.

Da Nang was one of the few U.S. bases which employed native Vietnamese to assist in the base cargo operations. There were four or five Vietnamese who would assist the loadmasters in pushing palletized cargo on and off the aircraft. Since Da Nang was one of our more frequent stopping places, we got to recognize these guys from one stop to another. The Vietnamese as a race are smaller and thinner than Americans and also have distinctive skin coloring and eyes which distinguish them from other Asian races. One of the Da Nang loaders was as tall as we were and had a lighter color and different eye characteristics than the other Vietnamese. We all noticed him and among ourselves figured he was a Chinese spy.

Three days after that, on 1 December, we left Clark at 9:30 in the morning and flew direct to the new marine base at Dong Ha, just about 10 miles south of the border between North and South Vietnam. The marines were taking over responsibility for the northernmost corps (I Corps) in South Vietnam. To get into Dong Ha, we flew up the coast from Da Nang some 60 miles. When we hit the large river which sat just south of the Demilitarized Zone, or DMZ, we turned due west. The runway at Dong Ha was virtually east-west in orientation, so there was very little deviation from the inbound heading to landing. The terrain all around this coastal area of I Corps was flat as a pancake, broken only by very low tree lines or rice paddies.

We flew two sorties from Dong Ha to Da Nang and back, hauling cargo and people, and then returned to Clark at 8:00 P.M. — eight hours' flying time in a 12 hour day. The U.S. buildup, now including a large marine contingent in the Northern I Corps, was continuing countrywide.

Once back at Clark, we learned of the new change in our own future status. When we had come to Clark in early October, there had been talk of the USAF sending a C-130 wing to Asia permanently as part of the Vietnam buildup. There had been plenty of rumors as to the location of the wing and which wing it was going to be. While we were on our two month TDY at Clark, the final decision had been made, partly on the results of our good ORI showing at Pope during the summer, that our Wing at Langley was the one to be moved to Southeast Asia.

The Wing would be split up into two separate two-squadron flying units. Two of the squadrons would be located at Clark and could bring their families with them for a two year tour. The other two squadrons and the Wing headquarters would be located in the southern Philippines at the bare base location on Mactan Island. Personnel at Mactan would serve a one year (13 month) tour without families. The choice of which base to go to was left up to each individual. In addition to the three squadrons in our Wing at Langley, additional personnel from another C-130B wing at Forbes Air Force Base in Kansas would be joining us to fill out the new four squadron alignment.

The first of the permanent personnel at Clark were now arriving on base as our replacements. We would go back to Langley for two months to celebrate the holidays and get our personal affairs in order and then come back and join a unit at Clark or Mactan. In the next few days, one or two aircraft from Langley landed at Clark bringing crews that would be stationed there for the next three years.

The last night at Clark, Captain Dunn, Hal and I went to happy hour at the club, which was packed as usual. In the crowd were some of our fellow Langley crews who had come to replace us at either Clark or Mactan. We had a few drinks at the then bar rate of 10 or 25 cents while trading stories of what was changing in Southeast Asia and what was going on back at Langley.

After a few drinks, we paired up with a newly arrived crew from our squadron for dinner. We'd been in the same unit for over a year and knew each other by name only. We had never spent very much time together, as we were in head to tail rotations. We were both relatively young crews. Their pilot was a year or two younger than Dunn and had always been an airlift pilot, whereas Dunn had earlier been a fighter pilot. In age, the copilot and navigator were within a year of Hal and me and we all had very similar backgrounds. We got along well.

We traded small talk as we sat at one of the tables in the dining room. Each table had an Oriental bowl with a candle in it as the center decoration.

After we all sat down the waiter lit the candle as he took our orders. Rather, he tried to light the candle, but no matter how many matches he used or how he tilted the candle, he could not get it to light. Finally the waiter put our bowl on another table and took that table's bowl over to ours. He again tried the light routine, which again did not work. While he was attempting to set a blaze with the second bowl, the original one burst into flame on the other table. At the waiter's suggestion, we adjourned to the other table, guffawing and hungry.

After dinner all of the others adjourned to return to our trailers. The new crew was unpacking and John and Hal went to pack up for our return to the States. I lingered in the club and went back to the large teakwood main bar, which was now virtually deserted. I asked the barman where the prettiest waitress was that night and he told me she wasn't working. So I told him I was leaving in the morning and wanted his recommendation on a special departure drink. He immediately came up with a Timberwolf. So I had a Timberwolf, which turned out to be a one glass combination of three or four shots of different liquor with a hint of schnapps or a mixer in with them. It was the type of drink which tasted very good, very smooth, but dried your mouth out as you drank it.

While my mouth was drying, I engaged the nearest barfly in conversation and told him my sorry tale of leaving and then returning in two months to win the war from Mactan (I had opted for the bare-base, or "remote," one year tour). He listened so well that I ordered another Timberwolf for the both of us. The bartender rolled his eyes, as one Timberwolf was usually enough for any thinking person, assuming that he could still think.

I was just starting my second glass when the barfly informed me that, while he sympathized with my sorry tale of reassignment, he had one of his own. He was a sailor on his way from Clark to Manila Bay, where he would board a communications listening ship and spend a year floating in the South China Sea with only occasional liberties onshore where he could lose his sealegs and have a libation or two.

Just my luck. My last drink at the end of a two month rotation followed by a one year tour to the same locale with a war starting up and I got beaten in my attempt to gain sympathy from a swab who came up with a story more sorrowful than my own.

I finished the Timberwolf, called a cab and left. The next day we departed, going home by way of Japan, Midway Island, Hickham and Travis AFB in California. By crossing the international date line, we landed at Langley a day and a half after we left Clark. My second Vietnam tour was over.

Between Tours Again

We went home for two months to get our personal affairs in order, enjoy the yuletide holidays and prepare to go back to Southeast Asia for thirteen months. Once back at Langley, there was very little flying to do. Most of the Wing had already left, and the eight or ten aircraft which we had available were mostly getting repaired and refurbished before we took them back.

We flew once a week, mostly short flights to keep us airdrop qualified and, once or twice, a checkout flight for one of the aircraft which had just been worked on. Since a lot of us were going home to see families and friends before leaving on our year tour, the Wing arranged to combine training missions with flights to central locations around the country. These flights took us home for the holidays and then picked us back up on a prearranged schedule.

One day after the holidays, I was in the squadron doing a small bit of cleanup and paper shuffling when someone brought in the word that a C-130 from Clark had been lost in Southeast Asia. A few hours later it was confirmed that the aircraft belonged to our Wing and that one of the crews which had just arrived in Clark for their two year tour had been down at low altitude near Pleiku and had run into the side of a mountain. I asked about this story later and have never been sure that it was correct. Supposedly they ran into a small hill (at most, several hundred feet high) which we knew as Pussy Mountain. Pussy Mountain was a small volcano-like cone with one side collapsed. It was duly named for its similarity, from above, to a certain part of a woman's anatomy.

What did not ring true was that one of our crews would have been down at low level in that vicinity. The mountain was 20 or 30 miles southwest from Pleiku in a direction which they would not have been making approaches from. Unless they were on an airdrop mission (which was unlikely because we weren't flying those in-country at the time), there was no reason for the airplane to be down low in that area. But, unfortunately it was.

The entire crew was killed in the crash. It turned out that the crew was the same one that we had had dinner with on the night they had arrived at Clark and we were leaving. As soon as I found that out, I recalled the incident of the candle that repeatedly would not light as we sat down for dinner. I'm not naturally superstitious; but to this day, the hair stands up on the back of my neck whenever I'm in a restaurant and, for whatever reason, the table candle won't light.

When the holidays were over and the aircraft were ready, what remained of the Wing assembled and we set off for our Southeast Asia locations. On the morning that I was to depart, I awoke in the local Holiday Inn. I put on my flight suit, gathered all my bags, and took them into the motel lobby. While I ate breakfast, the counterman called me a taxi to take me to the base. When I'd finished eating, I walked to the counter, paid my room and breakfast bill, and then headed toward the front door and the waiting taxi.

A tourist family of four with two small children was eating breakfast and listening to my conversation with the front desk as I was leaving.

"Are you leaving on a long trip?" the counterman asked.

"One year's worth," I replied.

"Not to Vietnam, I hope."

"Yeah, I'm afraid so," I answered as I walked out with flight helmet bag in my hand.

"Good luck," he said.

Absolute silence reigned. I can still remember the family as they sat silently at the breakfast table and watched me leave. They had taken part in one small moment of the Vietnam War, which they were probably otherwise unimpacted by.

The One-Year Tour

January 1966

U.S. Troops in Vietnam	U.S. War Casualties (KIA)
200,000	2,000

Our flight arrived at Mactan Air Base, Philippines, at 10:30 on the morning of February 11, 1966, after a three day Pacific crossing which featured stops at Hawaii, Kwajalein and Guam. Mactan was only a two hour flight from Guam, so we were refreshed and ready when we arrived. We were met by a base and squadron welcoming committee complete with stained red carpet stretched from the airplane crew door to the waiting bakery van-like truck which took us to Squadron Operations.

It was pouring rain.

Squadron operations was two wooden buildings with a small sidewalk connecting them. Across the street was a similar set of buildings for the other squadron which occupied the base with us. In between and all over the rest of the viewable area, through the very heavy rain, was a sea of mud and deep puddles.

It took about an hour to check into the squadron, leave our flight bags in a storage area, get a mailbox slot and be told which tent was going to be our home for the next year. Then the van took us and our clothes bags to tent city.

Our new home was a wooden frame hut about 20 feet by 30. It was built on blocks so that it sat a foot above ground level. Inside, the wooden walls turned to chicken wire above the 3 foot level. From there the wooden and wire frame went up to eight or nine feet and the top of the structure was a large, thick denim roof (somewhat like a circus tent) which was stretched and tied down to outside ground supports. Seven or eight officers lived in each tent. Each had a metal cot with a thin army mattress and space alongside the bed for a trunk or other small storage container or piece of furniture. My bed was separated from my neighbor's by large metal standup lockers where we hung flight suits and clothes and stored other clothing items. The center of the tent was an aisle, so that a row of beds was on each side of it. Dunn, Thorson, and I all lived together. We were joined in our tent by Major Ned Kahn, of whom more will be said later, and Capt. Curt Civil. Both were in our same squadron back at Langley. There were two empty beds, which gave all of us a bit more room.

After stowing our clothes bags, we set off collectively for the dining hall, where we were told the new crews would be welcomed. The dining hall was about a block from our tent. We walked up through a row of about ten sim-

Early 1966 — Mactan Air Base in the rain.

ilar tents on each side of "the street." "The street" was a lane of mud well-trodden by numerous other inhabitants of tent city. You had to walk carefully lest your boots became stuck in one of the deeper holes in the mud and threatened to entrap you. Wooden sidewalks were being built on both sides of the street, but they hadn't gotten to our neighborhood yet.

It was still pouring rain.

The dining hall was an enlarged tent with the same wood and chicken wire construction as tent city, except that it had a metal roof. At the door we checked in. There was a small fee for the noon meal and we had special tickets as new arrivals. We got a steak dinner. The meal was served on a large metal plate divided into thirds like a cardboard picnic plate or a frozen food tray. The eating utensils were similarly metal. The tables in the dining hall had plastic red and white covers on them and the servers and waitresses were all local Filipinos. After the newness of our arrival and the lousy weather attending it, the steak dinner was very good. Later in the month, when all the new crews had arrived, meals in the dining hall decreased in quality for a week or so. It turned out that the steak dinners for all the new arrivals had wiped out the food budget for the month. For a few days afterward, dinner was a piece of bread you could soak in tomato sauce for the main course. But that only lasted until the next month, and then a new food budget came in.

After dinner, we all took our metal plates and silverware outside in the rain. Behind the dining hall were several large, oilcan-sized containers of boiling water. You first scraped your plate and utensils into an empty trash barrel and then dipped both plate and utensils into the boiling water to sterilize them before taking them home for the next meal.

We trudged back to our tent home in the pouring rain. We had nothing else to do for the rest of that day, but the following morning we had a briefing at the squadron about our new methods of operation. At home in Pennsylvania, when it rained as hard as it had been raining since we arrived in Mactan, my mother had a saying that it wouldn't rain long because either the force of the rain was too high or the drops were too big. Both conditions were true of the rain then falling, but evidently Pennsylvania rules did not apply in the Philippines. It rained steadily just as heavily for the next 3 days.

The community bathroom for showers and shaving consisted of one large room with 20 different showerheads and 40 sinks in it. Officers and enlisted men showered together, which astounded some of the people who had gone to Clark when they heard about it. The water in the shower room was desalinated and came out of a big tank mounted in the center of the base. It was always freezing.

Later in the tour, we would come back from a week or two in Vietnam

Early 1966 — Mess kit hanging in the tent.

and reenter the Mactan showers only to find someone (it was always only one) leisurely soaping up and enjoying a lengthy stay under the stream. *Aha*, we would think, *they've added hot water while we were gone.* Turning on the previously useless hot water handle on the shower we would first stick a hand under the shower nozzle to see if indeed there was some heat there. In the meantime, everyone else in the shower would break out laughing: "Fooled 'em again!"

Very much later, like very near the end of my one year tour, they did indeed add hot water. By that time we all had skin like rhinoceroses.

As our first day on Mactan drew to a close in the pouring rain, we undressed and got ready to crawl into our cots for the night. Just then, several crews walked by on their way from the officers' club. Several of them were drunk as hoot owls, one of whom lost his footing and fell with a great splash and a curse right into the thoroughly muddied street. We laughed and were glad it wasn't us.

Mactan Air Base consisted of a 10,000 foot runway built by the U.S. as a recovery base for B-52s should a war with the Russians ever occur and the B-52s needed to land when returning from a strike on the Soviet heartland. Thankfully, it never came to that. There was a two story wing headquarters, a small dispensary (any major health cases would be taken to Clark), a chapel, maintenance hangars for the aircraft, the dining hall, two separate tent cities for the officers and enlisted men, two squadron operations complexes facing each other near the flight line, a base exchange about the size of a hotdog stand, with nothing in it, and a combined officers'/enlisted club just then being built. Mactan was just barely above sea level and the earth was largely coral broken in places with clay and small areas of soil. On base, most of the pathways, trails and designated roads were now mud. There were a few wooden sidewalks and there were plans to fill them with gravel or paving sometime in the near future.

Away from the base there were several small communities on the island. The largest was Lapu Lapu. Don't laugh, that was really its name. It had a boat landing where several ferries were available for the 30 minute ride to Cebu City, which was the second biggest city in the Philippines after Manila. Mactan was regarded by the air force as an "isolated" tour, which was the reason that the tour length was one year. Isolated meant that your family was not with you and you lived in a tent city. The base did not have a BX, commissary, hospital, or any of the other amenities which existed at Clark. But if you had to be isolated, being 30 minutes from Cebu was not all that bad.

Initially, the way to get around Mactan was to hire a pedicab, which consisted of a seat for two and a bicycle peddler providing the motion. Later there would be cabs, and many of the crews bought motorbikes, mostly Hondas which we could have someone buy in Japan and bring back on an empty 130.

Four days after we arrived, we were put on our first in-country shuttle of the tour. We had heard all about the new rules from the crews which had come to Mactan in November. Most operations now were flown out of our Wing's operations at Tan Son Nhut in Saigon. Crews stayed downtown in hotels or rented barracks and rotated back to Mactan after two weeks. The flying day for these crews had been 14 hours instead of the 12 we used to fly; and flights now went on around the clock, where previously we had flown mostly days.

As soon as we arrived, the old crews, who were already pretty tired of the routine, felt that we would take up some of the slack and that things would ease off. Wrong. As soon as we arrived and increased the number of crews and airplanes available, the flying day in-country went to 16 hours.

15 February 1966: We stumbled out of our cots at three in the morning, went to the shower room to shave (at least it wasn't still raining) and then caught the squadron crew van, which took us to squadron operations. We had a coffee, collected our flight bags, .38 pistols for in-country duty, and were briefed on our two week tour, the weather, and our planned itinerary for the day.

By five o'clock we were off the ground and on our way to Clark. We were the only crew on the airplane, although usually the daily plane which left Mactan for in-country carried several crews. We landed at Clark two hours later after over-flying the southern Philippines and Manila Bay.

We had one pallet to offload at Clark and then took on a full load of pallets as our outbound cargo. We ate breakfast at the flight line snack bar at Clark and rechecked the weather before filing our flight plan for in-country. This would be our standard operation for going in-country. It was almost always through Clark, and flight times and procedures became routine. Clark was always overloaded with cargo that had been brought in by strategic aircraft and commercial flights. They would offload there and we would pick up the loads and take them and a lot of people into Vietnam and Thailand.

We crossed the South China Sea in the usual three hours and landed at Cam Ranh Bay. Cam Ranh was now much bigger and had a larger building effort underway, both on the flight line and in the living and support areas nearby. Plenty of metal and wooden hangars and facilities were going up everywhere, and there were many more people than had been there three months previously.

From Cam Ranh, we took some air force personnel to Bien Hoa. From there we had a short 15 minute flight to close our day at Vung Tau. We landed at Vung Tau at ten minutes after five. We were going to operate out of Vung Tau rather than Tan Son Nhut because of construction in the C-130 parking area at Tan Son Nhut.

Vung Tau had been a weekend vacation resort for the French during their time in Vietnam, and now it had resumed that activity. At the base operations counter, they told us to go downtown and we'd have rooms waiting in one of the old resort hotels which had now been taken over by the U.S. The army ran activities in Vung Tau, and when the crew van dropped us off downtown we found out that we really had no rooms. The town was filled with army types in all varieties of time off, from leave to weekend pass to

AWOL (Absent Without Leave). The hotel told us to go up the street a block to one of the civilian hotels, which we did.

The recommended hotel was actually an old house with several rooms spread over three floors. Baths were shared on each floor by the people staying on that floor and there were probably 20 or more people staying in the place. We checked in, changed clothes and then went back to the resort to get something to eat. We had a five o'clock get-up again the next morning, and after we ate we went back to the hotel to get some sleep.

We each had a room to ourselves with a mosquito-netted bed in it. We got to bed early just as the sun was going down. Shortly after that, we began to hear increased numbers of people — men and women — walking and talking in the hallways and stairs outside of our rooms. This seemed to go on continually; then there were lights in those areas going on and off. Once or twice someone banged on my door or tried to enter my room. None of us got very much sleep. In the morning we compared notes and concluded that we had just spent our first and last night in a Vietnamese whorehouse.

By prior arrangement over the phone, the crew van came and got us at six o'clock A.M. and we proceeded out to the air base. Our support for daily flights out of Vung Tau came from a small ALCE that was there to control the C-7 Caribous that normally flew out of Vung Tau. The Caribou was a small, two engine turboprop that was owned by the army. It had a 3 man crew and carried two pallet equivalents for a cargo load.

There were two different caribou outfits at Vung Tau, and one of them was Australian. We were the only C-130 there at the time. The Aussies had a small contingent supporting the war and maintained a reputation, much as they appear to have done in all wars, of a loose disciplined but highly enthusiastic force. As we stood at the counter on this particular early morning to get our flight orders and file for the day, one of the Aussie crews was doing the same. There was no difference in the procedure and we were going through the same routine simultaneously.

Now, it was customary in our outfits, when available, that each crew member got a 2-ounce bottle of whiskey at the end of a flight day from the ALCE personnel. We had gotten one yesterday when we checked in prior to going downtown. We were really surprised, however, that after the Aussies had filed their daily flight plan and were about to exit the ALCE, the controller behind the desk reached under the counter and handed them a fifth of Bourbon. They took it, laughed and walked on out to begin their flying day. We stood there, openmouthed. I never did find out what they did with the bottle, or whether or not that was their normal procedure.

19 February: We left Vung Tau at 8:30 for the short flight to Tan Son

Nhut. We offloaded a pallet and then went into the new C-130 operations building that had come into being while we were home in the States. It was a two story, rectangular, wood and metal building. The operations staff manned the second story and did their load, flight, schedule and maintenance planning there. We never went up to the second floor. The ground floor had a bathroom, crew waiting area with some couches and chairs and a large bar-like desk in the front where we got our daily flight schedule and logged in and out. The C-130 parking and loading area was directly in front of the C-130 ops building. The parking/loading ramp was also just in front of the taxi-way to the main runway.

On this day, we were going to fly a base inspection mission with no load on the airplane. John Dunn got to be a spectator for the day as the in-country wing commander took over the piloting, accompanied by a flight examiner who was going to give him his semi-annual flight check during the day's flying. Our first stop was a new field in the North of Vietnam called Khe Sanh. As we flew upcountry towards Khe Sanh we could see that there were many fires raging everywhere. At first we thought that they might have been the result of air strikes; but gradually it became clear that Vietnamese farmers were clearing their fields by burning off the ground cover.

It took us two hours to get in the vicinity of Khe Sanh. The weather was clear and we could easily make out this laterite strip that ran east to west on the top of a low plateau. To the east was a large valley that sat several hundred feet lower than the airstrip. To the west, and quite close to the strip, was a forested mountain range that rose steeply.

We had the coordinates of the strip and several radio frequencies that were supposed to allow us to talk to the people on the ground. But the frequencies were wrong or their radios were broken or turned off, because we couldn't talk to anyone. We could see people alongside the runway with a few vehicles and they waved to us as we flew by; but we couldn't talk to them.

The purpose of our visit was to ascertain that this strip was suitable for C-130B operations and we couldn't do that without landing. Since we couldn't talk to anyone, we weren't sure of how long the runway was. The two pilots guessed about it and I tried to figure it out roughly by timing our passage down the runway in the air and then mathematically combining the time and our ground speed as indicated on our Doppler. At best, we were operating on a big estimate; but we all agreed the runway was between 3 thousand and 4 thousand feet long. Plenty of length for an empty C-130B. Still, we weren't quite sure.

Col. David Lewis, who was flying the plane, decided to minimize any errors in our calculations. When a C-130 lands, the pilot puts the turbo-

1966 — A C-123 in the loading area at Khe Sanh (from the collection of Fred W. Straub).

props into reverse shortly after the plane is solidly on the ground and the pilot is sure of being in control of the landing, thus slowing the aircraft in conjunction with the brakes. In this instance, Lewis reversed the props while we were still 3 to 5 feet off the ground. What followed was the hardest landing I ever sat through. We stopped flying and crashed into the ground vertically. All of us were slammed into our seats. We easily stopped within the length of the runway. We were the first C-130 into Khe Sanh; but we wouldn't be the last. (Others claim they had been in Khe Sanh earlier, but those claims may relate to C-130As or marine C-130s, which might have conducted their own base inspection in a similar fashion.)

We turned around on the runway and then taxied back to meet the base personnel who had been watching us. They hastened to tell us that they had been sure the runway was long enough, but had to wait for a verification flight (which was us) to prove it. While they and Col. Lewis discussed the base's qualifications, I set off on a tour of the runway and the base. There wasn't much to the base. A single story operations building adjoined the runway at about the midpoint, and that was about it. The remainder of the plateau on which the runway sat had been cleared and stood out in the blazing red laterite and clay which marked much of Vietnam. I walked to the eastern end of the runway and stood on the edge of the plateau. Several hundred feet below was nothing but dense green jungle. After a few minutes of looking at it and out into the vast valley beyond, I began to think about what kind of target I made to anyone on the forest floor below. Standing on the brink of the steep bank and with the clear blue sky behind me, I could be a chip shot for someone like a Viet Cong lurking below. With that in mind, I stepped back and retreated to the airplane.

We stayed at Khe Sanh for 45 minutes. Col. Lewis agreed with the base residents that it was suitable for C-130 ops, but he cautioned that they needed to add overruns to both ends of the runway and put taxi stripes down for the parking area. We took off to the west and proceeded to another new airstrip north of Bien Hoa. We only overflew the second place, however, as the runway was still being worked on, the approaches had to be cleared of trees and there were vehicles all over the strip and its parking area. At this location we did have contact with the ground personnel over an established radio frequency so that all these suggested changes were passed on verbally.

On return to Tan Son Nhut, Col. Lewis and the flight examiner were dropped off and we flew back to Vung Tau. We had flown for eight and a half hours in an eleven hour day. That night we ate at the dining hall on the airbase and slept in the aircraft on passenger seats which we put down along the sides of the plane. We never spent another night in downtown Vung Tau, preferring the quiet and safety of the base to the pleasures of another night in a whorehouse trying to get some sleep. The aircraft was hot. The seats were a very hard bed and we had to wash and shave in the men's room at base operations, but it was better than the downtown alternative.

The next day we left Vung Tau at seven in the morning and flew to Tan Son Nhut, where we were assigned the mission of flying a passenger shuttle for the day. In rapid succession we flew to and left Cam Ranh Bay, Nha Trang, Qui Nhon, An Khe and then back to Tan Son Nhut. All of the places that we stopped at were then involved in a construction or expansion role, as the number of U.S. troops at each of them, and in-country in general, was rapidly increasing. We then flew a round-trip from Tan Son Nhut to Pleiku before returning to Vung Tau for another night in the plane. We had done six hours of flying time in a fourteen hour crew day.

This mission, or one very much like it, was a standard daily flight schedule for the Tan Son Nhut-based shuttle. One (or several) C-130s a day would be rigged for passengers only and then fly a counterclockwise (east to west circle) or clockwise route to all the U.S. bases, dropping off and picking up

U.S. troops at each stop. Since there was no cargo to on- and offload, time on the ground was short at each stop. Flying the passenger shuttle was much like a peacetime airline job, except for the absence of stewardesses. Since it was usually finished in less than a twelve hour day (our last trip to Pleiku was extra), it was one of the better missions to appear on the daily Tan Son Nhut mission schedule.

The following day we returned to Tan Son Nhut before nine o'clock A.M. and embarked on a cargo haul for the day. First we went to new location: Kham Duc in the Western Highlands, some two hours from Saigon. If Khe Sanh had been an interesting place to visit, Kham Duc was more so. It sat several hundred feet high, almost on the Laotian border west of Da Nang surrounded by nothing but jungle.

The runway ran east to west and was located directly against a forested mountain that rose on its north side. The runway was just a long slender laterite strip with no taxiway beside it. Turnarounds were made on the runway and then a plane taxied halfway back up it and turned 90 degrees before taxiing a further quarter mile to the offload area, which consisted of a small one story building, a forklift and a few tents.

What really made Kham Duc interesting, however, was the fact that two-thirds down the runway there was a hole in it, as if an artillery round had landed and blown the surface away. The hole, according to the residents, was not a shell hole at all, but the result of that part of the soil collapsing and running downhill. On landing and taxi, a plane had to swerve around the hole while still staying on the runway and not running a wing tip into a tree or the high earth bank on the north side.

The combination of the small runway, small base camp and remote jungle location, together with the very close proximity of the runway to the rapidly rising and dense jungle made your first thought on Kham Duc to be, *Good God, when is Charlie going to overrun this place?* Like Khe Sanh, Kham Duc's principal reason for existing was to serve as a listening and reconnaissance post with regard to Viet Cong operations in Laos and the western jungle along the Ho Chi Minh Trail, which the communists used to supply their forces further south in South Vietnam. In talking to the Special Forces troops stationed there, we found out that the airfield had served as a remote fighter operations base for the Japanese during World War II. It had also been noted as a tiger hunting resort for both French and Vietnamese high officials during earlier years.

We offloaded our cargo at Kham Duc, taxied back onto the runway, swerved around the hole in it and soared off to the east and Da Nang, which was a short flight away. We were delayed getting into Da Nang because of low clouds near the field and heavy air traffic. We had to approach from out over the ocean in conjunction with several other planes, including air force fighters and navy and marine transports. Da Nang was now a very busy place compared to the somewhat sleepy old operation we had first seen just eight months previously. There was an air force F-4 fighter wing in Da Nang now and increased navy and marine activities offshore and in the I Corps region north of Da Nang. All of this heightened air activity contributed to congestion and parking delays in and near Base Operations and the passenger offload area.

We finally got a cargo load onboard, together with a small number of passengers, and set off for one more new stopping location. Dong Ha was the marine base just short of the DMZ up in I Corps. As we approached the DMZ and river we lowered our altitude so as not to appear as a target on North Vietnamese radar screens and turned west, flying along the river until Dong Ha was sighted. There was a profusion of vehicles and tents all around the small Base Operations building and aircraft control tower. The marines were moving into the I Corps area in earnest. We left Dong Ha and flew directly home to Vung Tau for another night in the aircraft. We had flown 4½ hours in a 13 hour day and had seen two new bases in the process.

The following day was almost a repeat of the day before, except we did not return to Kham Duc. We were up about six and took off at eight on another passenger run, visited Tan Son Nhut, Dong Ha, Da Nang, Pleiku, Tan Son Nhut and then back to Vung Tau: Five hours of flight time in a fourteen hour day.

The next day, 21 February, started in much the same fashion. We were up at 6:00 and in flight by 8:30. On a cargo mission for the day, we stopped at Tan Son Nhut, Bien Hoa, Da Nang; and then from Da Nang we flew a half hour due south to the new base at Chu Lai. Chu Lai was a marine fighter location with varied types of aircraft and frequent visits from navy aircraft. It was another major aircraft location in the rapidly expanding U.S. buildup. We left Chu Lai after a short, 30 minute stop and flew east over the South China Sea for Clark. Our first in-country shuttle of the new tour was over after only six days. We landed at 9:30 at night with 6 hours of flight time in a 15 hour day. After a rapid shower and clothes change, we left our overnight trailer and adjourned to the officers' club.

This first shuttle was indicative of the changing pace and size of the increasing U.S. activity in Southeast Asia. There were now U.S. bases all over South Vietnam, with the army dominating in the lower three corps regions and the marines running the northernmost I Corps. There were large and constant calls for airlift to move people, equipment and vehicles throughout the country. As a result, we were putting more aircraft into shuttle operations from a variety of bases. Our crews and aircraft were now operating on a 16 hour crew day, with continuous 24 hour operations out of Tan Son Nhut. The next day, we left Clark in the early afternoon and flew direct to Mactan.

After a one day rest we were assigned to fly our first low-level training and airdrop mission at Mactan. Such missions were usually four hours long, beginning with a one hour low-level route that ended in a practice paratrooper or cargo airdrop. The airdrop load was simulated by a training bundle which weighed about 10 pounds, but was released from the aircraft and floated to earth with time and drift characteristics which resembled the real loads. We only got part way around the first route when an engine problem caused us to terminate the training and return to base. The very next day we were back on the road again: an 8:30 A.M. takeoff. We got to Clark at 10:30 and had lunch at the club, with a few drinks by the pool, before retiring early.

25 February: At two in the morning, we were off the ground and headed for Thailand with a load of palletized cargo and passengers. We flew across the East China Sea, over Da Nang and across the southern tip of Laos into Thailand — no more flying around the coasts of Vietnam and Thailand in order to get to the U.S. bases in Thailand. The first stop was Korat, where we were on the ground for an hour and then on to Bangkok. We landed in Bangkok at seven in the morning after a five hour flying time day. Our Wing now had a regular daily mission to fly cargo into and out of Thailand from Clark. Bangkok was the stopover point for the shuttle. There was usually one or two of our aircraft on the ground in Bangkok daily, waiting for crews to come out of crew rest, with two others in the air, one coming and one going.

We got a whole day off in Bangkok and revisited the gem stores, the hotsi bath and downtown restaurants. The following day, we took off on the outbound leg of the shuttle but had to immediately return and land after one of the engines began to act up.

Recently, one of the Wing's crews had had a night on the town in Bangkok and had failed to reset a circuit breaker in the aircraft before engine start the next morning. The circuit breaker had been pulled to stop an oil leak problem that had occurred on the previous flight, which had been flown by another crew. Had this crew reset the breaker, started engines and then repulled it, there would have been no problem. But, by not resetting the circuit breaker and attempting to start engines, they were effectively starting the engines with the oil system not functioning properly. In less than a minute, all four engines burned up.

Two hours after that, we were in the air again with a different aircraft. The load, once more, was a mix of cargo and mostly air force personnel. We spent about an hour on the ground at each stop letting people on and off at Takhli, Udorn and Da Nang before proceeding on to Clark, which we got to at midnight after a 16 hour crew day. The following day we were up at noon for the two hour flight back to Mactan.

When we got back, we found out that the reason we had been flying nearly every day since our arrival was because many of the other new crews that had joined the Wing needed theater and base indoctrinations before they could assume their flight duties. Since we had been in the theater previously and were flying the same aircraft that we had at Langley, we didn't need the training. Essentially, we had spent the last three weeks flying ours and other people's missions.

Most of the new Wing members were C-130 Troop Carrier trained veterans from a wing similar to ours that had been based in Kansas. With the buildup in Southeast Asia at a peak, they had become members of our Wing and shared our tents and crew spaces on an as-required basis. With their indoctrination now complete, they were patched into our crews as necessary and the then fully formed crews picked up some of the slack in the daily flight crew missions and shuttles. As a result, we got the next two weeks off from flying.

For one week, instead of flying, our crew divided up into day and night shifts and manned the flight operations counter at Squadron Operations. I pulled the night shift, while Hal and Capt. Dunn worked the days. Each night, I logged returning crews in, collected their weapons, told them as much as I knew about the forthcoming schedule and saw that our squadron van took them to their tents. Our loadmaster and flight engineer alternated driving the van on 12 hour shifts.

When we left Langley and the Wing split its personnel between Mactan and Clark, we got a number of new people into the squadron. Many of them had little or no previous C-130 or Tactical Airlift experience. A number had come from the Strategic Air Command, where they had been involved in nuclear operations and continual training flights in and out of their home base only. Several such officers were senior in rank to many of the more qualified airlifters who held the same rank. Accordingly, we had a number of new people in supervisory positions with whom we were not familiar. One was our new squadron commander.

The old commander had retired rather than make the move to Southeast Asia. The new commander was an ex-SAC type. He was about six feet, four inches tall and built like a lumberjack. What he had in brawn was more than made up for, however, in brain power. Of that, he had very little. It was said that every day when he walked from the squadron mailroom to the operations building he would hit his head on the wooden beam over the doorway into Ops. The door had been put in by Filipino building crews who may not have ever seen a man over six feet tall before we got there, but our leader forgot that every morning. Early on he was given the nickname "Big Stoop" from a character in the *Terry and the Pirates* comic strip. The name fit.

During the second week off, we got to tour Mactan Island for the first time. It had a variety of small villages along the dirt roads in and out of the main town and port at Lapu Lapu. The base sat in the center of the island. On the other side of it from the town was a nice sand beach, although the sea floor was sharp coral with virtually no surf. Mactan had a number of small neighborhood cafes and bars that, according to the natives, sat among "banana farms."

There were several thousand people who lived on the island, and the hourly ferries to Cebu City across the bay were usually full. Most of the population spoke very good English. By the time of our arrival, the local population had gotten used to the base and the American airmen who populated it. The crews who had come two months earlier than us remarked how they were first greeted with cries of, "Hey, Joe," as if they were World War II GIs. One airman lost his wallet on the way home after exiting the ferry, and the next day a local on a bicycle returned it to the base complete with all his money and cards still inside. The atmosphere was somewhat more wholesome than that found at many other U.S. base locations at the time.

The same could be said for Cebu City. Cebu was the second largest city in the Philippines, after Manila. It was a twenty minute ferryboat ride from Mactan. The ferry ride could sometimes be quite exciting or interesting. The ferries were large, flat bottomed vessels with canvas roofs. The passenger section had 40 people sitting on wooden slat seats around both sides of the center mounted engine. Since the ferries were usually very busy and safety regulations were near minimum, another 40 to 60 people stood in the center of the boat. Many of the passengers had chickens or other live creatures along with them. The boats rode about two feet above the surface of the bay, and in storms or choppy weather the seated passengers could get quite wet by the time the ride was over. It was something like a cheap variant of the log mill ride at Disneyland.

Downtown Cebu began at the harbor, which was dirty, busy and not a place to spend a lot of time. But only a short walk or cab ride brought you to the center of town, which featured restaurants, movies, bars, hotels and shops. There were no large department stores, shopping centers or anything that would remind you of a major American city, but it was relatively clean and safe.

Early 1966 — Mactan Harbor.

Our first night in town, Hal and I had dinner at a Chinese motif restaurant in the center of town. The restaurant was on the second floor of a building above a store. You rode an elevator to get to it. The tables were ringed around a dance floor and each table had an umbrella above it like a seaside resort. A rock and roll band played starting at about seven in the evening. The menu had about 200 different items on it, all Chinese and all described in English. We weren't too familiar with any of the entries. But none of them was too expensive, so we decided to each order five or so and then both of us would eat whatever looked good since they would certainly be small portions because the prices were so cheap. When the food was delivered, we discovered that each dish we had ordered came in a quantity suitable to feed a family. At least half of them were good. We felt like fools, as the table was jammed full of more food than we could have eaten if we had stayed there a week. Evidently, expensive dining wouldn't be much of a problem for us in Cebu. The Chinese restaurant became a favorite of ours and of many others from the base.

With our tour as duty crew over, and having had over a week to adjust to Mactan and complete some ground training, we were off again from Mactan to Clark. Having left Mactan early (9:30 A.M.), we were into Clark by 11:00; but we spent several hours at Clark waiting for a palletized load to be put on and a minor maintenance fix was made to one of the engine instruments. Neither action got done on time due to a variety of problems and miss-ordered parts. We finally went into crew rest at six o'clock in the evening.

The next morning we were up at four and flying out of Clark at six-thirty. We arrived in Da Nang at ten o'clock and spent two hours on the ground waiting for a forklift to get the pallets off of the aircraft. Da Nang was now very busy, with navy, marine and air force aircraft of all shapes and sizes moving in and out. From Da Nang, we returned to Clark and then proceeded south to Mactan, getting back at seven-thirty in the evening. What was to have been a short two day trip turned into a long two day trip due to maintenance and loading problems. The U.S. force buildup was continuing, but remained disjointed.

16 March: We left Mactan at 7:00 A.M. and landed at Clark at 8:30. In a replay of our previous trip, we spent four hours on the ground at Clark again waiting for a load. We finally left Clark just after noon and landed at Phan Rang at 3:30. Phan Rang was being developed as an F-4 base. It was about 20 minutes' flying time southwest of Cam Ranh Bay. We were on the ground at Phan Rang for an hour and then left for a one hour's flight to Tan Son Nhut to start another round of shuttling.

While at Phan Rang, we had been joked with by the ground controller on the radio. The airplane we had taken from Mactan was one that had been recently painted in camouflage by air force orders. The green and brown, random patterned camouflage was painted on the top of the plane and the underside was grey. We were never sure if the planes were supposed to be camouflaged against an enemy looking down at it from above (the North Vietnamese had no aircraft in the South), or the Viet Cong shooting up. At any rate, painting the C-130 fleet cost a small fortune and took most of a year to complete.

We were evidently the first camouflaged C-130 to land at Phan Rang. When we cleared the runway and called for parking and load information, the reply was, "This is Phan Rang ground. C-130 on the ground and calling for parking, please identify yourself. I can't see you. Are you invisible?"

After we had checked into C-130 Ops at Tan Son Nhut and left our bags, we called for a cab to take us to our assigned quarters in the Globe Hotel. The Globe was almost in the center of town, on one of the main wide thoroughfares. The hotel was six stories tall, had its own restaurant, bar and snack bar and had reasonably comfortable rooms, each of which had fans for cooling.

The family that owned the Globe also owned the Mercedes franchise in Saigon. They lived on the uppermost floor of the building and were frequently seen moving about the hotel's corridors, but they didn't mix with the cus-

Late 1966 — The author on a scenic Saigon terrace.

tomers. They had several children, including a "cowboy" son, who sped around town on a motorbike, and a teenage daughter who seemed to specialize in the briefest of underwear beneath her transparent ao-di. The other notable resident of the Globe was a Pakistani or Indian who spoke pidgin English and doubled as the doorman and baggage carrier. He was much larger and darker than the Vietnamese and easily the hardest working member of the hotel staff. To us, he became "Pakistan Pete."

A military carpool cab came and got us the next morning about seven and we were back on base in half an hour. We got our first mission of the day, filed the flight plan, checked the weather and then went for breakfast at a small, igloo shaped metal hut which had been added about 100 yards behind 130 Ops. There, with paper plates and cups, we got a coffee and a ham and egg breakfast. After breakfast we walked back to Ops and out to the aircraft.

The new snack bar facility we had eaten breakfast in went unnamed for some time. There was, however, a small stream that flowed near it, oozing out of the laterite clay in the adjoining cargo storage area behind 130 Ops. One day someone with time to spare put a small, ground-staked, hand-painted sign proclaiming the stream "Shit Creek." The dining facility then quickly became the "Shit Creek Snack Bar."

The C-130s parked right in front of the Airlift Operations building in eight parking spaces. The cargo storing area was between those parking places and the snack bar we had just walked from. There was constant traffic here of people, forklifts, airplanes and vehicles. The planes were backed and driven in and out with the aid of wing walkers and ground personnel who used hand and light signals to tell us that the airplane was clear on all sides. The vehicles, forklifts and people were on their own to avoid being run over or running into each other. It was hectic and especially so at night or when it rained; but I don't remember any accidents.

In my previous tours, Tan Son Nhut had large areas of the base where there was no activity or aircraft parking. Now, virtually everywhere on base was a site for activity of some sort. There were air force units and joint service units and Vietnamese units all operating on base. There were also reconnaissance aircraft (F-101s) and C-130s based there and transiting strategic airlift (C-141s, C-135s, C-124s) in addition to the commercial flights which were bringing new people into the theater. The base was a beehive of activity 24 hours a day. The permanent aircraft all parked in spaces were separated from each other by fences of corrugated metal so that a single Viet Cong rocket or mortar round would not set off chain reaction explosions if it hit one aircraft.

Mid 1966 — The author and Pakistan Pete.

Another thing which distinguished daily life in Vietnam from similar activity in the Philippines was the presence in every men's room of written or carved sayings and pictures in every toilet stall. In World War II, there were cartoons of "Kilroy was here." Now there were cartoons, sexual drawings of various parts of women's anatomy, poems and jokes. Eventually, these scribblings got to be so numerous that places like the officers' club painted the walls of the stalls in the restroom and added a large piece of paper toweling to each stall so that the doodlers could continually make new products without defacing the permanent walls. That didn't work either. The walls still got written on.

From Tan Son Nhut, we flew into the highlands and landed at Kontum, where we offloaded people and cargo. As we flew north on the way to Kontum, we were warned to avoid flying in a "hot area" just off to the right of our flight path that would be active in ten minutes and would remain so for a period of 30 minutes. The weather was clear below us but overcast above. Right on time, ten minutes after the warning we could look off to the east near the Cambodian border, and down through the overcast about ten miles distant came a load of bombs. The hot area was for a B-52 drop. We could see the bombs drop through the clouds above and impact in a straight line, but we never did see the planes that dropped them.

Kontum was a provincial capital north of Pleiku, and our flight was in support of the continuing U.S. Army buildup in the Central Highlands. After an hour on the ground, we flew two hours back to Tan Son Nhut, where we spent two more hours putting a new cargo load on the aircraft for Ban Me Thout. It was then one hour of flight to Ban Me Thout, one hour on the ground off and on-loading. From Ban Me Thout, we flew for an hour and offloaded some Vietnamese cargo and passengers at Vung Tau. We flew back to Tan Son Nhut and were done after a 12 hour day.

The following evening we went on the night shift. We rode from the hotel to the officers' club in late afternoon, ate at the Club and then went on to 130 Ops and did our flight planning. We left Tan Son Nhut at 7:20 in the evening and flew to Da Nang, where it again took us two hours to offload cargo due to loading problems. Even at night, Da Nang was jammed. Our offload area at Da Nang was directly in front of the small ALCE and Base Operations area, but on all sides of it and its rectangular taxiing area in and out were large and small aircraft jammed together. Some of the smaller navy transients were parked under the wing of the large USAF transports that were also spending the night. We flew back to Tan Son Nhut, landing just after midnight, and that was the end of our flying for the day.

En route to Saigon, we were flying at 20,000 feet on a clear night. Ahead of us on the route was a C-141 strategic airlifter which was probably carrying pallets of stateside loaded cargo in Tan Son Nhut. Suddenly, the night sky lit up directly above the C-141 with several bright pops much like fireworks displays. Quickly after that, we heard the C-141 call into Saigon control and report that they had just been fired on by enemy antiaircraft artillery (AAA), or Surface to Air Missiles (SAMs).

In actuality, what had happened was that the C-141 had been over flown by a reconnaissance aircraft returning from a mission over the north. The recce pilots delighted in releasing their unused photo flash flares over lazy and sleepy airlift crews. Lest the report be accepted as true and restrictions get placed on airlift operations in South Vietnam, we immediately called Saigon approach and asked them to cancel the enemy actions claim and chalk it up to accidental friendly action.

There were 12, maybe 14, C-130s operating on the shuttle at any one time and 20 or 23 crews flying the airplanes, together with 2 crews which rotated for desk duties. There were, similarly, some 18 missions scheduled each day, roughly one every one and a half hours. The usual method of assigning crews to missions was one of the worst ever hatched by the mind of mortal man, but it was an attempt to be fair to all concerned. All of the planes flew in the daytime providing that they were in-commission. Then about half of them would fly at night while the other half underwent maintenance to be ready for the next day.

A new airplane and crew, or two crews, arrived every day and an equal number went home every day to Clark or Mactan. The new crew usually got into Tan Son Nhut about four or five in the afternoon after a direct flight from Clark or one stopover somewhere in-country. That meant that they got the first daytime mission the next day, usually a seven or eight o'clock morning takeoff. Whatever time they got back in the afternoon and had finished their flying day, they would get credit for 12 hours of off duty time to eat, get to and from the hotel, and sleep before returning the next day and taking up the next scheduled mission. That meant that ideally your "day" was continually slipping forward one or two hours during the two weeks you were on the shuttle.

After about a week of flying every day, a crew would get one day off and then find that their day had completely reverted from daytime to the night shift. It was almost impossible for your body to adjust to this schedule, no matter how fair it was intended to be. Being human, you wanted to start and stop work and sleep at approximately the same time every day. Under the airlift rotating start program that was impossible. The day to night transition was particularly difficult. Because of heat, noise and other nonstandardized distractions, it was almost impossible to stay awake for an extra half day so you'd be so tired you could sleep in the daytime and be ready for that first night flight. Most people couldn't accomplish that trick and so started out on the first night more tired than they would normally have been. And then each night following it got that much worse.

The hours between three and five in the morning were the worst. Only owls are meant to be awake at that time of day and your body always seemed to want to go to sleep in the hours just before dawn. The aircraft had a small galley near the cockpit where coffee and water could be heated in metal containers. Both the coffee and the water were usually several days old, but a lot of the stale, iron tasting coffee got consumed on the night shift.

Many of the aircraft scheduled for the next day's daytime missions were broken and in maintenance. The aircraft we had flown was in good condition, but there wasn't a full load to be taken to any one base at the time, so we got the rest of the night off, while the in-commission aircraft was kept for the day's daylight flights and possibly higher priority missions.

We got the next day off and spent the afternoon touring downtown Saigon. We stopped in a bar and bought a Saigon Tea (which was colored water) from one of the bar girls, who babbled pidgin English and tried to look sexy in her very slim, transparent ao-dai and French underwear. Then we walked the main street, had a beer at the previous French hotel, with its sidewalk café adorning the corner of the main downtown street, and finished the evening in the U.S. officers' club atop the Hotel Rex.

The Rex was open to all services. You could get a real U.S. steak, which you barbecued yourself at bargain prices. One additional feature of eating at the Rex was that the dining room had a large open air porch which looked out over the west side of Saigon. The scenery wasn't that great, but on the outskirts of the city, which weren't too far away, you could watch the new U.S. C-47 gunships shoot up large areas. Such a gunship was called "Puff the Magic Dragon" (after a then popular folk song). They had so much firepower (3 mini-guns, each of which fired 6,000 rounds per minute) that, even firing every sixth or tenth round as an accuracy measuring tracer, their line of fire looked like a laser beam. We sat and ate our steaks and watched the gunship show, which was almost continuous. Once again you had to wonder what kind of war this was where the gunships were that active every night right outside the capital, while we were bringing in and supplying forces all over the countryside.

The C-47 gunship was the original in a line that kept getting bigger, with more guns and constantly improved targeting and firing options. The C-47, which was largely a visual targeting and aiming gunship, was replaced by the larger C-119, which was up-gunned and also began the process of mechanizing both finding targets and shooting at them. By the end of the war, there were C-130s flying the gunship missions not only around cities in the south, but also over the Ho Chi Minh Trail. The 130s were up-gunned yet again and even included a 105 millimeter (mm) howitzer.

Later in my career, I flew with a pilot who had flown the C-130 gunships. He told of one night over the Trail when they had flown all night with their night scopes and automated targeting equipment but hadn't seen one target worth shooting at. Accordingly, when the time came for them to leave their orbit and return to base, they still had the initial round of shells in all the guns. Not wanting to land with the guns loaded, the procedure was to fire off the basic rounds and then return empty to home base.

On this occasion, they chose one of the loaders in the rear of the aircraft to designate where they should fire the rounds. He randomly picked a radial and distance from the aircraft and all guns were then fired there. Miraculously the entire night lit up from the impact of the guns and the simultaneous secondary explosions which they had ignited in the dark jungle below. Purely by luck, they had hit an NVA storage area after a night of having found no targets with the latest hi-tech sensors and aimers.

Another story relating to the gunships involved the navigator who fell out of one. This also occurred later in the war. When the gunships took up station, they orbited depressurized at altitudes under ten thousand feet. As part of the depressurization, as well as the need to clear the plane of smoke from the firing guns, the forward crew door was also left opened. The crew door was directly in front of the stairs leading from the cockpit to the rear of the airplane. The steps were bordered by tiers of electrical equipment, most of which had hooks and wires extending from the ends facing the stairs. Crew members wore chest pack parachutes as a safety measure in case they took ground fire during the mission.

This particular navigator needed to go from the cockpit to the rear of the airplane to use the urinary tube located there. He got on the interphone and informed the pilot and the rest of the crew that he was going to do so. On his way down the stairs, however, his chest parachute came in contact with one of the hooks on the electrical equipment trays and the parachute opened. He could not stop the silk from unraveling before it got caught in the slipstream from the open door at the bottom of the stairs. He was, accordingly, pulled out of the airplane by the deploying parachute. One logical question is how he managed to miss impacting with the propellers on the left side, but he did.

The next thing anyone knew, the pilot got an interphone call: "Joe, can you hear me?"

"Sure," said the pilot, recognizing the voice, "where are you?"

"I'm down here. Down in the jungle," came the reply.

In short order, the missing navigator informed the pilot how he had fallen out of the airplane and that he was on the ground below talking over his emergency rescue radio. It is said that on the floor at the bottom of the steps one could see fingerprints and fingernail slashes in the tar and shingled panels just inside where the front door latched. At any rate, the pilot called Air Rescue and gave them the point of the C-130s orbit. They pulled the navigator out of the jungle in the dark and he was back at his home base before the rest of the crew had completed their mission.

20 March: We were up at one in the morning and rode a van out to the base, ate breakfast in the snack bar, filed and were airborne at 3:45. We hit Da Nang, and then Qui Nhon. By the time we left Da Nang at seven in the morning, it was light and we then stopped at another new installation, Tuy Hoa.

Tuy Hoa was an army installation that sat in a large plain on the coast halfway between Qui Nhon and Nha Trang. There were eventually two airfields there, Tuy Hoa North and South. A major road, Highway 78, ran from Tuy Hoa to Pleiku and the Central Highlands, so the base was the eastern end of an in-country logistic net.

On the night/early morning shuttle, all of the loads were cargo so that the ground time at each stop was an hour or more minimum. From Tuy Hoa we flew to Cam Ranh Bay, dropped off two pallets and went home to Tan Son Nhut. We landed at 1:30 in the afternoon and our first night/day was over. The next day, March 21, we flew out of Tan Son Nhut three hours later than the previous day, at seven in the morning. We carried cargo to Nha Trang, picked up some cargo there and flew it back to Tan Son Nhut and then carried some more to the army at An Khe. We flew back to Tan Son Nhut and our day was over at three in the afternoon.

Since it was early in the day, we journeyed to the officers' club to have a few drinks before dinner and our return to the hotel. At the bar in the club, John Dunn met an old fighter jock friend of his who was stationed in Saigon and was flying F-101s on reconnaissance missions. The pilot and John had flown F-100 ground attack aircraft together and now both were "new guys" in different aircraft and totally different missions. The recon pilot was ecstatic about what a great aircraft he was in and how good the missions were.

The F-101 was originally designed as a fighter and bomber escort for high altitude, high speed flight. Once it got to its operational altitude of 50,000 feet or more, the F-101 could go supersonic and was virtually untouchable by any aircraft below it. On reconnaissance photo missions they would fly fast, straight and level, take their pictures and go home. We had a few drinks and dinner together while the ex-fighter pilots traded jokes and war stories. Then Dunn and I called for our van and retired to the Globe for the rest of the evening.

The next day we were again off the ground at seven in the morning, but this time we didn't get very far. One engine started acting up as soon as we got airborne. We flew one loop in the Tan Son Nhut traffic pattern and then landed, out of commission for maintenance. We had flown all of 15 minutes.

Maintenance said they'd have us fixed in two hours, so we retired to the C-130 Ops building and read the girlie magazines and newspapers which littered the waiting room while the plane was being worked on. The two hours turned into four and then into six.

About noon, while we sat waiting, some six or eight crews came in from an airdrop mission in the delta, south of Saigon. Several of the crews were from Mactan. They were all laughing and described the mission as an operational disaster or comedy with regard to airlift procedures. (All my later attempts to identify this mission as part of a ground operation or code-worded sweep have failed. Nor have I ever heard anyone else comment on it later. It may have been a training drop in support of the ARVN paratroopers.) Whoever planned the mission miscalculated the distance needed for the aircraft to slow to drop speed from en route speed and low level flight. On the first pass they couldn't drop because their airspeed over the drop zone (DZ) was too high. They then flew a racetrack over the DZ, which eliminated all chance of surprise crucial to a contested airdrop.

When the time came for the Vietnamese paratroopers to stand up from the seats and line up at the aircraft's jump doors, they were so short in comparison to U.S. troops that they and their long back chutes and equipment packs kept catching on the seats as they walked forward. Because of discrepancies like these, each plane had to do multiple racetracks over the DZ in order to get all their troopers out. In a final glitch, on the last pass a rain shower broke out and the drop had to be completed with individual aircraft dodging clouds.

One final humorous sidelight involved a navigator who kept asking what his drop score had been. On stateside training missions, after a drop a ground controller on the DZ would radio the formation and tell each aircraft the direction and distance that their drop had landed relative to the desired Impact Point (IP) on the DZ. Now, mistaking training procedures for reality, this navigator wanted someone on the ground in hostile territory, in a rainstorm, in the midst of a badly botched operation, to give him his score. "Give yourself a perfect," one of the more experienced fliers in the same formation told him.

For lunch, as we continued to wait for our airplane to be fixed, we wandered back to the snack bar for a hamburger and Coke. The snack bar had become so popular now that a small barbershop, run by a Vietnamese, was located next to it.

After seven hours of waiting, we reboarded our aircraft for a flight to our original destination. Again, we taxied out, took off and ... again the same engine (or one of its instruments) acted up and threatened to stop running.

It was now mid-afternoon and there were a lot of arriving and departing aircraft in the pattern, so we had to extend our approach as we returned to base a second time for landing. This time we got 25 minutes of flight time. We landed, taxied back to the same parking area we had been in all day and left the aircraft.

There was no other in-commission aircraft readily available since they were all out flying missions. The repair time for the one we had aborted in twice was again put at several hours, and the estimate was that by the time it came back into commission our remaining crew day would be so short we wouldn't have time to fly anywhere. We were done for another day. Again, we retired to the club for drinks and dinner.

The next morning, March 23, at 8:45 A.M. we flew to An Khe with two small vehicles and a pallet or two for the army. It was late in the morning, but An Khe was socked in by weather and its radar approach was out of order. With a 500-foot hill sitting next to the runway, An Khe was not the place to try to land without guidance in fog and light drizzle. We were about to return to Tan Son Nhut or take the load to Pleiku when the control at An Khe came on the radio and asked if we would attempt an approach as they had an emergency medical case that needed to be taken to Tan Son Nhut as soon as possible.

Accordingly, we began an airborne radar approach (ARA), with me doing the directing using our onboard weather radar as our guidance. The radar clearly painted the hill next to the runway and dimensions of the valley in which An Khe sat. The runway itself, made of pierced steel plating (PSP), was less clearly indicated. We lined up on the first approach and flew to the ARA's 500-foot altitude minimum; but the field was not visible in the rain, fog and cloud.

Hal informed the tower of our missed approach and told the army we would try again due to the urgency of their medical evacuation. We headed away from the hill, climbed around to the north and began another ARA. This time, at 600 feet above the runway surface, the field and its lights broke out of the weather just in time. We landed and were met by an ambulance and several doctors and nurses in addition to the stretcher-borne patient. We also picked up a small pallet and a few other passengers and returned to Tan Son Nhut. We were back on the ground at noon and then spent six more hours waiting for a load to be put on. Due to a lack of forklifts and some screwups as to which loads needed to go first on the priority basis, we never did get reloaded.

The air force liaison officer to the army division at An Khe turned out to be an old acquaintance of Dunn's and he called into C-130 Ops and said he had filed papers recommending our crew for the award of the Distinguished Flying Cross (DFC) for making the emergency patient evacuation in the bad weather conditions without a ground approach aid. We quit for the day about six o'clock and retired to the Club and the bar.

The following day we were off at 7:30 in the morning. We landed at Qui Nhon an hour later and then spent four hours on the ground waiting for a load. Clearly, aircraft maintenance and forklifts for loading and unloading were getting to be major problems within the airlift elements as the U.S. buildup went on. We were back in Tan Son Nhut by two in the afternoon, and again our day was done. We never got another load but spent several hours in the heat waiting for one. It was after five when we got to the officers' club.

25 March: We showed up at noon. This was our day to return to Mactan from the shuttle: except the plane we were to return in wasn't ready to fly and we couldn't leave anyway until our replacements landed. Usually the replacement aircraft was in by mid afternoon, but this time they had trouble getting out of Clark on time due to a maintenance problem. By the time they did get in, around five, our airplane was still not ready to fly, so we waited a bit more. Finally, by ten at night we were ready to go. We carried several pallets into Cam Ranh Bay and then, because our whole schedule had gotten so late, we flew direct to Mactan rather than going through Clark as would have been the normal pattern. We'd completed our second shuttle with a 15½ hour day.

Three days later, 28 March, we took off at ten in the morning and flew to Clark. We got into Clark at 11:30 and went into crew rest when it developed that they were having trouble loading all the aircraft on the ramp. We spent the rest of the day at the Clark Officers' Club, in the bar and around the pool.

In the course of the day, I met one of our old squadron members who had opted to go to Clark rather than Mactan when we got PCS'd at the beginning of the year. We went over to his apartment on base before going back to the club for dinner. He had a two-room air conditioned apartment in a five story building on base that was certainly nicer than our tent back at Mactan. I'm not sure it was worth an extra year's separation from the U.S., however. While I was in the apartment, I noticed that he had a small plastic display case on his dresser. In it was a MacDonald's Big Mac hamburger that he had brought with him from the States and was maintaining as a memory of stateside living. It was covered with moss, turning green and didn't smell too good. A mental memory might have been better.

The same friend also told me of the hazards of being a crew member at Clark. It seems that one morning the lieutenant who was on the duty desk for C-130s was visited at 1:00 A.M. by none other than the three star general commanding Twelfth Air Force, whose headquarters was at Clark. The general was an ex-fighter pilot and was not in a very good mood on arrival. After finding a refrigerator full of beer (which was kept for the crews returning from the Vietnam shuttle) in the operations area, he quickly put himself into a worse mood. The general began kicking beer cases around the area and verbally assaulted the young duty officer, who was terrified. It took the base air police and a quickly awakened squadron commander to calm the general down and send him back to headquarters for the night. Henceforth, the cold beer was kept in another area.

We left Clark at 10:30 the next morning and flew in-country, making stops at Da Nang and Qui Nhon before returning to Clark at 7:25 in the evening. We then spent a second consecutive night in the Clark club for dinner and drinks. The following day, we flew from Clark back to Mactan, arriving home at 12:45 in the afternoon.

While we were back in Mactan, we saw, in what passed for the base paper, a report that two American lieutenants stationed on the base had had a double wedding with two local Filipino girls from the higher society levels of Cebu. Their pictures were in the paper. We had been in Mactan for three months and the crews that had come ahead of us had been there for five months. The Filipino brides looked lovely in the pictures, but I found it hard to imagine that a mere five months could cause men to forget what corn fed American girls looked like.

April 1, April Fools Day, we were up at 5:00 in the morning setting out on another shuttle. We left Mactan at 7:00 in the morning and got to Clark at 8:30. There we got caught in a maintenance problem on the airplane, followed by a loading problem. We were supposed to be the input airplane for the Tan Son Nhut shuttle and be in-country by the early afternoon so that another plane and crew or crews could go home. Instead, we went into crew rest about noon.

We left Clark the next morning at 4:00 A.M. with a cargo of five pallets of 500 pound bombs. That morning's *Stars and Stripes* newspaper, which was readily available at Clark but less so elsewhere, had carried a story that the U.S. was said to be running low on bombs due to the war and had had to buy some from the Germans. Supposedly the German bombs had been sold to them by the U.S. at low NATO prices, but were now being sold back to the U.S. at a profit. The story noted that the Department of Defense denied any such activity.

Halfway across the South China Sea, Carl Gross, who spoke and read German, called up on the intercom and said, "Remember today's newspaper story about the German bombs? Well, guess what! All these bombs we're carrying have safety warnings and notations all over them in German and none in English. Ain't that funny?" Well, it wasn't comically funny, but it did make one wonder about the public veracity of the defense department and the Johnson administration.

We landed at 7:30 and offloaded the bombs at Bien Hoa before going on to Saigon, where we checked into 130 Ops at 9:00. The crews which had had to remain an extra day because of our overnight stay at Clark left as soon as we landed. We were going to spend another shuttle staying in the Globe hotel. Our squadron commander, Big Stoop, had accompanied us from Mactan and was now checking into the hotel at the same time we were. The Vietnamese clerk behind the hotel desk was a small woman who told Big Stoop that he would have to turn in his revolver and a copy of flight orders in order to stay. He blew up at this and tried to shout her down and rescind the order. John Dunn told him that this was a normal procedure and that we did it all the time. Having lost the fight to the small lady, Stoop then angrily turned on me and told me to be sure and do the same thing. I guess in his embarrassment he felt he had to take it out on someone and I was the closest, lowest rank. What a sweet fellow and inspiration to us all he was.

Since we had gotten in so early the previous day, we started the shuttle on the night shift. We took off from Tan Son Nhut at 1:30 in the morning on April 3, carrying cargo to Nha Trang. From there we went on to Da Nang. We spent two and a half hours on the ground in Da Nang getting a load on. From there we flew to Qui Nhon, arriving after sunrise. From Qui Nhon we carried a load into Pleiku and then returned to Tan Son Nhut just after noon.

The next morning we should have had a 7:00 or 7:30 takeoff if everything had gone right. Instead, we had a sick aircraft. When maintenance declared it required too long to fix for that day, we went to another aircraft the night shuttle had just returned. We finally took off at 2:15 in the afternoon and flew one cargo load into Ban Me Thuot. When we got back to Tan Son Nhut, our crew day was up.

While we had been on the ground waiting for maintenance to fix our first aircraft, I happened to run into the wing maintenance officer, who was checking planes and signing off maintenance repair work. I'd heard a story about a meal he had eaten in Saigon and asked if the story was true. It was, he said. He and a shuttle crew had gone downtown one evening and stopped to eat at a restaurant which was recommended for its food and atmosphere. As the restaurant had been a renowned French bistro, the officer began the meal with some French onion soup, one of the house specialties. In keeping with the house rules of how to best savor the soup, he gently pressed down on the cheese layer on top so that the soup and the onions in it flowed over the cheese and into his soup spoon. When he had gotten to the bottom of the bowl, he proceeded to cut the cheese layer with his spoon preparatory to eating it. That was when he lifted the edge of the cheese layer and saw beneath it, in the bottom of the bowl, a dead mouse. He laughed when he told the story, but I still think of it whenever I'm eating onion soup.

The next day, in keeping with the progressive daily start policy of 130 Ops, we showed up at ten in the morning for what should have been a noon takeoff. Instead, we arrived to find that we had no airplane to fly since more than the usual number were still in repair. Accordingly, we sat around 130 Ops waiting for a plane and a load. We finally took off at five in the evening and flew to Da Nang with a cargo load and then returned to Tan Son Nhut. Our one-flight day was over at eleven in the evening.

It was becoming quite clear that our maintenance and loading crews were becoming less and less efficient. The C-130 operation had been very busy supporting all aspects of the U.S. buildup since our first permanent crews had arrived in November of the previous year. Now we were paying for it with longer loading times on the ground and lower aircraft readiness among the in-country fleet.

6 April: We arrived at ten in the morning. Our mission was to fly a passenger run; however, the aircraft was in need of maintenance and we did not take off until two in the afternoon. Despite the late start, we made the complete route of Pleiku, An Khe, Qui Nhon, Nha Trang, Cam Ranh Bay and back to Tan Son Nhut in three hours and fifteen minutes of flying time and six hours of total clock time. Our shortest ground time was ten minutes from landing to takeoff and the longest was thirty minutes, whereas each cargo stop was a minimum of one hour and possibly as long as two.

The passenger loads were always large and nearly filled the plane at each stop. For as many people who got off, there were as many more waiting to get on. The travelers now were almost all U.S. military, although there were some Vietnamese; but the passengers were predominantly military men. There were few of the families or children we had seen earlier. We called into the ALCE at each base prior to landing and gave them our best known estimate of how many people would be getting off and how many seats we would have for replacement passengers. The ALCE then counted heads, and the people for the next leg were waiting for us when we taxied in. Passenger runs were one of the easier missions we got on a two week shuttle, although we usually got only one on each two week shuttle. Many of the passengers, particularly Vietnamese civilians, became anxious when the plane's doors and rear ramp were closed on the ground during engine start and the air conditioning was turned on. The cold air turned to frost in the hot interior of the airplane and many of the passengers thought they were going to be gassed.

On one of the legs that day, one of the passengers was a young and rather pretty Vietnamese female all dressed in her ao-dai. She was so pretty we arranged for her to sit up in the bunk in the cockpit with us as we flew from Nha Trang through Cam Ranh Bay and then into Saigon. On the last flight from Cam Ranh, we were climbing to altitude when suddenly an emergency siren and a warning "Door Opening" light came on. This indicated that one of the door seals had slipped or was not fully fastened and there was some danger of depressurization or a door flying open.

Our loadmaster was standing on the steps near the crew entrance door when the light came on and the young Vietnamese damsel was sitting on the bunk just above him. When the warning came on he dove up the steps and groped for the bunk, as there was a danger that the crew door could fly open and he'd be sucked out. His leap up the stairs fell a bit short, however, and his face landed squarely in the young lady's lap. She panicked, probably imagining rape, or something worse, at the hands of these cunning Americans. Her eyes got as big as saucers and tears flowed immediately. Since she didn't speak English, we had a heck of a time calming her down and trying to explain what had transpired.

Our next mission was a night run, since we had worked our way back onto the night shift. We left in the dark at 9:30 P.M. and an hour later were inbound to Da Nang. The weather at Da Nang was clear, with a thousand foot ceiling, and the base put us on an instrument approach to ensure separation from other aircraft. The approach would be with ground radar giving us heading and altitude directions to landing.

We were about 25 miles from Da Nang and inbound on a northern heading at 5,000 feet in accordance with the radar controller's instructions. Suddenly, up from below and about 2 or 3 hundred yards in front of the aircraft's nose came a hail of orange tracer bullets. Evidently Charlie was listening in to Da Nang approach control and firing into our traffic pattern with as much accuracy as he could.

John Dunn immediately turned the aircraft east, toward the sea. Hal Thorson told Da Nang approach that we were being fired on and would fly inbound over the ocean and make a visual landing. The existing weather at the base was well within our visual flight rules criteria (500 foot ceiling minimum). Our rerouting took a little longer than usual for us to get on the ground, but we did so without any further difficulty. We unloaded and uploaded cargo pallets and left Da Nang after an hour on the ground.

Our next stop was Qui Nhon, which was now operating at night rather

1966 — A Vietnamese girl sits in the cockpit on a flight from Nha Trang to Saigon.

than just in the daylight. We landed there at 1:20 in the morning and left an hour later. Cam Ranh Bay was the next stop, and after an hour's ground time, there we were back in Tan Son Nhut at 4:45 in the morning.

We got the following day off to again go from the night to the day shift and spent the morning sleeping late at the Globe. It was a Friday, so we set off late in the afternoon to go out to the base and have dinner and a few drinks at the club. When we got there, we found that we were just in time for the joyous opening of the new bar and dining room.

For some time the club had been under construction, with a lot of wood and wallboard barriers put in where the outside walls used to be. The old club had proven too small to accommodate the increased number of troops on the base, so a newer and larger one had come into existence. What had been the entire interior of the old club was now just the dining room. Beyond the dining room was a new bar and slot machine room that was at least half again as big as the entire old club used to be. Once, we ate and drank in some measure of a hurry in the club in order to allow seats and space for other diners and drinkers. Now there was enough room to spend leisure time in new and comfortably upholstered chairs and bar stools.

Also, one whole wall of the bar consisted of huge air-conditioner outlets. Rather than the constantly sweltering atmosphere (80 plus degrees?) of the old establishment, this entire new club was at a civilized 70 degrees or so. It really felt a little bit like back home — to us, that is. The Vietnamese bar girls and waitresses were totally at odds with this air-conditioned atmosphere. On this first day of operation, half of the air conditioners had to be shut down because the girls were freezing and couldn't work in the cold. The next day, they all showed up for work in sweaters.

9 April: We left Tan Son Nhut at 7:50 in the morning and landed at Vung Tau, where we were again involved in an Army search and destroy operation. We loaded up with U.S. Army troops and vehicles on a 20 minute flight to Bung Bung, which was a small, newly created airstrip north of Saigon and Bien Hoa located in rubber plantations. Each flight was 20 to 25 minutes long, with an hour's ground time at Vung Tau loading up with cargo, vehicles and people. It was one more army search and destroy mission trying to find, surprise and wipe out the Viet Cong.

By two in the afternoon, we had hauled all of the forces at Vung Tau into the operation and we were done for the day. We'd flown eight roundtrips for three hours and five minutes of flight time for the day. Dirty, dusty, hungry and thirsty, we retired to the Tan Son Nhut bar. On the last flight out, a French speaking priest, complete with beads, cassock and wide black hat, asked for a ride into the capital. No one else could understand him, so in pidgin French I translated his needs. We took him and he disappeared into the base crowd on landing.

Frequently now, when we first got on an aircraft to preflight it or when cargo was loaded at a stop away from Tan Son Nhut, there would be a large canvas sack with an orange placard on it saying, "TV film, High Priority." Somehow, when we were carrying troops, bodies, families and ammunition, TV tapes didn't seem to be high priority in our point of view, especially when we knew that the TV networks back home were not entirely in support of our actions in the war. Many of the high priority tapes were continually left on aircraft rather than being turned over to the cargo handlers. A few others were known to have been thrown away. Eventually the powers that be threatened to court-martial anyone who mishandled the tapes, but the bags' self-proclaimed High Priority was always a sore point.

The next day was support for another large search and destroy operation. The army was really stepping up its offensive operations, and those operations were all centered on the jungle and rubber plantations north of Bien Hoa towards the Cambodian border. This time we left Saigon and operated the rest of the day out of Bien Hoa. Again, we loaded up with U.S. Army troops and vehicles and then flew 20 minutes into the Iron Triangle north of Bien Hoa.

We flew eight round-trips between Bien Hoa and Nui Bara, a just created dirt strip with only enough parking space for one or two aircraft to be

1966 — A search-and-destroy operation in progress north of Bien Hoa.

on the ground at a time. Several of our sorties resulted in holding over Nui Bara while aircraft on the ground unloaded and took off to leave room for us to land. The air was filled with red clay dust stirred up by aircraft propellers and hundreds of army vehicles roaring off into the surrounding jungle and rubber plantation. It was another 90 degree day in Vietnam, but around Nui Bara the heat and humidity feel like 150 degrees. The cockpit air conditioner in our airplane was broken. When we got on the ground and opened doors, the temperature in the cockpit climbed above the top limit on the temperature gauge that sat above my desk and pegged out at 140.

The director of the airlift operation was a full colonel. He was dressed in a flying suit, with a large pair of plastic goggles shielding his eyes from the dust. Otherwise, he was covered from head to foot in mud and red clay dust and grime. He could do little more than wave aircraft in and out of the parking area after they landed. There was no ground control other than him, and all takeoffs and landings were run on a visual basis. The colonel was filthy and already tired when we first talked to him in the morning. Late in the day, on one of our last runs, the colonel came up into the cockpit to get some water out of our water jugs. The water was old, stale and hot, but he really enjoyed it. When he took the goggles off to drink, the white of his face around the eyes stood out from the dust, dirt and grime as if he were a blackface comedian in a minstrel show. Someone asked if this was the worst job he'd ever had. The colonel laughed and said, "No sir, I did the same thing a week ago in Khe Sanh and wondered how I was going to get out of there."

We had a spare pilot with us all day, one of the senior operations people out of the Wing airlift operations in Saigon. He was a previous member of our Langley Wing named Ernie, and he came along to see how smoothly the operation at Nui Bara was run. Now, as we are hurried to unload and get out of Nui Bara, he disappeared. It was hot, other planes were calling for us to get out of the parking area so they could land, and we were running out of crew day. Five minutes we waited, ten. Finally it was fifteen minutes we'd been on the ground. Dunn ordered the crew door closed and we started to taxi. We were leaving. Ernie could find his own way back to Bien Hoa or Saigon.

Just then Ernie pulled up in an army jeep. The door was opened again and he scampered aboard. "God dammit, Ernie; where the hell were you?" Dunn rasped. "Hey," says Ernie, filthy in red dust and sweating, "I went and got all of you some cold sodas off the army." As he handed them out, we didn't know whether to continue cursing him for wasting our time or to be embarrassed that we begrudged him an intended good turn.

11 April: We left Tan Son Nhut and stopped at Qui Nhon to offload

1966 — In the rain, one C-130 takes off over another on a search-and-destroy operation.

cargo. At 10:30 P.M. we were in Clark offloading. We left Clark and flew the standard hour and a half route back to Mactan, landing just after midnight, another shuttle done.

On arrival we found that the Wing had instituted a new policy for crews back from the shuttle: we got a free, two day stay in Cebu's best hotel, the Magellan. Each crew got three rooms in the hotel paid out of squadron social funds. John Dunn stayed by himself; Hal and I doubled up and so did the flight engineer and the loadmaster. Two days aren't a lifetime, but a clean room in a first class hotel makes a big difference in morale around the flight line. The Magellan had good rooms. It was a relatively new hotel in one of Cebu's best neighborhoods, near the golf course. It had a garden, a restaurant, cab service to all of Cebu. It also had a large bar down in the basement with its own homegrown bar girls and prostitutes.

Several other things had changed in Mactan since we had left on the last shuttle. There was a story going around about the young captain police officer who took it upon himself to patrol the waterfront in Cebu and enforce the off limits restrictions which the U.S. had imposed on several bars there. Unfortunately for him, he decided to do the enforcing by himself rather than with a posse, like John Wayne would have recruited.

In one of the first places he entered, he found two airmen enjoying the San Miguel and forbidden nightlife. One was a short white mechanic. The other was a large, tall, heavy, black cargo loader. When confronted by the civilian clothed vigilante, the two airmen took the law into their own hands and inflicted a major beating on him. All three were later taken to the Cebu City jail. The captain went back to keeping Mactan safe and the two assailants went to a U.S. jail after rank reductions were imposed.

Another interesting event at Mactan was that it had come to the attention of the powers that be that there were probably too many motorbikes owned by the officer corps on the island. Nearly half of those who owned one had crashed it in one way or another. Many of those were crew members who had to be taken off flight duty until their injuries healed.

Riding the bikes at high speed on Mactan and Cebu's unpaved but stone covered roads could become very painful when the driver literally hit the road under the influence of San Miguel or the scantily clad Filipino lady riding behind him on the bike. Because most of the bikes were purchased in Japan and hauled to Mactan in the back of empty C-130s, the powers that be ruled that bikes could no longer be hauled. Accordingly, the Japanese manufacturing companies cleverly broke the bike into four packages which could be stamped for U.S. mail and rapidly reassembled on delivery. The C-130s then continued to take the bikes into Clark and Mactan, until one crew refused a valid load in order to take their bikes home. After that, bikes were refused in toto as cargo regardless of whether they were in one piece or not. Due to depleted renewal supplies and a number of additional crashed bikes, the bike population was much diminished the later we got into this one year tour.

A story was making the rounds in the squadron that our squadron commander, Big Stoop, went on a shuttle as an extra pilot. One of our instructor pilots flew with him since this was his first time to actually fly in-country. They made a landing on a dirt strip during one of the army's search and destroy combat offloads and, once the plane was stopped, Big Stoop ran to the back, took off his flight suit, wiped his ass and threw his underwear out into the jungle. He had shit in his pants during the approach and landing. The story was told as if he had defecated due to fear, but more than likely he had a touch of dysentery like a lot of the rest of us. The same thing happened to me one day when we got delayed taxiing in to offload due to an aircraft with a flat tire on the taxiway in front of us. I was fighting to hold my bowel movement until I could get to the latrine near the Shit Creek Snack Bar; but the delay went on too long and I ended up shitting into two coffee cups while still in the cockpit.

We also heard by rumor that our tent mate, Capt. Civil, got sent up to Korea to fly some ROK soldiers home from Vietnam at the end of a shuttle. From there he flew over to Japan, where the airlift headquarters for all of Southeast Asia was located. Civil was known as a real self-fulfilling individual. (He was a member of an Air Force sports team and annually managed to get a month off to compete in inter-service events at the expense of others doing his flying time.) Somehow, in Japan, he managed to make it appear as if his C-130B was available for alternate missions, when in reality the Wing expected it to come immediately back from Korea. He and his crew remained up in Japan, flying out of Tachikawa for about a week. When he returned to Mactan, it was said that he got his ass chewed by the wing commander as well as Big Stoop for falsely and deliberately assisting the headquarters in Japan to appear confused about his availability. Civil was in the doghouse for the remainder of his stay in Mactan. Three days after our shuttle, we picked up a one day mission ferrying cargo from Mactan to Clark.

18 April: Flew from Mactan to Clark and spent the day in crew rest. We had a good relaxing time around the Clark pool and eating real meals at the Officer's Club. The next day we were up at five and left Clark at seven. We were back on the shuttle. On the flight over the South China Sea, a large radar blip appeared just ahead of us about 100 miles past our west turn at Corregidor. It was a perfectly clear day and we soon visually made out an aircraft carrier chugging its way westward.

After sighting the carrier, we continued on to the Vietnam coast. As we approached the coast, I noticed that the radar on this airplane was particularly sharp in its ground display. Wonder of wonders, what should appear on the scope as we neared land but a train running along the coast north of Qui Nhon. The Viet Cong had long ago destroyed South Vietnam's train service and this was the first and only train that I ever saw running in the country. The radar return on the train even from 50 miles away was so sharp that I could distinguish individual cars.

When we got to Tan Son Nhut I told the maintenance officer there how impressed I was with this particular radar. He told me that they had just received a load of new radar equipment at Mactan and that one newly assigned airman was particularly good at working radars. When a new aircraft is originally contracted for and accepted by the air force, the first editions are flown and maintained by civilian personnel working for the contracting company (Boeing, Lockheed, etc.). There is always a decrease in the performance of some of this equipment when the whole fleet is built and dispersed to regular air force units and the maintenance is done by low ranked air force trained technicians. The new technician at Mactan was tuning the radars, like this one, to near original requirement specifications. A week later, while still on the same shuttle, we flew the same aircraft again. The radar was completely inoperable. Even the best work didn't suffice for long under the conditions we were working in.

We landed and offloaded cargo at Binh Thuy, which was in the delta, south of Saigon. The army was still deep into search-and-destroy operations. We made only that one stop but then went on to Tan Son Nhut. As the replacement shuttle crew, we were done for the day at noon. After room assignments we were back in the Globe for another week or two.

We showed up the following day early in the morning, but our assigned aircraft was broken and it never did come back into service by the time the rest of the crews were arriving for their pre-scheduled missions. We sat around in the C-130 Ops building for most of the morning anticipating a repaired airplane, but it never came. We went back into crew rest about noon without having accomplished a thing all day and retired to the officers' club for lunch before returning to the Globe for a night's sleep.

The officers' club was now humming with business and prosperity after its enlargement and upgrade. In the afternoon you could eat lunch in the dining room in a civilized fashion, and after all the headquarters types had gone back to work, settle into the enlarged bar for some serious drinking. On this day, John Dunn and I (Hal having left us to go back to the hotel early) adjourned to the bar, where a flyboy we didn't know began to engage us in conversation. We both looked at each other. Who was this guy who seemed to know us, but was unrecognizable?

Well it turned out he was John's old fighter pilot buddy who was assigned to the Tan Son Nhut reconnaissance squadron and was flying F-101s. From the alert, happy, energetic pilot we had encountered a few shuttles earlier, he was now aged, worn, pessimistic and deeply into booze. His early flights around South Vietnam and southern North Vietnam were standard learning trips into a deeper web. From those areas where there were no enemy defenses, he was gradually introduced into the ever more threatening regions of North Vietnam and Laos, which were divided into different "route packages." Each route package was a standard flight over hostile territory for a reconnaissance aircraft carrying a prescribed load of collective assets (cameras, sensors, etc.). Each route package also had a standard set of enemy defensive assets which could attack the airplane as it flew the standard route. Defensive assets included MIG aircraft, which most often could not catch the F-101 but might fire, or attempt to fire, air-to-air missiles at it. Next came the surface to air missiles (SAMS) which were ground launched but attacked the aircraft with little or no warning and could meet or exceed the plane's flight altitude.

Having flown a few missions into the northern route packages, and having seen and dodged SAMS on a nearly daily basis, the previously enthusiastic and highly motivated fighter pilot had rapidly aged and much more booze ridden than when we had previously seen him not too long ago. He only had some 80 or 90 more missions to go before he could return home, but he wasn't looking forward to those experiences.

The following night, April 20, we were up at midnight and, after a slight loading delay, got airborne at 3:30 in the morning for a day of cargo hauls to Cam Ranh Bay, Da Nang, Pleiku and then back into Tan Son Nhut at eleven in the morning just in time for lunch at the officers' club: Four hours of flight time for an 11 hour day.

The next day, we were up at five to fly the western passenger run out of Tan Son Nhut to Phan Rang, Nha Trang, Qui Nhon, Pleiku (we were directed away from An Khe by a helicopter accident near the runway), and then back to Tan Son Nhut. We were back to Tan Son Nhut by one in the afternoon, so we had another good afternoon of the lunch meal and drinks in the bar before going back to the hotel. We ended up with three and a half hours of flying time for an eight hour day.

The following day we were not so lucky. The army was still doing search-and-destroy missions north of Bien Hoa. We went back to flying shuttles from Bien Hoa to Nui Bara all day long. Each flight was a load of army personnel and vehicles going into the rubber plantation country. It was here we found out that the U.S. government was paying the French plantation owners for each rubber tree or plantation installation which was damaged or destroyed by our attempts to defeat the Viet Cong insurgency. I resolved then and there to never buy a Michelin tire for the rest of my life. Such are the costs of alliances, diplomacy and combat. We quit at 7:30 in the evening after a fourteen and a half hour day in heat, dust and frustration: Eight flights for five hours of flying time.

Our following launch time slipped to three in the afternoon. But, in the meantime, we heard that when several of the loadmasters from the previous day's missions into Nui Bara had returned to Tan Son Nhut and attempted to eat in the enlisted dining hall, they were arrested for being "filthy in uniform." These guys had worked harder than anyone yesterday in loading, unloading, crawling under and tying down and releasing chained vehicles. Now they were declared enemies of the people for cleanliness. The head of C-130 Ops went down and bailed them out of jail, but should have chewed some ground pounder's ass for an ignorance of combat operations. As far as I know, that did not happen. Such are the stupidities of warfare, even among the warriors, when daily eight to five deskbound, stateside-oriented warriors run into conflict with others who are working 14 or 16 hour days to get a job done.

Ever since we had come back to Vietnam on this 13 month tour, we had noticed how much the context of the war had changed from what it was in the summer of 1965 on the first tour. Then we used to fly to main bases in daylight; now it was 24 hour operations, 7 days a week. The loads at first were all palletized cargo and a mix of U.S. troops and Vietnamese families and troops. Now it was mostly U.S. troops and Vietnamese troops, with very few families. In 1965 we frequently added single people or small U.S. contingents to a planeload when we had room and they were taking beer or food back to small detachments. Now all of our loads were centrally managed by the ALCE or a passenger control station at each base. We were no longer allowed to add anyone or anything to the load.

A few days later, when we pulled into Da Nang, someone called over the radio requesting that a limousine meet the airplane to take some dignitary to a meeting. "Roger," came the reply. "We'll have the marine protocol office take care of that." The Protocol Office, for Gods sake! The war was already getting over-organized.

We were back on the western passenger run, with a late takeoff. The majority of the passengers were air force personnel, and, accordingly, so were the bases we stopped at. We hit Cam Ranh Bay, Nha Trang, Qui Nhon, Da Nang, Pleiku and Tan Son Nhut all within a ten hour day. For that, we got a day off before going on the night shift. We ate lunch and dinner in the Tan Son Nhut Officers' Club and spent the afternoon drinking at the air conditioned bar. In the midst of that afternoon activity, one slot machine player got a high-speed rhythm going between putting coins in the slot and pulling them off. He pulled off a jackpot before it could register and pay off. Shortly thereafter, in a rage, he retired to the bar.

25 April: The day started with a 5:00 A.M. get up and a 7:30 takeoff. Somehow, we had again gotten the counterclockwise passenger run. This time it was Phan Rang, Nha Trang, Qui Nhon, An Khe, Pleiku and then back to Tan Son Nhut. Most of the day's passengers and stops were U.S. Army. Three

June 1966 — Offloading a search-and-destroy operation, possibly at Loc Ninh.

and a half hours of flying time in an eight hour day. That's the way the passenger run was supposed to go. We got another day off and spent it lounging around the Globe and going downtown to the Rex Hotel for a steak early in the evening.

The following day, April 27, we were going back home to Mactan on the rotation aircraft. We got out to Tan Son Nhut about noon, and when the replacement plane got in about two we were airborne. We made one stop at Qui Nhon to offload several pallets of cargo, and then for a change we flew straight to Mactan rather than going through Clark. We were back in our tents at "home" by nine that evening.

We were expecting to get a two day stay over in the Hotel Magellan with some hot and cold maid service, but it was not to be. After one day off to pick up some fresh clean clothes and read our mail, we were back on the shuttle again. The Wing had picked up some additional missions and, together with more than the usual load of broken aircraft needing maintenance and some crews on leave or sick, we were unlucky enough to pick up two shuttles in a row. On Sunday, May 1, we are headed west again on the usual route through Clark. We got off about four hours late due to a maintenance delay and didn't get into Tan Son Nhut until seven at night: Five hours of flying time in a fourteen hour day. Once again it was downtown to the Globe, our home away from home.

Because we got in so late the day before, we started the shuttle on the night shift, taking off at 5:30 in the afternoon for Qui Nhon, with a second stop scheduled for Udorn in Thailand. For Udorn we were told we would be carrying some very high priority cargo that we would onload at Qui Nhon. We were in and out of Qui Nhon in 45 minutes after uploading the mysterious air force cargo. The vital cargo was a box about 6 inches cubed. It was also the only cargo that we had onboard as we flew to Udorn. We got to Udorn at nine at night.

A truck met the airplane, and without a word the vital box of cargo was hand transferred. We still had five hours of crew day left, plenty of time to fly back to Saigon, but they didn't have any cargo to go out until sometime the next day, so we spent the night. There were no empty barracks on the Udorn fighter base, and we were sent downtown or somewhere off in the jungle in the dead of night to find a place to sleep. Arranging the night's stay and getting to the hotel took over two hours and we had an early get up and go scheduled for the next day. The hotel was very nice; it was clean and even served a sort of breakfast with coffee and eggs late the next morning while we waited for the taxi to take us back to base.

Once on base, our priority for getting a load was very low. Possibly all the loaders were involved in the daily fighter operation. We sent Hal to the local hamburger shop to pick us up some early flight meals in the late afternoon. Carl, our loadmaster, was one of those strange people who did not like lettuce and he had an enhanced sense of when it was ever in contact with something he was going to eat. Hal got us all a hamburger or two, plus some sort of fries and a Coke. The short order cook, a Thai, didn't understand the request for the part of the order without lettuce, so before Hal gave Carl his he took the lettuce off and threw it away. When Carl finished putting the load on the aircraft, which he was doing when Hal came back, he opened the hamburger and just smelled it; then he declared it once had lettuce and refused to eat it. Some days you just can't win. Carl went hungry rather than eat the lettuce-cursed burger. We didn't leave Udorn until 8:15 that evening. We landed at Tan Son Nhut fifteen minutes after midnight: Three hours of flying time and a lot of hot ground time in a twelve hour day.

We got all of that day off and we needed it. Despite the heat and the noise, we slept late in the Globe, going out only later in the day to the base to eat. We then immediately went back to the hotel and went to sleep again. The pace of the war and our swift return to this second shuttle were beginning to tell on us physically. The late arrival at Udorn, and having to be taxied to the off base hotel, together with an early get up the next day, followed by waiting all day in the heat for a load hadn't helped either. We were all pretty tired when we finally got in the air and headed back to Tan Son Nhut.

Halfway through the return flight, I nodded off while sitting at the navigator's station. The next thing I knew, I heard someone calling us by our call sign. I woke up. It was air traffic control in the Central Highlands asking about our location. I looked around the cockpit and waited for John or Hal to respond. No answer. In the darkened cockpit, with only the instrument lights on, everyone was asleep and the plane was on autopilot. I spoke loudly and asked Hal to answer the radio call. Slowly everyone awoke and we got back to normal crew operations. Flying along with everyone on the aircraft asleep never happened again; but it was scary.

The following morning we were up at four A.M. and had breakfast at the Shit Creek Snack Bar (ham and eggs on a paper plate) on base. That day we were again on the eastbound army passenger run, Phan Rang, Nha Trang, Qui Nhon and then An Khe. At first, everything went well, with all stops being less than 50 minutes. At An Khe, the stop turned into an hour and a half due to the army's inability to get their onboard passenger list in order. We went thru Pleiku in short order and were back in Tan Son Nhut by 1:20 in the afternoon.

The next day, May 6, our place in the shuttle schedule shifted forward

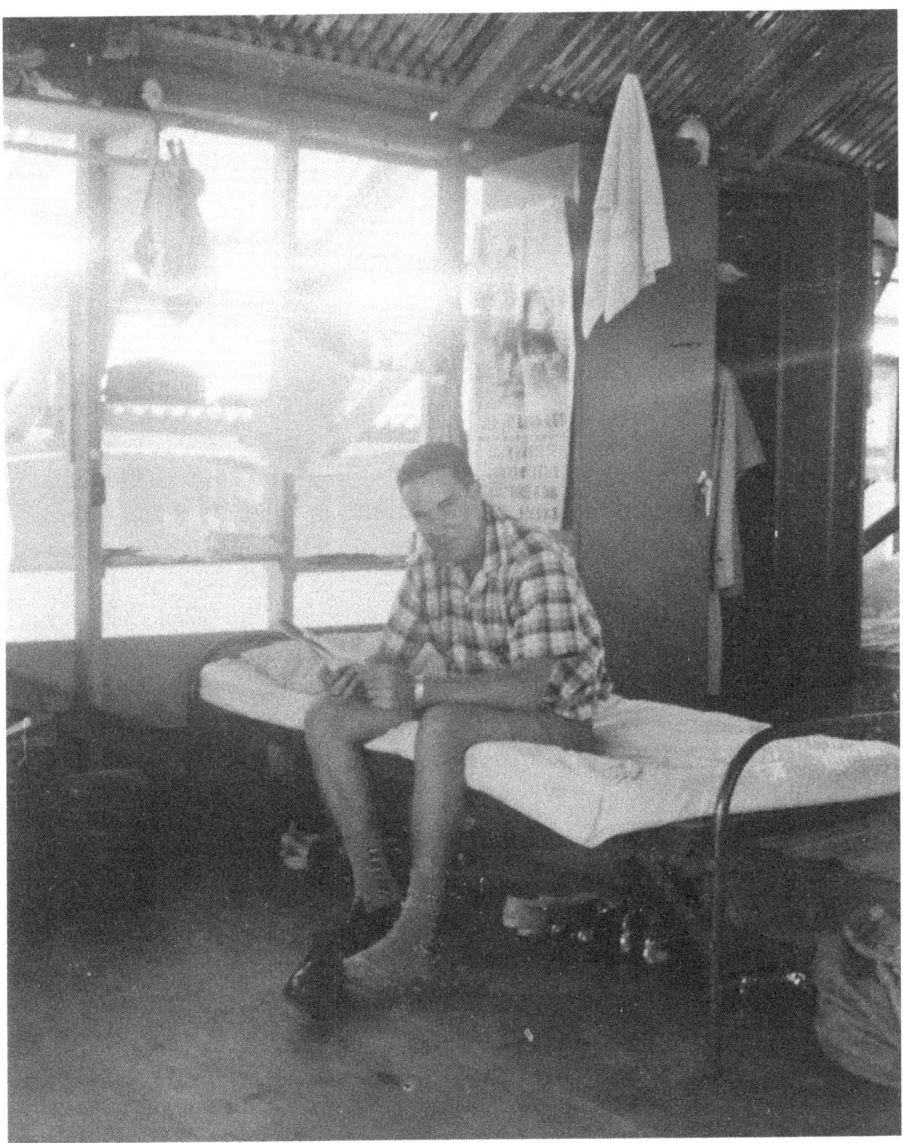

Late 1966 — The author at his Mactan cot.

by eight hours to a noon takeoff. We hauled army cargo in and out of An Khe, Bien Hoa and finally into Tay Ninh. Tay Ninh was north of Saigon almost on the Cambodian border where the army was starting another of its large search and destroy operations. We left Tay Ninh and were back in Tan Son Nhut with another day complete at six in the evening.

The day after that, we were again deep into support of the army operations around Tay Ninh. We hauled three mixed loads of pallets, vehicles and troops from Tan Son Nhut into Tay Ninh from 3:30 in the afternoon till 10:00 in the evening. On our last sortie, we left Tay Ninh and went to Binh Thuy in the delta, where some army personnel were quickly let out the back door with the engines running. We went back to Tan Son Nhut at 11:40 in the evening. Carl, the loadmaster, was in bad need of rest when the day was over. The mixed loads keep him continually busy on the ground working with pallets or chaining and unchaining vehicles for the succession of short, 20-minute flights.

We got another day off and then returned to the shuttle at three the following morning. That day we hauled cargo to Chu Lai, Da Nang and Phan Rang and were finished at one in the afternoon. Since it was early, we went to the officers' club for a late dinner rather than go straight back to the Globe. Hal ate quickly and then caught a ride downtown. John Dunn and I stayed to have a drink or two in the bar, which was largely deserted since it was now mid-afternoon on a Monday.

Somewhere around four o'clock, there were ten or so people in the bar and another ten scattered through the slot machine section. The dining room was closed and things were quiet, with nothing other than the slots and small, dark, and serious drinking going on. Suddenly, into this quiet atmosphere came a young lady and her escort. One quick look told us that she was part of a USO troupe which was touring the theater and had probably just gotten into Saigon. This lady would stop traffic in a major U.S. city: Short, good-looking, busty, dancer's legs and wearing a tight—I mean tight—T-top, and really short shorts. Her escort was thin and flakey, probably a fellow dancer in the same group, dragged along to keep her company in this all male atmosphere.

Within 5 minutes she had ten drinks sitting on the table in front of her and was talking to a young instant admirer lieutenant who had just proposed marriage. She laughed him off, but he was shortly followed by two more swains. The scene was getting funny and the crowd she drew was growing as the late afternoon shift began to come in for food and drinks. We'd like to have stayed and seen more of the action, but tomorrow's duty called. Never underestimate how horny and foolish otherwise reserved young men can act when in extreme circumstances. Or, as the navy saying goes, "any port in a storm."

10 May: We were up and out on base at noon to be the rotation crew going home. Naturally, the replacement aircraft was late and didn't get in on time. We finally left at six in the evening and made one stop to offload cargo at Qui Nhon. We then went through Clark in an hour and were back in Mactan at one in the morning, another shuttle done.

This time we did get to spend two days in the Magellan Hotel when we got back. The Magellan was a nice hotel with good food and comfortable beds and a large bar downstairs that was open all night and featured its own hostesses. It was a good break from the routine, which was starting to get to be too much, with the short back-to-back shuttles.

When we got back from the hotel, there was still more time off: A day to go to the beach, although the beach really wasn't all that good. It was three or four miles from the base and you rode your motorbike there, if you had one (which I didn't), or you took a cab. Once at the beach, there was very nice white sand, but no surf. The coral seabed extended quite a way out and you had to wear tennis shoes in the water to keep from cutting your feet. Also, the water wasn't very deep and there were no waves.

There were beer salesmen on the beach, just like at a ballgame back home. San Miguel is the Philippines' best known beer. It was a nickel a bottle. The main San Miguel brewery was in Manila. It brews beers that are sold worldwide and has a pretty good reputation for quality and production control. All the San Miguel sold in the northern Philippines and around Clark, for instance, came from the Manila plant. A second San Miguel brewery was right across the harbor from us in Cebu. Its reputation for quality was not quite the same. Since the beer was a nickel a bottle, you could buy a case for one dollar. You bought one case one week and it was so weak it tasted like Mexican beer or lite beer (which didn't exist at the time). If you bought another case a week later, it might be so strong it almost blew your head off. So much for cheap beer and quality control.

16 May: We were up at four in the morning and off the ground by six. We staged through Clark and dropped off a few passengers. We also had a maintenance problem while on the ground at Clark and then some trouble getting our load on. We didn't take off from there until four in the afternoon. After a three hour flight, we landed in Kadena Air Base on the island of Okinawa, where we stayed overnight in base quarters.

The next day we loaded up with palletized cargo and flew from Kadena to Udorn in Thailand. It was a six hour flight and on the way the weather threatened to make us fly over the Chinese island of Hainan. (I recalled an academy instructor I had who described a similar experience during the Korean War. He claimed they overflew Hainan by accident and could look down and see MIGs taking off to intercept them before they flew into clouds and escaped.) Instead, we picked our way through the clouds and storm and only got close enough to get a good visual of the place as we went by. We landed in Udorn at six at night and got out of there with no load an hour later. We were back in Tan Son Nhut for another shuttle at eleven in the evening.

We stayed downtown in the Globe Hotel again and left there early the next evening to go to the base and eat at the officers' club. From there it was the normal routine of going to C-130 Ops, checking the weather and filing a flight plan. We took off at eight and went to Da Nang with a load of cargo. Then from Da Nang we flew to Pleiku where we off- and onloaded cargo. We landed back in Tan Son Nhut at 2:40 in the morning and called it a day. We had had engine trouble on the flight into Tan Son Nhut and the airplane was going to need maintenance before it could fly again. Rather than park in front of 130 Ops where all the loading took place, they told us to park the plane out in the "bomb dump." The bomb dump was a large open area across the runway from the aircraft loading and parking areas. It was where major maintenance was done and also where bombs and other munitions were stored and loaded. It was located quite a distance from the normal parking and loading areas, just in case one of the munitions went off.

After leaving the aircraft, we waited in the bomb dump several hours for a crew bus to come and get us. For some reason, one never came. Whether it was broken, 130 Ops forgot about us, or something else intervened, we didn't know. At any rate, after waiting longer than we cared to, we gathered up our crew bags and decided to walk from the bomb dump into 130 Ops, which was about a mile away across the runway.

We hiked through the bomb dump and got to the runway. It was now about 4:00 in the morning and there was not much, if any, air traffic. Still, we didn't want to get run over crossing the main runway, so we checked both directions and overhead to make sure nothing was about. Then we hurried across, bags in tow, and made it into the Ops building, where they swore a bus had been sent some time ago. Tired and disgruntled we retired to the Globe for half a night's sleep.

A month later, while working on the night shift, I witnessed a base-wide intruder alert at Tan Son Nhut. Without warning, all the base sirens went off and the air police emerged in full combat gear with their jeeps and other vehicles to close off all entrances to the base and the aircraft parking areas. I noticed that one of the first things they did was secure the runway and immediately fire automatic weapons up and down it. Seemingly, our earlier, unannounced walk from the bomb dump, across the runway, could have been a disaster.

The next day, May 20, we had reverted to the day shift. After breakfast in the Shit Creek Snack Bar, we took off at noon and flew one load of combat passengers into Luc Thinh. After offloading the army through the rear cargo door with the engines running, we went back to Tan Son Nhut; but the aircraft had had steering troubles at Luc Thinh and we went back to the bomb dump when we landed. We sat around for three hours in the heat and isolation waiting for maintenance to come, which they never did. Finally, about 5:00 P.M., 130 Ops called and said we were running out of crew day and should call it a day so we could appear that much earlier the next day. Apparently they were still having trouble matching crews and aircraft to meet the daily schedule with all of the army's search-and-destroy missions still going on. The next day we flew the army counterclockwise passenger run to Phan Rang, Nha Trang, Qui Nhon, An Khe, Pleiku and then back to Saigon. We had started at four in the morning and were done by eleven thirty.

Our early quit got us an early start the next day. We left the Globe at two in the morning and were off the ground by four hauling cargo to and from Cam Ranh Bay, Pleiku, Da Nang and Chu Lai. Our crew day ended at three in the afternoon, just enough time for a few beers and dinner in the club before retiring to the Globe for the night.

23 May: We left the Globe at four in the morning. Our mission was to serve as the carrying platform for an Airborne Command and Control (ABCCC, or AB triple C mission, in air force terminology) platform. In later years, the air force would have dedicated aircraft for such a mission, with all communications and coordinator seats built into the airframe. But this was an early version of the same thing. They loaded a triple palleted communications building into the aircraft and then tied it down like cargo. The walls were whitewashed plasterboard and there was room inside for 6 or eight people. There were about 10 or 12 people who spent the entire flight in the back of the aircraft either in the palletized building or sitting out of it on breaks on the strapped seats we used to carry passengers. Several of them spoke various Asian languages and dialects and we were given to know that some were spooks (spies, etc.) of some sort that we shouldn't try to talk to.

We took off at 7:00 in the morning and proceeded at 20,000 feet to a spot due east of Da Nang along the Laotian border. We then took up an orbit at that point using the TACAN at Da Nang to keep track of our location in orbit. John Dunn and Hal took turns flying the aircraft, and I gave up my seat to one of the ABCCC people who used our aircraft radios to talk to varied headquarters on the ground and fighter flight crews in the air. Once in orbit, we shut down two of our engines to save fuel. Ten (more or less boring) hours later, when our fuel began to run low, we broke out of orbit and went back to land at Tan Son Nhut. That day's mission ended at 5:45 in the afternoon. We had flown ten hours and forty-five minutes for the day.

The next day we got the clockwise army passenger mission. The night after that we left Tan Son Nhut at seven in the evening and flew two round-trip cargo runs into Cam Ranh Bay. We had worked our way through another shuttle. We got to the base the next day, May 27, at noon and ate in the club and flew the rotation airplane out at 2:20 in the afternoon. We stopped to offload cargo at Cam Ranh Bay and then flew on to Clark. We spent two hours on the ground at Clark and then flew on to Mactan, which we reached at eleven that night. The flight from Clark to Mactan was all after dark and there were several large tropical thunderstorms along the route on the way down. We circumvented the storms using the aircraft's radar. In the dark, several of the lightning displays over the islands were spectacular, or would have seemed so if we hadn't been so tired.

We got another two day stay in the Magellan, and again it was very nice and relaxing. However, that is all we got. The Wing was short of crews due to lots of new recruits coming in, and the crew members who were instructors had to train them. All the new crews needed aircraft and theater checkouts. Most of the initial new crew training was done locally, which meant there were that many fewer qualified crews to support the shuttles. We went off to Clark on our third day back. It was supposed to be a quick, short day; but it instead turned into seven hours on the ground at Clark waiting for a load. We flew back to Mactan at six in the evening.

Our crew was now included in the Wing plan to train additional instructors. With a one year (13 months) tour for all personnel, there would be a 100 percent turnover at Mactan in just eight more months. Many of the people now coming into the base as replacements were not experienced C-130 or Tactical Airlift personnel. They were a mix of Strategic Air Command (B-52, C-135) flyers who had just passed through the basic conversion course into the C-130, plus others recalled to flying from desk jobs and staff positions. They would have to be screened as to qualifications and trained for in-theater procedures before they could fly by themselves. Thus, John Dunn and I were going to be upgraded to instructors in order to help train the new guys, and Hal would be upgraded from copilot to pilot as part of the same scheme. Our crew would be broken up. Crews at Langley when I first got there in 1965 were among the most experienced in C-130 Operations and the instructor and flight examiner positions in the Wing sometimes took five or ten years to move into. Now, as a result of the one year tour rule which the military had put on Vietnam experience, that rotation and passage of corporate knowledge would be reduced to several months within the 13 month total tour.

One of the new arrivals in Mactan was Capt. Jaime Montez. He was assigned one of the empty bunks in our tent, thus becoming the sixth member of our little community. Jack was an ex–SAC, B-52 navigator. He was also a single American of Filipino extraction. He loved Mactan because all of the local girls thought he was a rich Filipino and not an American at all.

It was now May 31 and we were up early for a local training mission. The airplane broke and we sat around until three in the afternoon before flying a local training mission with two short low level routes and much pilot landing practice. Two days later, we repeated the same pattern, even down to the late takeoff. This time, however, we also quit 40 minutes early because the airplane needed maintenance.

Once having passed our own check rides, we began the upgrade training of others, which was kind of a breeze. Flying between Mactan, Clark and Vietnam, we could get all the upgrade over-water training that we needed just flying normal cargo/passenger haul missions. The low level/airdrop missions flown out of Mactan were much easier than those we used to fly out of Langley. Back in the States, every other turn in a low-level flight path was frequently hard to identify due to terrain and forestation. Here, virtually every turn could be seen well in advance since most of the routes were over-water and involved small island landfalls that were easily identifiable far in advance on radar.

The routes went in a variety of directions from Mactan before finally turning back to it and leading to the DZ, which sat next to the runway. Many of the routes went south from Mactan and passed or overflew Bohol Island and the Surigao Strait, which was the site of a famous World War II naval battle in 1944. On a clear day, when the sun was at a proper altitude and direction, you could look down and see the remnants of the Japanese Fleet lying in the water.

Initially, one of the low level routes used a point of land on Bohol as a turning point because it stood out prominently on a map. In actuality, however, the point was not a smooth beach protruding into the water as it looked on the map. It had a higher rock promontory overlapping, and anyone trying to touch the point and turn at 500 feet would have run right into the side of the mountain. This would have been especially hazardous at night. Soon after the route was first flown, the turning point was changed.

The Japanese ships in the sea claimed one more American casualty from Mactan. This fellow went scuba diving on vacation with some local Filipinos from Cebu and they dived down to investigate the ships. It developed that they dove too deep and stayed too long and then, after surfacing and refilling their oxygen tanks, they repeated the dive. When coming up on the second attempt, the U.S. diver developed a severe case of the bends and had to be emergency evacuated through Clark to a naval facility in the Pacific that had a pressure chamber that might have been able to reverse the effects of his diving. When last heard from, he was still alive but he was paralyzed over much of his body.

We got three days on the ground in Mactan for some upgrade training ground school. It turned out that during this time the Filipinos had decided to make some money and also improve the nightlife of the Mactan Base. Two local bars were built just outside the base perimeter. Both were open almost all night (or at least long after the clubs on base closed), and both featured bands, dancing, and cards in addition to booze. It turned out, however, that one of them was owned by the local police chief, who was also responsible for base security. His bar remained easily accessible to the base through an open gate. His competitor, however, soon had a barbed wire fence put in front of his establishment so that, in order to get in, someone on base would have to walk an additional half mile, go out the base main gate and then walk back the half mile in order to patronize his establishment. In short order, the second establishment was out of business. Three days after our local flights, we again flew back and forth to Clark in one day, partly to pickup cargo and partly to get instructor training with live students. It turned into a full day's work due to spending seven hours at Clark waiting for a load.

During one of our following off-days, I ventured over to Cebu in mid-afternoon. No one else was interested in going, so I decided to take in the local cinema. One of the features was *Doctor Zhivago*, which I had not seen. I got there just before the feature started and succeeded in getting a seat up in one of the last rows in the balcony. Despite the fact that this was a weekday, the theater was packed. It was also not air-conditioned. The heat in the balcony was stifling and the movie was over three hours long. In many of the scenes, Zhivago was out in the Russian wilderness, up to his neck in snow and undergoing freezing temperatures. During those scenes, the theater was completely silent. In the boiling balcony heat, I was convinced that I was the only one there who had any concept of snow and freezing temperatures. Once the feature was over, I climbed down from the balcony and headed straight for the nearby Chinese restaurant for a few San Miquels in order to reacclimatize myself.

Two days later, we left Mactan at ten in the morning and proceeded to Clark. Dunn and I had been upgraded to instructors and we had students flying along with us. Hal transferred to another crew, where he continued his upgrade training and got his own crew. We flew into Clark just before noon and then spent five hours waiting for a load which never came. We went into crew rest and introduced our students to the wonders and comforts of Clark, its officers' club and bar. The next day we were up at 4:00 and off the ground by 7:00 in the morning. We flew cargo and passengers in and out of Da Nang and Qui Nhon and then proceeded back through Clark and then on to Mactan. We landed in Mactan at ten in the evening. In an eighteen hour day we got eight plus hours of flying time and the students got a lot of flying time, over-water training and theater indoctrination. Two days later, we spent a sixteen hour day flying two round-trip shuttles between Mactan and Clark.

After this somewhat hectic period of local flying, there was a down period of a full week in which I did no flying other than showing up for a local flight one morning and then having it canceled for lack of a flyable airplane after several hours of waiting. There were, however, important things happening on base during this period. The Catholic chaplain, who had only recently arrived, turned out to greatly enjoy going to the beach each and every day. It turned out that his interest was not only in the beach, but also in a lovely young Philippine lady who swam there and lived nearby in a "banana farm." He was soon gone from the base, possibly off to a less exotic locale.

One evening I was sitting at the bar in the officers' club, which adjoined the enlisted/NCO club. The officers' club sat on a flat concrete slab and consisted of a bar and some 20 tables distributed around the room behind it. It served no meals. The door to the officers' club sat just between the bar and the start of the tabled area. Directly across from the officers' club door was the door to the adjoining NCO/enlisted club. The lower ranks club sat on a raised two foot crawl space so that there was a two step stairway leading up to it. The NCO club featured a bar, snack bar and dance floor.

The officers' club was rarely more than half full on any night other than Friday, when all the Wing personnel congregated there before going over to Cebu. The NCO/enlisted club was usually full every night. On this particular evening, I had barely settled in my seat at the bar in the O club, where the door was habitually left open, when suddenly the door to the adjoining NCO club flew open and rolling out of it down the stairs came two combatants. It was a good old, U.S. Western fistfight for about two minutes before someone broke it up and the air police arrived in pursuit of the pugilists. One of the fighters was a well known staff sergeant who was one of the best aircraft crew chiefs in the Wing. He had, however, also gotten a record of numerous boxing extravaganzas such as this one, and when next seen, he was an airman again and no longer a staff sergeant.

In the heat of the tropics, and after an extended period there, young men were known to do stupid things, especially under the influence of drink. There was, of course, never such a violent outbreak of savagery in the officers' club. Occasionally a single drunken punch might be thrown or the would-be combatants would stagger back to their tents to conduct a punch-up; but there were no fights in sight of the lower ranks. One reason the door between the clubs was left open, I guess, was to spread civilization and culture to the lower ranks of society.

19 June: After a week of not flying, we left Mactan at 9:00 in the morning on our return to the shuttle. We passed through Clark, as usual, and picked up a load of cargo and passengers for Da Nang and Tan Son Nhut. We landed in Saigon as the daily replacement aircraft at 6:30 in the evening.

Hal was now in training for his upgrade; and John Dunn was flying with another crew as part of his upgrade, so I was with a completely different crew. The copilot was an ex–SAC flyer just breaking into C-130s. He was an older captain and would probably end his career as a copilot. The pilot was a new major who was in our squadron at Langley, but I had never flown with him before. He was an instructor pilot, but he was also known as a "mission hacker," one who is in search of glory, medals and making a name for himself and his career. Such people deliberately volunteered for missions that others avoided. In their own minds, they were the living embodiment of Errol Flynn, John Wayne and other Hollywood heroes. In the minds of other people, including their crew, these hackers were egotistic assholes and stupid glory seekers.

We left Tan Son Nhut and checked into the Globe. Unfortunately, the hotel was all but full for the first time, and since rooms were short, our crew checked into just two suites rather than three rooms. The two enlisted members stayed in one suite and we three officers checked into another. It was a time for real togetherness.

The next day, we headed out to the base about noon but found that our aircraft was being worked on by maintenance. We drew a version of the passenger run as our first mission, but it was four in the afternoon before we got off the ground. We flew clockwise to An Khe, then Chu Lai, Da Nang, then back to Chu Lai because there was a large marine influx in that area all of a sudden. Then we went to Da Nang to pick up a cargo load, which we took back to Saigon. It was fifteen minutes after midnight when we finally landed and shut down the engines.

The next day, we left the hotel at noon and ate on base at the officers' club. We checked into 130 Ops and were scheduled for a cargo hauling mission with a 4:30 takeoff. Our first stop was the army base at An Khe, where we picked up cargo and passengers. We flew from An Khe in the Central Highlands due east to the coast and then south to a new army base which was being established at Tuy Hoa.

Tuy Hoa sat in a large plain on the coast. To the north of it was a river clearly identifiable on my radar. The base itself, however, was not a good radar target, as the runway blended into the coastal plain and, other than distance from the river, there was nothing to distinguish it from the plain itself. We quickly offloaded the cargo and troops through the back door and ramp with our engines running, and were airborne again in five minutes. It was still daylight, but the sun was setting and the field had a low cloud cover over it which appeared to be decreasing in height. It was also lightly raining.

It was only a 20 minute flight back to An Khe and we returned there to pick up another similar mixed load also bound for Tuy Hoa. It took 40 minutes to get the new load onboard and we again set off for Tuy Hoa. When we got abeam Tuy Hoa this time, it was beginning to get dark due to a combination of the time of day and the steadily increasing cloud buildup and rain around the base. Again, we landed visually, offloaded quickly and got airborne in less than five minutes.

Now, with an empty aircraft, we flew 25 minutes down the coast to Cam Ranh Bay, where we were supposed to pick up cargo and take it to Tan Son Nhut. It took us nearly an hour to get offloaded and put a pallet on at Cam Ranh Bay. We then took off and proceeded east for a return to Saigon. Just after we were airborne, the Cam Ranh Bay ALCE called and told us that things had taken a turn for the worst back at Tuy Hoa and we were to turn around and go back to An Khe for another load to take into Tuy Hoa. As directed, we turned around and flew back to An Khe.

It was now dark in the An Khe valley and the base's approach radar was again out of commission. There was a low cloud layer over the base just a hundred or so feet above our minimums. We first attempted a prescribed letdown, flying with the base radio antenna as our guidance; but when we hit our minimums the runway was not in sight. My radar was working, so we next attempted another radio approach with me giving final guidance and altitude levels using the radar as the primary aid. The base runway showed up well on the radar, but the valley was not all that big and had a 3,000 foot mountain less than ten miles south of the runway. Right next to the runway was a 500 foot high karst hill. We made our approach in a southerly direction, staying to the east of the hill just as we had earlier when I was flying with John Dunn and we evacuated a medical case. In the event of a missed approach, the pilot was to immediately climb to 1,500 feet, thus keeping us above the hill while circling counterclockwise to avoid the mountain.

On our second radar assisted approach, we broke out just in time to see the lighted runway, but we were not lined up with it so we climbed back into the clouds and circled for another attempt. The third attempt was successful. We were on the ground after an hour of shooting approaches to get down in the weather and black night. The flight would usually have taken 25 minutes. It took an hour for the army to load us up with pallets of ammunition and then we were off again for Tuy Hoa.

We were inbound to Tuy Hoa in twenty minutes, but now it was also night over the South China Sea. Night, it was still raining, and the cloud layer had thickened. Just as at An Khe, we were just 100 or 200 feet above our minimum approach altitude. Tuy Hoa did not yet have a radar or even an approach radio to use for a landing aid. We were cleared for an approach, again using the radar and me as our main aids. The radar, however, did not paint the field at Tuy Hoa; so the approach was planned as a turn so many seconds after we came abeam of the river, which sat a half mile to the north of the Base. The river did give a strong radar return. Tuy Hoa sat just inland from the coast and the nearest mountains were ten or fifteen miles east of the runway. Our missed approach plan was to climb straight ahead to 1,000 feet and then circle to the south and back out over the ocean for another attempt.

On the first approach, we let down over the ocean in the dark and flew south, 90 degrees off the heading of the Tuy Hoa runway. At 1,000 feet, we couldn't see anything on shore because the rain and cloud layer had blocked out all light. Twenty-five seconds after the radar showed me that we were abeam the river, we turned to the runway heading. I corrected the heading to make up for drift, which read out on the Doppler above my desk. We then descended at 150 feet per mile, hoping to break out of the clouds in time to see and line up with the runway. On the first attempt, we didn't break out by the time we hit our minimums at 500 feet. We began our go-around turn and suddenly, off to the right, we could see three lights or flarepots set up on the extremities of a barely visible runway. Two lights marked the approach end and the last light sat in the middle of the runway's far end.

We climbed back up to 1,000 feet and proceeded out over the ocean and repeated our approach pattern. This time we turned 20 seconds after passing the river on radar. We hit 600 feet altitude and suddenly broke out of the clouds and rain. In front of us, in good visibility, were the three lights perfectly aligned. But as we moved in closer, the lights begin to shift. Suddenly the three evenly spaced lights were now bunched to the right. We weren't lined up, and the light at the far end moved toward the light at the right front. We now initiated another missed approach. Three lights of approximately equal size and intensity can take on numerous designs and undergo rapid shifts if you are not lined up exactly with them. We all knew this from having practiced numerous night paradrops where the drop zone was marked by the same light pattern as the Tuy Hoa airbase. But we had just learned the lesson again in the rain and fog.

Our next approach followed the same pattern, except we turned at 23 seconds past the river. Now we broke out again at 600 feet, but this time we could clearly see that we had lined up with the runway. Again we were on the ground after an hour in the air on what would normally have been a 20 minute flight. The army rapidly unloaded the ammunition pallets. Artillery was firing just off to the side of the parking area as we turned back on the runway and proceeded back to An Khe. It again took two tries to get on the runway at An Khe due to the low cloud base and the lack of any nighttime approach aid except our own radar.

At 1:15 in the morning, we took off with another load of ammunition. As we approached Tuy Hoa from over the ocean, we could see that the rain had stopped and the cloud layer had thinned out and lifted. We proceeded in and landed visually with no further problems, using the three marking lights as our landing reference. The army was still firing artillery off as we unloaded, but the pace was much reduced from the previous landing. After fifteen minutes on the ground, we were unloaded and back in the air.

An hour later we landed at Tan Son Nhut and called it a night at 2:30 in the morning. The combination of the bad weather at both landing sites and the lack of any reliable approach aid other than our own radar made this an interesting and hairy night of flying. Each nighttime approach was hazardous. We could have all used a drink before turning in; but the club was closed, so it was back to the Globe for an attempt at a night's sleep.

That evening we were again airborne at 9:30 and shuttled with cargo between An Khe, Da Nang and Chu Lai. We got back into Saigon at 5:00 in the morning. On landing we were told that our crew had been submitted for a medal citation to each receive a DFC for the previous night's flights into An Khe and Tuy Hoa.

That was the second DFC I was recommended for. I never got either one. Everyone in the air force who flew collected Air Medals for every 25 missions that they flew in Vietnam. I eventually collected eight or more of those. But the higher rated DFCs I never got.

The first DFC recommendation, for flying into An Khe in the weather and using an ARA as the approach aid while evacuating a sick or wounded GI, was denied. The air force said that the paperwork was done incorrectly and the AF liaison officer to the army division at An Khe did not have the authority to make such recommendations. The second submission, for flying multiple ARAs into An Khe and Tuy Hoa at night and in the weather, was denied because, at the time, the C-130 crews were all supposed to get a DFC incorporating all the missions that they flew in their one or two year tour. Several of the first crews to complete their tour and return to the States, those who had arrived in November 1965, did get such DFCs, but by the time we left in March 1967, the practice had been discontinued.

There were a great many medals given in the Vietnam War. Proportionately to the forces involved, there were more than were given in World War II and Korea. Many were given in an effort to improve morale or show support for what became an increasingly unpopular conflict. We were all given and allowed to wear a Vietnam Service Medal, which was awarded by the Republic of South Vietnam. In previous conflicts, U.S. personnel were not allowed to wear foreign decorations they were awarded. After Vietnam was over, I met people who were awarded DFCs and even the higher decoration, the Bronze Star, for actions much less hazardous than either of the two flights I'd been involved in leading to DFC recommendations. Winning a medal wasn't always a case of performing a heroic act alone; it also reflected the rules at the time you did the act and how well the paperwork was filled out.

The next day was almost a repeat of the day before. We left Tan Son Nhut at nine in the evening on a cargo haul. From there we flew to Kontum, Kontum to Tuy Hoa twice, then Cam Ranh Bay. Cam Ranh was now a fully operational 24 hour base and it took us two hours of ground time to unload and take on more cargo. Again we were back in Saigon at 5:00 in the morning.

25 June: We were out of Tan Son Nhut at 3:20 A.M. and landed at Bien Hoa fifteen minutes later and spent an hour putting on a load to take back to Tan Son Nhut. An hour after that, we were off to Cam Ranh Bay, and then back to Tan Son Nhut followed by a trip to Dalat. The aircraft was empty as we flew to Dalat, which was a district capital 50 miles inland on a direct route from Saigon to Nha Trang. Dalat was in the mountains and had a noticeably cooler climate than Saigon or the delta. It was an up-country vacation site and also was the location for the hydroelectric plant that provided Saigon with electricity.

When we landed at the civilian airport, we were told to park near the control tower and await our load. For 45 minutes nothing happened. Then suddenly a limousine pulled up and one man got out carrying a suitcase. A U.S. diplomatic official came up and told us that this one passenger was our load and we were to take him to Saigon. We did as directed. He sat in the back of the aircraft on our 35 minute flight and was met on arrival at Tan Son Nhut by another limousine. We later heard that he was the province chief at Dalat and had left in a hurry after receiving death threats from the Viet Cong.

The next day was somewhat of a typical one. We left the hotel at 7:00 in the morning in the crew van. After checking the weather and filing the flight plan, we grabbed a quick snack breakfast at the Shit Creek Snack Bar and then headed for the airplane, which was being loaded. We took off at 10:20 and immediately had wild engine fluctuations. The pilot shut it down and we entered a short left-hand turn back to the runway. C-130 Ops told us to park in the bomb dump, as we would require a good deal of maintenance on the engine. We left the bomb dump as maintenance took over the airplane. Once in Ops, they got an estimate that put the plane back in commission too late for us to fly anywhere for that day. By noon we were in the officers' club having lunch and a beer or two before returning to the hotel. We got ten minutes of flying time in a six hour work day. Except for the heat, dust, and location, it was almost as good as an eight to five civilian job in the States.

There was somewhat of a crisis in the officers' club. It seems that the scheduled shipments of various brands of U.S. sodas had somehow failed to arrive. The only shipment that had recently been received was Sprite. There was nothing else, no ginger ale, no orange, no Coke or Pepsi, not even seltzer water. If you wanted a soda, you had to drink Sprite. Also, if you want a mixed drink, you had to drink your favorite alcohol and Sprite. This situation led to many strange, new and not very tasty drinks being tried until the day the missing alternative sodas did appear.

I also found another sign of the increasing bureaucratic trend of the war's course. A few weeks before, I had read in the *Stars and Stripes* that the services in Vietnam were eliminating any traces of rank on uniforms except for black rank patches. At that time, I had started to cut my white lieutenant's bar off my fatigue cap, intending to replace it with a black bar that would be stitched on in its place. I got the job halfway done and stopped because I remembered that I didn't have a replacement black bar yet.

I was standing in a line at the bank on base at Tan Son Nhut with my fatigue hat on and the half remaining white bar prominently displayed on it. I was there to convert some dollars into Vietnamese script. There were about ten people in line in various uniforms. Right behind me in the line was a major wearing a flight suit and a blue flight cap with metal rank on it. As I was waiting, I heard someone say, "Major, don't you think you need to buy a new cap?" The major turned around and found an angry lieutenant colonel from the joint headquarters chewing him out because the braid on his hat was fraying. I never turned around. I could just imagine what he would have said if he had got a look at my half cut off fatigue cap. I suspect the lieutenant colonel was on his lunch hour and was mad because the line was so long. Or maybe he was just mad about being in Southeast Asia.

Thanks to our early quitting time, we got an even earlier show time for the next day. We were up at 3:00 in the morning and again took the crew vehicle to the base. Same routine as the day before, but this time the airplane worked and we were off to the small runway at Song Be and another Army "search-and-destroy" operation. Song Be is some forty miles North of Saigon. The bare runway with no parking area sat just adjacent to a 200 foot mountain in an otherwise flat plain. Loc Ninh is some 15 miles due west of Song Be and both sit within ten miles of the Cambodian border.

All day we made seven shuttles between the two sites, hauling army troops and equipment in rapid onload/offload operations where the troops and vehicles rolled on and off through the rear ramp and door while our engines were running. It was hot and dusty and the aircraft's broken air conditioner would not have been of any use on the short flights anyway. Halfway through the day we returned to Tan Son Nhut for fuel and an hour on the ground. We finally landed back at Tan Son Nhut for good at 10:30 that night. We logged five and a half hours of flying time in an eighteen and a half hour day with 12 separate individual sorties flown.

It was late June and we were now nearly halfway through our assigned thirteen month tour. The variety of loads that we were carrying was in some ways funny and in others amazing. Probably only the C-130 could safely accommodate them all, and that is in spite of the many errors and miscalculations that kept them from having any kind of "ordinary." Largely for these reasons, the Tactical Airlift mission and its crews became known as "trash hauls and trash haulers" since, like garbage men in the states, they would haul anyone and anything.

When we picked up a load from the army, it was their responsibility to identify the load and correctly indicate its weight and contents. Many army loads included large metal conex containers, which they used to store everything from ammunition to the personal belongings of units which were moving or going into the field. We were used to moving the containers to storage areas or to the deploying unit's next location.

Many, many times the loading data for the containers gave an incorrect weight for them. On other occasions the weight was given for an empty container when in fact the container was loaded to the fullest with something or other. Sometimes it became apparent that the container was mislabeled when the forklift putting it on the aircraft had trouble lifting the listed weight. At other times, several palletized containers might be loaded and each of them would weigh more than listed, but not enough to, individually, indicate that something was wrong.

The same could be said for many of the army trucks, jeeps and trailers that we loaded and carried. Our loadmaster planned each load according to

May 1966 — The author in the rain in the Tan Son Nhut cargo area (note the Conex containers).

the listed weights so that the airplane maintained the best center of gravity for performing according to standards for both flying and takeoff and landing. When the actual load was widely off from what was listed, the aircraft would either tilt on its tail or give indications of sinking on its front nose wheel. Many times we had to raise our legs to get in the crew door on the steps which should have been resting comfortably on the ground. On occasion I've even had to physically climb up the steps to get in the door. Thank God the C-130 handled so well and was so forgiving.

One load that we had was a five pallet shipment of army boots packed in large cardboard boxes. The boxes were oversize commercial moving containers about four feet square by five feet high. They were stacked two high and tied down so that twenty or so boxes were on each pallet. The pallets had been sitting in the Tan Son Nhut cargo storage hangar for some time. Once we were in-flight carrying the boots to an army base, several of the boxes collapsed inward or caved in. Some were completely empty and others had half a load of boots in them. Between their original destination and our flight to their final one, they had been looted. I doubt if the whole load had more than one-quarter of the number of boots in it that we cited on the loading document.

Another time, our load was the cannon barrels for 155mm or 175mm guns. Each of the guns sat on two wooden frames, which they fit into on each end of the gun. They were palletized on three interlocked pallets and secured to individual pallets by metal bands running over the wooden frames. Carl figured out the proper loading for them as far as the plane's center of gravity was concerned. They were long and heavy, and with the loading end larger than the firing end, an unusual load. When the loading crew pushed the triple palleted guns onto the aircraft, the metal band on the rear pallet of one of the guns broke when crossing the point where the rollers on the rear door of the plane met the body. The long narrow end of the gun pivoted upward, held in place only by the metal band on the opposite wooden frame, which was on the first pallet inside the aircraft. As the gun barrel swung upward, it stopped just short of going through the ceiling of the aircraft.

Another load to be avoided was a plane full of Vietnamese troops when they were "combat loaded." Usually when we carried troops or passengers of any sort, they were seated in nylon strap seats which folded down from the side walls of the C-130 or were secured by ceiling mounted stanchions and straps. But when we carried Vietnamese troops in combat gear, we usually put five pallets on the floor rollers and stretched nylon straps across them secured to the sidewalls. By doing this, we could get twice as many troops on board (more than 150 versus 92 seated) as we could by giving them individual seats. When this mass of humanity got onboard, however, if someone needed to go to the rear of the aircraft for any reason he had to wade through them in-flight. That was not a pleasant experience, since our allies, the Vietnamese, liked to goose, fondle and sexually stroke male flyers in that atmosphere. They also shared an Asian affinity for holding hands when there were two males together in close proximity.

During the conflict, the C-130 carried a variety of loads under all sorts of conditions, from normal operations as well as emergency introduction and extraction missions in the face of combat, poor weather and sometimes both.

I can recall during 1965 and 1966 that some of the passenger and troop carrying runs included chickens and little potbellied pigs. Later in the war, when the Vietnamese organized a loading organization and the issuance of flight passes, creatures such as these were no longer seen.

The all time champion animal load, however, has got to be the elephants. This was one that neither I nor our squadron was involved in, but it made the papers in the theater. Everyone in the airlift force knew of it, and most of them laughed. After the war, a movie was made of the incident, but it was Hollywooded-up and was not the true story.

As I recall, a small Vietnamese village somewhere in I Corps, up near Da Nang, had a lumbering operation as their main industry and they used elephants to do their hauling. Somehow or other, deliberately by the Viet Cong or as the accidental result of firing, all of the local elephants were killed and the village was left without a livelihood. Enter the U.S. Civil Affairs folks, who saw restoring the village to prosperity as one means of winning the hearts and minds of the people. The elephants were slated to return and the C-130 was chosen to deliver them.

Spring 1966 — U.S. Army Capt. (Chaplain) Fred Straub visiting with an elephant in the Central Highlands near the Laotian border (from the collection of Fred W. Straub).

Vietnamese elephants are of the Indian variety — thank God, because their African relatives are considerably bigger. At any rate, the Civil Affairs group procured two elephants and delivered them to a nearby Airlift Control Element. The animals were then put to sleep with injections. Once out cold, they were strapped down on pallets just like giant sides of beef and rolled onto a C-130A like any other palletized load. They were then flown to the nearest C-130 capable airstrip to the logging village, offloaded on pallets by forklifts and then played their role in the village seeking to win the war for the good guys.

28 June: We got a day off and the following day reported out to Tan Son Nhut to rotate back to Mactan. We took off at 1:30 in the afternoon and flew to Qui Nhon with a cargo load that took two hours to download. Instead of going to Clark, we flew direct to Mactan and arrived there at 8:00 in the evening. Another shuttle was over with.

We got our two day stay in the Magellan Hotel, but just barely. The morning of our third day back, I was again airborne on another shuttle input. The crew syndrome was now badly disrupted by the additional personnel training and upgrades going on. The rest of the crew was my basic one, but the pilot became Major Kahn, who came from Langley and lived in our tent. He was another ex-fighter pilot and still maintained a lot of the aggressive and enthusiastic outlook to flying which seems common to such types. We flew through Clark and took a load to Bien Hoa, and then from there we went on to Tan Son Nhut with the daily replacement aircraft. We got in Tan Son Nhut at 5:00 in the evening because we had a five hour ground delay in Clark getting the load for Bien Hoa on.

The next day, July 3, we took off at 4:20 in the afternoon and went to Dalat, where we picked up a load and took it back to Saigon. Once on the ground at Tan Son Nhut, we reported a broken airplane due to leaking hydraulics. We waited four hours for maintenance to make repairs but the plane was still out of commission at the end of that time. C-130 Ops sent us back to the hotel.

The following day our schedule and takeoff slipped to five hours later in the day. We took off at 7:40 in the evening and flew to Cam Ranh Bay, where we picked up a load and took it back to Saigon. On the ground at Tan Son Nhut, we landed in a broken airplane. Maintenance came out and took a quick look at the engine and engine gauges and issued a several hour repair estimate involving a trip to the bomb dump side of the base. C-130 Ops decided we should again return early to the hotel and forfeit what was to be the rest of our schedule for that day.

5 July: Fourteen hours later we were back on base and getting ready for another flying day. We took off at five in the evening and carried air force cargo and an assortment of passengers to Phan Rang, then Cam Ranh Bay, then Da Nang, followed by Nha Trang. Having spent most of the time flying up and down the East China Sea, we returned to Tan Son Nhut and went into crew rest at eleven in the evening. Four hours and ten minutes flying time in an eight hour day. For the first time in three days we got a somewhat easy cargo hauling effort with no broken airplanes.

The next day, we took off at six in the evening and hauled cargo to the marine base at Chu Lai, then Da Nang and finally into Hue. Hue is the old Vietnamese Imperial Capital and it had two bases. One was inside the city itself and close to the Citadel, which is a pentagon shaped fort dating back to the French possession of the country. The Citadel airfield had a short runway and was used only by U.S. planes with smaller load and takeoff needs than us. We operated out of the Hue-Phu Bai base, which is outside the city on the coast. When we got to Hue it was midnight and the ground loading personnel seemed to have taken the rest of the night off. We couldn't find anyone to get us offloaded. Major Kahn didn't want to spend the night there waiting so he commandeered a forklift which was standing nearby and unloaded our palletized cargo himself. We were back in Tan Son Nhut and called it a night at three in the morning.

The following day, we stumbled into 130 Ops at midnight and went though our routine of filing and then eating at Shit Creek. We took off at 3:00 A.M. but got only thirty minutes in the air before the aircraft developed an engine problem. We returned to Saigon and landed an hour and a half after we left. We then sat on the ground for another two and a half hours while maintenance switched our load onto another aircraft. Finally, at 7:00, we took off again in the second aircraft and flew to Pleiku with the cargo. We were back in Tan Son Nhut at 9:30 in the morning and went into crew rest.

The rest of that day was spent in downtown Saigon walking the streets, having a beer on the patio of the Caravelle Hotel, eating a steak at the Rex Officers' Club and then back to the hotel. The next day, we left at midday on the rotation aircraft, stopped at Cam Ranh Bay with a load on the way out. Then we went straight back to Mactan, getting in at 4:30 in the afternoon. Another shuttle over.

We got another stay in the Magellan and an extra day off to collect fresh clothes and enjoy the communal tent on Mactan together with the charming officers' club. On our fourth day back, we were again airborne and heading for another shuttle. We left at 6:45 in the morning and were in Clark by 8:20. Three hours and fifteen minutes later (Clark was very busy and we were a low priority for getting a load on) we were airborne and flew to Ubon Air

Base in Thailand. It took an hour and ten minutes to download cargo at Ubon and we flew from there to Tan Son Nhut. We checked through C-130 Ops at 6:30 in the evening and went downtown to eat an Asian hamburger in the Globe Hotel at 8:00. That was a fourteen hour day, since we got up at Mactan at four in the morning.

15 July: Naturally we were put on the night shift the following evening. We flew a two leg mission from Saigon to Pleiku and then from there went to Cam Ranh Bay and back to Tan Son Nhut. We quit at 2:00 in the morning after three hours of flying time and a total day of eight hours. Some of the airplanes were in pretty bad mechanical condition at this time, and to get a complete fleet ready for the daylight missions the next day we were sent home early rather than trying to fly anymore of the less productive night sorties.

The following evening we showed up at midnight only to find that there were no airplanes in commission for us to fly. We sat around for five hours waiting for one to become available, but that did not happen. At six in morning we went to the Tan Son Nhut Officers' Club for breakfast and then retired to downtown for a casual afternoon of touring Saigon again. We had a drink or two on the veranda at the Caravelle Hotel on the main street and ate steak for dinner at the Rex Officers' Club. This time there were no C-47 gunships shooting up the outskirts of Saigon. We could almost imagine that we were winning the war.

Up at 5:30 the next morning, we took off from Tan Son Nhut at 8:20. After a twenty minute flight, we landed at Bien Hoa for the start of another operation in support of army "search-and-destroy" operations. All day long we flew from Bien Hoa to a small single runway and limited parking area landing zone known only as VVLE. As usual with these operations, it was a long, hot and dusty day. The only thing possibly worse would have been a long, hot and rainy day. The troops and vehicles rolled on and off the back of the C-130. There were no palletized loads and no need of forklifts.

Each stop at Bien Hoa to upload took about an hour, as we had to wait until the landing field at VVLE was clear lest we create gridlock on the ground there. Each flight to VVLE took fifteen to twenty minutes. We often had to circle or hold in orbit until the runway was clear since each landing plane must stop on the far end and then taxi back to the small, offload area, which had room for only one or two C-130s at a time. Once we landed and taxied to the offload area (often taxing in just as one of the waiting aircraft taxied by us to take the runway), we were on the ground for a maximum of ten minutes as the troops and vehicles exited out the rear ramp and door just as quickly as they got on. Then it took fifteen minutes to get back to Bien Hoa and an hour for another load. We spent all day in the aircraft at temperatures between 95 and 110 degrees, except for the two times we refueled while on the ground at Bien Hoa. We flew six round-trips between Bien Hoa and VVLE before returning to Tan Son Nhut at 7:30 in the evening. As usual, our loadmaster was exhausted and filthy dirty from rolling around the cargo deck of the C-130 all day, chaining down and then unchaining vehicles during each twenty minute flight.

A day later, 19 July, we were back on the night shift. We flew two cargo lifts out of Tan Son Nhut, one to Binh Thuy in the delta and another to Nha Trang on the East China Sea. It was cooler and more relaxing at night, and the ground times were longer because there was only a skeleton shift at the bases working the cargo on- and offloads. We got three hours of flying time in a ten-hour day and were back on the ground at 5:15 in the morning. We went for another breakfast in the Tan Son Nhut Officers' Club.

We got the rest of that day off and the following day we left the hotel at three in the morning and took off from Tan Son Nhut at five. We flew to Da Nang and spent four hours on the ground waiting for an onload. When we finally got cargo, it was for the marine base at Chu Lai just a twenty minute flight down the coast. We offloaded at Chu Lai and took on a pallet to go back to Da Nang. At Da Nang we took on three pallets of rice and flew them back to Saigon.

While we were en route to Saigon, our loadmaster started reading a note written on one of the rice loaded pallets. It said that this load was hauled from Saigon to Da Nang about ten days earlier. The loadmaster had heard from some of his compatriots that they had started marking some of the loads we carried because they were finding out that they had been carried multiple times to the same or different locations. It appeared that we were keeping our records of tons of cargo hauled up by continually hauling the same loads back and forth! Such jacked-up cargo hauling records helped the air force in justifying the need for so many transports in Theater.

In another cargo fiasco, Major Kahn, our tent mate, was almost made a criminal. The cargo storage area behind C-130 Ops was usually crammed with pallets of C-rations. Since we were forbidden to prolong our stops anywhere by going to eat lunch or dinner, each crew usually carried three or four cases of C-rations with them. Each case had 12 boxes of ready to eat or heat meals, together with cookies, crackers and fruit. It seems that Kahn's crew had exhausted their supply, so the good major went back to the cargo area and lifted several cases off a pallet. As he was walking back to the airplane with his booty, he was stopped by several MPs and a lieutenant colonel who informed him that he was guilty of stealing government property. It was just his luck that a stateside inspection team was in Tan Son Nhut at the time looking into the theft of U.S. war materials, which was rampant. Kahn's semi-innocent act of taking C-ration cases was just what they needed to fill out their trip report and show that they had captured a major criminal. Ned was subjected to several paper charges which flowed down through the squadron, but the whole issue eventually blew over with no permanent damage done.

We were back in Tan Son Nhut at 3:00 in the afternoon and retired to the officers' club for a few beers and dinner. We flew the rotation airplane home the next day, but the route was a bit out of the ordinary. Instead of flying to a base on the coast and then going on to Clark or Mactan, we first fly to Korat in Thailand. From there we flew back through Vietnam to Qui Nhon on the coast and let off a few Army passengers and a pallet of cargo before flying direct to Mactan. We landed in Mactan at 10:45 in the evening.

We got to enjoy our two day stay in the Magellan in Cebu and then returned to Mactan for an extended stay. Due to the low in-commission rate of the aircraft flying in Vietnam, the Wing was trying to keep its flying hours total up to normal by flying more hours on local missions. There was also a problem of increased crew upgrades and training for new personnel, both of which required instructor crews and working airplanes.

In a four day period we flew three days on local training and upgrade flights. During this period of sustained local training I was upgraded to instructor navigator. I also took a thirty day leave and, with a set of somewhat illegal orders signed by our squadron night duty officer, (who was authorized to sign orders giving us the right to fly on any theater aircraft when necessary to get from place to place for further flights, although this authority did not extend to other theaters or other commands), I set out across the Pacific to the U.S. I begged, borrowed or bummed a ride on numerous aircraft coming and going. But that is a story for another time and place.

In late August, I returned from leave, and my first flight duty was to serve as the navigator on a mission to Thailand with staff officers from the Wing headquarters flying in all the other crew positions. While I was in Bangkok with the Wing Weenies I heard a good story about visits to the Bangkok market. It seems that one of the C-130 crews from Taiwan spent a day in Bangkok, and at the market one of them bought a habu. The habu is a local Thai version of the cobra. It is relatively small and has the somewhat curious habit of liking to live around people, since it dines primarily on rats.

Habu are for sale in the Bangkok market, as are a number of other snakes. Since the buyer meant to keep this snake as a pet, he bought it alive and had its fangs removed as a safety measure. The officer who bought the habu took it back alive on his plane's flight to Taiwan since their baggage was not usually inspected on return from military trips. He then took the habu back to his apartment in downtown Taipei, which he shared with three other flyers.

In the apartment, the snake was kept in a glass enclosure like a fish bowl with a mesh top. As luck would have it, one evening one of the apartment mates returned to his bed drunk and knocked the habu enclosure over. The snake was never found, but no one worried since it had been defanged.

Several months later, one of the apartment dwellers went on another trip to Bangkok and, in the course of an evening on the town, related to a local about the missing habu. Everyone laughed until the local commented that, of course, the storyteller knew that a habu which had been defanged grew its fangs back over a period of several months. As I said, the missing habu was never found.

Four days after my return to Mactan, on September 6, I flew a local training mission at Mactan with John Dunn, Hal, and our whole old crew. Also attached to us were a newly arrived pilot and a navigator. Before these new personnel could be allowed to fly by themselves, they had to train with us and be certified as Theater oriented. Our crew was back in business together, at least for a little while.

Two days after that, on September 8, the complete old crew left for a shuttle with both trainees accompanying us. When we landed at Clark to pick up a load, there was a notice on the flight messages board saying that flights going to Thailand could now only go via the route over the South China Sea into Bangkok from the south. This was because a Surface to Air Missile (SAM) site had been reported in the vicinity of the route into northern Thailand, directly west of Da Nang. I was startled by this, since that was the route we had just flown on my last Bangkok mission.

Just then I happened to meet one of the C-130 crews who flew shuttles out of Cam Ranh Bay. Since I hadn't flown a shuttle in over a month due to my leave, I asked one of the shuttle crew's pilots I knew from the academy: "What's going on? Has the air war in Vietnam now been extended into the south, since this is the first mention of SAMs in South Vietnam?" He assured me that there was no such SAM site reported in the notices in South Vietnam. Together, we went to the intelligence and message center at Clark and, after bringing the situation to the attention of the duty officer, the SAM message was deleted at Clark and crews going in-country and into Thailand resumed normal routes and operations. Evidently the fighter pilots coming back with excess flares from recce missions over the North spooked another C-141 crew, or an airliner, and their report of SAMs or antiaircraft artillery at high altitude over the South was accepted as enemy action.

We had to wait for a load at Clark and were delayed five hours. As a result, we didn't get into Tan Son Nhut until 8:30 P.M. instead of mid-afternoon. We were sent into crew rest at new quarters close to Tan Son Nhut and were once again on the in-country shuttle after a break, for me, of over 40 days. The new quarters were in a recently built multistory brick building that was about ten minutes driving time from Tan Son Nhut. It had over 100 rooms in it and a shared multi-person bathroom, shower room and toilet on each floor. It appeared to be filled only with air crews, and van service to and from the base ran regularly at half-hour intervals.

We started the next day on the late afternoon shift, and took off at 3:30 and delivered loads into Phan Rang and Cam Ranh Bay. We then returned to Tan Son Nhut, where loading delays kept us on the ground for four hours. When we took off again, we went to Pleiku, Da Nang, Nha Trang and then back to Saigon, getting in at 2:10 in the morning — a pretty efficient 6 hours and 45 minutes of flying time in a 12½ hour day.

That got us a day off, which we spent lolling at the quarters and getting a steak dinner in the Rex Hotel before reporting at 3:00 A.M. for our return to the morning shift on the following day, which was a short day with stops in Chu Lai, Da Nang and Phan Rang before we quit at 1:00 in the afternoon.

We followed that up with a one flight day on 12 September. We flew in and out of the 1st Cavalry base at An Khe and then quit for the day when the airplane developed mechanical troubles. The maintenance estimate of time to be repaired extended into the evening and we were let go and moved up only two hours in the flying order for the next day.

On our approach into An Khe on that single mission, we had taken a radar approach from the An Khe controller through an undercast cloud formation. We were landing to the north on a new An Khe runway which was to the south of the main base. We were at medium altitude over a mountain range when he cleared us to begin descent to an initial approach altitude.

Just as we left flight altitude and headed down to the directed approach altitude, my radar scope went black. I immediately told Dunn to hold his altitude, and only when I again began to get radar returns in front of the aircraft did I recommend we start the descent. Just then the weather in front of us cleared and sure enough, right below us was the sharp face of the mountain range which fell away into the An Khe valley.

Evidently the new approach radar at the base wasn't exactly calibrated with regard to altitude and starting point over the mountain — either that or the operator misread one or the other of his limits. An immediate response to the controller's command with a steep descent would have run us right into the mountain about 8 miles from the end of the runway.

The following day, the 13th of September, proved to be unlucky 13 with regard to mission accomplishment and flying time. We took off at one in the afternoon but made only one cargo hauling flight into Qui Nhon. When we got back to Tan Son Nhut for another load at 4:00 P.M. the aircraft had developed engine trouble and we were done for the day. The combination of two short flying days and early quits moved us back instead of forward on the schedule and we started the following day at five in the morning. It was another cargo hauling mission to Qui Nhon, Bien Hoa and Dak To before quitting at six in the evening. That quitting time made it convenient to have dinner in the Tan Son Nhut club before we returned to quarters for some sleep and the next day off, which was again spent wandering the streets of Saigon prior to our departure for Mactan the following day on the rotational aircraft.

At the time our Wing had been given the movement orders from Langley and had been assigned to the Far East, I made up my mind that one acquisition I would try to make while in that part of the world was a tiger painting of some sort. After dining in the Rex Hotel on our free day and wandering the main streets of Saigon before going back to the quarters, I took in some of the shops and souvenir stands on the main streets.

One recently opened site featured furniture and artworks which looked like they had been looted from homes somewhere in the war zone. And there, in the center of the display as you walked in the door, was a five foot by three foot painting of two tigers drinking. The shop wanted $150 worth of Vietnamese piastres for the painting. After several minutes of haggling and threatening to walk out, the price was down to $75, which I agreed to.

The only problem was that I didn't have $75 on me. Luckily, the navigator trainee who accompanied us on this mission had a few extra bucks, which I borrowed. I then walked out with the unwrapped painting and carried it back to the Rex to catch the bus to our quarters. As we were at the end of another shuttle and possibly had imbibed too many 25 cent highballs at the Rex, both the trainee navigator and I got off the bus and went to our rooms in the BOQ without taking the tiger picture off the bus with us.

By morning, my head was a little clearer and I got concerned that I probably paid $75 for a painting which was now lost somewhere in Saigon. Lo and behold, however, when the bus came to take us from the quarters into C-130 Operations, sitting in the back of the bus on the last seat was my painting. It had been riding around Saigon all night.

We left Tan Son Nhut at 9:30 that morning, passed thru Bien Hoa and Clark on the way home and settled into Mactan at nine that evening. Another shuttle was over, and that meant a two day stay in the Magellan earned. Just like old times.

2007 — The once missing tiger picture.

21 September: Our crew flew a four-hour local training mission at Mactan again with students on board. The squadron now had a temporary surplus of people. Many new arrivals were being trained and none of the original company had yet left, nor were they scheduled to for another two months. As a result, we got more time between flights and shuttles.

It was very easy to spot the new arrivals prior to meeting or being introduced to them. Most were sweating heavily, especially the older ones, in the hot and humid Philippine climate. Others hadn't yet grasped the fact that living on base at Mactan differed somewhat from the stateside lifestyle. When told to go to his assigned tent, unpack his bags and then return to the squadron for indoctrination briefings and training the next day, one new arrival refused to walk to the squadron area from his tent and instead waited all day for a bus to take him there. As a result, he disappeared from the ranks of the known and identified for over a week before someone noticed he was missing. Once refound he was rewarded by a good ass chewing from the operations officer and became somewhat of a joke around the squadron.

25 September: Off again on another shuttle, and with another new navigator along to break in. We were several hours late getting out of Mactan due to maintenance (11:00 A.M.); but we made our mandatory stop at Clark to pick up cargo and passengers and then went thru Bien Hoa for 30 minutes to let off passengers and then on into Tan Son Nhut. This time we were assigned to newly leased quarters southwest of the airport in the Cholon district of the city.

The next day we began on the mid-afternoon shift with a cargo run to Qui Nhon. We encountered a loading delay in Qui Nhon and got back to Tan Son Nhut at 10:00 P.M. That was the end of our day. One flight and we were back into crew rest.

While we were on the night shift, we heard that the day operations were rather restricted. It seems that there was an army operation about 20 miles outside of Saigon that required a number of airlift sorties for support. Since it was only 20 miles, someone decided to use the operation to set an airlift record. For most of the day, almost all of the loading equipment at Tan Son Nhut was devoted to supporting one aircraft that kept making repeated shuttles to the same place. Within a few days the *Stars and Stripes* newspaper reported that they had set a single-day record for one aircraft with regard to weight of cargo hauled. What the article never said, however, was how they did it by reducing all other operations for the day to almost zero. From such efforts in the midst of wartime are great records set. Great and meaningless.

The next day, we reported two hours later. Our mission was to fly the daily counterclockwise passenger run which was moved back in the schedule for the day due to an earlier aircraft breakdown. We were airborne at five in the evening and made four stops en route (Phan Rang, Cam Ranh Bay, Da Nang, and Nha Trang) and were back in Tan Son Nhut and into crew rest at 1:00 A.M. Seventeen hours later we flew exactly the same mission with the same four stops. We left at 6:00 P.M. this time and were back at 1:20 in the morning. We were getting more efficient every day it seemed — starting later but finishing the same run in less overall time.

We got one free day off to transition to the night shift and then reported at 2:30 in the morning for cargo runs supporting the marines in I Corps. Taking off at 4:40, we made stops in Chu Lai, Da Nang and Quang Nai and were back in Saigon at 1:00 P.M., done for the day. We all retired to the officers' club for lunch. The others departed for our quarters or downtown, but Dunn and I remained to sip a few cold ones.

1 October: We had worked our way back into the early daylight clockwise passenger run. We were off the ground by 8:00 A.M. and then picked up and dropped people off at Pleiku, Da Nang, Hue and then back through Da Nang, Pleiku and in and out of Cam Ranh Bay before returning to Tan Son Nhut at 6:30 P.M. Time for another meal in the O club with a few after-dinner drinks before grabbing the bus to our quarters.

On the first two legs of this day's mission, we had a load of passengers that included a USO troupe and the senior navy chaplain, a captain, for Southeast Asia. Through a process of natural selection and consideration for rank, a female dancer from the troupe and the navy chaplain were invited to fly up in the cockpit on the bunk seats next to the navigators' section. Shortly after takeoff from Saigon, the dancer ended up sitting on the student navigator's lap and making en route radio calls to the ground stations along the way. The result was pretty funny. One ground station member asked incredulously, "Are you a girl?" She enjoyed the humor and the attention. So did the student navigator.

At the same time, I stood with the chaplain behind the flight engineer's seat and pointed out to him where we were and how what he was looking at relative to the history and course of the war so far. After our Pleiku stop, the chaplain and I were seated on the bunk and the dancer was again entertaining both the student navigator and the en route reporting points. The chaplain turned to me and asked, with a slight hint of condescension in his voice, "How old do you think she is?" Not being an expert in such matters, I hazarded the guess that she was about 30.

"Must have had a hard life," said the chaplain. From this I guessed that the chaplain did not like the dancer nor appreciate the humor in her talking to the ground station operators, who had probably not seen an American woman for six months or more. You can imagine my surprise when, on arrival at Da Nang where they both exited our aircraft, the navy chaplain captain rated a limousine pick-up to take him to the officers' club for lunch and invited the dancer to accompany him there. Evidently chivalry was not dead.

On the following day, we had a 3:10 afternoon takeoff but made only one stop, at Nui Bara, a small base just outside Saigon, to offload cargo. We immediately went back to Tan Son Nhut, where the airplane was taken over by maintenance due to engine trouble. Our day was over at 4:25 after one hour and five minutes of flying time. Off we went to another meal and some drinks in the officers' club.

While we were waiting to take off on our flight for the day, Dunn and I walked back to the Shit Creek Snack Bar to have a soda and a sandwich. When we got inside there were five or six people sitting around the tables in the dingy, hot interior. I lifted a Seven-Up off the counter, paid for it and retired to an empty table to drink it. As usual, since there was no ice in the place, the soda can was warm. I began pulling the snap cap off it. As I walked to the table the hot soda had gotten shaken up. Before I could get the whole cap off, the can flew out of my hand and hit the floor with a hissing sound not unlike a lighted fuse. All six of the people at the other tables hit the floor as soon as the sound occurred. They thought we were under attack.

That was not unlike what a friend of mine had told me about the Sunday morning when he went to church in the Catholic cathedral in downtown Saigon. The church had a large, high, wooden door, not unlike those found in many old European cathedrals. At one point during the service, everyone was standing to sing a hymn when the wind blew the wooden door shut with a loud bang. He said the whole congregation hit the floor together. When you are in a combat theater where guerrillas plant bombs, you tend to take somewhat comic sounds and situations seriously.

The following day, we were airborne at 4:40 in the afternoon and hauled cargo to Qui Nhon and Phan Rang. While we were waiting for takeoff at Tan Son Nhut on the initial flight to Qui Nhon, we heard a Vietnamese T-28 trainer/attack plane call in to the tower that he needed an emergency landing. He had a hung bomb (one which did not drop on activation and was now hanging on the airplane uncontrolled) as well as a runaway propeller going at a constant uncontrollable speed. The tower told him to exit the traffic pattern and go to a horse racetrack which adjoined Tan Son Nhut and try to jettison the bomb as well as get control of the engine and propeller.

A U.S. instructor pilot who was in the backseat of the T-28 joined in the conversation. The instructor was the better qualified pilot, but he could not reach the controls from where he sat. As we exited the traffic pattern after takeoff, both the Vietnamese pilot and the U.S. instructor pilot in the T-28 were still carrying on conversations with the airport control with regard to their emergency.

When we got to Qui Nhon we took on a mixed load of two pallets of cargo and some 40 passengers going to Phan Rang and Saigon. While the passengers were boarding, a Vietnamese male in combat uniform tried to bypass the passenger control agent and get on the airplane without having a numbered pass to do so. In short order, his attempt was stopped by weapons pulled by the control agent, an MP standing by, our loadmaster and me.

Months earlier, a navy C-130 disappeared on a flight between Cam Ranh Bay and Okinawa. Sabotage was suspected. In the same time period, a loadmaster found a coffee cup turned upside down in the back of a parked C-130, which on further inspection turned out to have a hand grenade with the pin pulled lodged inside the cup. Luckily, the grenade turned out to be a dud. Accordingly, we were all on heightened alert with regard to who turned up as passengers on passenger runs and what they carried onboard or left behind.

We landed back in Tan Son Nhut at 9:30 in the evening and called it quits. Before departing the base, we found out that the T-28 that had an emergency earlier in the day had crashed on the racetrack infield and both occupants were killed.

4 October: We were scheduled to go home the next day and were all up at six in the morning with all our crew and clothing bags to ride the bus to C-130 Ops and fly home to Mactan. The bus was full as the crews for the early morning missions were also on it. Everyone noticed that one of the quarters workers carried out the bags of the young 2nd lieutenant who was my student navigator and placed them on the bus. This was noteworthy because all the rest of us had carried out our own bags.

Once the bus began moving, I asked the young officer how he got such privileged service. Well, he says, he didn't know but the worker seemed particularly grateful when he, the lieutenant, had paid him some $40 worth of piastres, as his room rent, for the shuttle. I couldn't help laughing because we always paid our BOQ fees to C-130 Ops at the end of a shuttle and they then reimbursed the housing authority. Sometime in the processing procedures the lieutenant hadn't been listening to details on who got paid when. He had just paid $40 for a bag carry.

The rest of the day went like clockwork. We took off at 9:40 and went through Pleiku and Clark on our way to Mactan, which we reached at 6:30 that evening. As a result of finishing our ten day shuttle, we also collected our free, luxurious, two-night stay in the Magellan Hotel in Cebu City.

Since our last stay there, the Wing had introduced a new policy whereby crews from Clark were coming down to Mactan to fly local training missions because the Mactan low-level routes were new and better and there was so much less air traffic at Mactan than Clark. Several crews would come for a week and alternate flying the planes they brought with them. This was the first visit to Mactan for most of the crews at Clark, including those who had previously been our Wing and squadron mates at Langley.

The Clark crews did not begrudge us our tents, showers or living conditions on base at Mactan. They were impressed, however, with the Magellan Hotel and with the local country club and its golf course, to which most of us belonged and to which they could go as guests. Soon, the word began to get around at Clark that Mactan was not quite the wilderness it was rumored to be and that, in fact, it wasn't a bad place to bring your family for a holiday. More and more of the visiting Clark crews began to bring their families to Mactan and put them up in the Magellan Hotel for a week or several days while they were flying local missions. It was thus only a matter of time before one (or more) of the Clark families was in an elevator in the Magellan going up to their rooms after a leisurely dinner when who should step in but one of their old, married, neighbors from Langley, together with his Philippine girlfriend of the evening. Numerous letters, cables and phone calls began to flow between Clark, the U.S. (Langley area) and Mactan. A short time later, the Wing discontinued the local training of Clark crews at Mactan; the reason given was lack of funding.

In the interim, I got two weeks of ground duty to perform. Dunn and company went off on another shuttle, but I stayed behind to write the Squadron history for the past year. When we were at Langley, I had been assigned as the squadron historian, which amounted to keeping monthly records of flights made, cargo hauled and personnel coming into and out of the unit. Some two months previously, when I had upgraded to an instructor, I had been notified that I was no longer the historian as that job had been given to one of the new arrivals.

Somehow, probably in a backdoor deal I was left out of, the squadron commander (Big Stoop) was tasked by the Wing to present the history on short notice. He then forgot, or chose to forget, that I was no longer responsible for the history, sent the guy who was supposed to write it on the shuttle, and chewed me out for not having it done. It took me about a week to find the records that should have been kept and put them in the fairy tale format and language which passed for the desired history. Although I voiced my opinion of this episode at several instances to several higher ranking people, Big Stoop never seemed to accept that he and not I had screwed up in bringing the situation about.

While on the ground for that two week period, I was witness to one of the great scientific breakthroughs of the twentieth century, not to mention of Oriental-Western relations. Ever since we had begun operating out of the Philippines, everyone had been stymied by our inability to tell exactly how old any of the Filipinos were especially the females. They seemed to have no recognizable aging pattern or middle age. They just went from youth to old age.

Two of the barmaids in the officers' bar in the Mactan Club were twins. They were also somewhat pretty, spoke excellent English and were seventeen years old when first hired, which was one year below the legal limit, according to the club's charter. Naturally, with their other assets, no one bothered about the age discrepancy. There names were Lalu and Lupa. One evening, in the course of an after dinner round of drinks in the club, one of the young officer members proclaimed that he had solved the mystery of Filipino aging, at least in the Mactan/Cebu area. The magic age at which a transition from youth to maturity occurred was 35. How, asked another member, was this determined? The answer was, "Lalu and Lupa took me to their house last night and I met their older sister. She was thirty-five."

Also, one of the unit's premier motorbike riders accomplished a new record over the period. A young captain who had been one of the new arrivals about a month before had purchased one of the older member's motorbikes. In short order, returning from a banana farm one evening, he crashed the thing and made high speed impact with his face on the unpaved but stone covered road leading back to the base. His face was a mass of cuts and contusions.

Almost exactly a month later on the same road and in nearly similar conditions, he managed to repeat the very same engagement and impact. At that time, his face had just begun to heal from the previous impact. By this time, his face was heavily crusted from the first accident, so that he looked somewhat like the Creature from the Black Lagoon rather than a human being. In the second impact, the rock road scraped the scabs and puss of the earlier creation and turned him into a true monster. He could have charged admission for viewings, but he instead opted to spend more time in his tent and less on the road.

This same individual was, like me, a favorite of Big Stoop. On one occasion, he had been scheduled for a flight to take him on the next day's shuttle with his crew. When show time for the flight came, he was absent — not in his tent, said the shuttle bus pickup driver. Another poor navigator was roused from his cot and sent on the mission for the day.

When Big Stoop was informed about two hours later, he went into a rage and was heard to threaten court-martial. The next day, when our squadron didn't have a shuttle flight, Big Stoop happened to be in the operations room at exactly the same time as show time the previous day. In walked the absent captain, fully clothed for flight and with all his bags. "Where the hell have you been, Captain?" thundered Big Stoop from behind the 4 foot high Ops counter. When informed that he was a day late, the offender looked at his watch and calmly replied, "I guess I just missed a day, Sir." Somehow the remainder of the staff restrained Big Stoop from murder, but then again, it is possible to miss a day on an island in the tropics.

On 18 October, I got back in the cockpit and flew off on a Bangkok run with a mixed crew of old guys and trainees. We flew to Clark late in the day after waiting for maintenance to repair our aircraft. When we got to Clark, the same problem resurfaced and we spent a free day around the swimming pool and in the Club. We were up at 3:00 in the morning the next day and in the air promptly at 5:25 A.M. We reached Bangkok at 3:35 in the afternoon after Air Force passenger stops at Cam Ranh Bay, Nha Trang, and Ubon and Udorn in Thailand. All in all, that was a pretty efficient seven hour and twenty minutes of flight time in a 12½ hour crew day.

We weren't quite so fortunate on the return trip, which included stops at Korat in Thailand and Tan Son Nhut where we had a four hour loading delay. By the time we got to Clark early the following morning, we were out of crew day and went into crew rest there. After a leisurely day of drinking John Collinses by the side of the Clark swimming pool and dining in the club, we returned to Mactan the next day in early afternoon after a six day odyssey.

There was a medical emergency on Mactan. One of the loadmasters in the other squadron checked into the hospital feeling exhausted. On examination they determined that he had somehow contracted (possibly from a native) a form of encephalitis, also known as sleeping sickness, or possibly extreme mononucleosis. The individual involved was air-evacuated to the Clark hospital, but in the meantime we were all subject to catching the thing. Not only was this a disease not heard of in the U.S. for nearly 50 years, but it was also very contagious and could be passed by normal social contacts.

The result was that everyone on base had to go to the medical clinic and get a shot in the ass. Until this was done, no one could leave the base lest the medical scourge be spread. No flights left for several days, including the shuttle, which was taken over by the Clark crews in the meantime.

Finally, serum arrived on base and we all trooped down to the squadron where the medics were waiting for us. The anti-encephalitis shot is really a dandy. The shot itself was as thick as Elmer's glue and sat under the skin on your ass for about a day before it dissolved and spread throughout the body. But, at least we were healthy and free to fly again.

On October 28, we flew a one day round-trip with cargo, people and mail between Mactan and Clark and then left the next day for another shuttle. Hal and I are assigned as veteran in-theater crew members to fly with a major who had just arrived in Mactan and had been through the checkout program. We were along to help see him through his first shuttle on his own as the pilot/aircraft commander.

We arrived in Tan Son Nhut, after stops in Clark and Tuy Hoa, in the early afternoon and were put on the schedule for about that same time the next day. Once again we were quartered in the Globe Hotel. On the following day, however, we arrived at C-130 Ops to find that the aircraft they assigned us was too sick to fly. After sitting around for five hours, we were told to go back to the hotel and reappear the next day. By this time, the aircraft which we brought with us from the States back in November and February were beginning to show the results of constant flights. They were having more mechanical problems than they used to.

Frequently, flights were made without air conditioning in either the cockpit or the cargo hold or both. The planes were also very dirty both inside and out. Many of the cargo floor rollers in the rear of the airplanes were contaminated with hydraulic fluid which had been used as an emergency lubricant on some mission or other. It worked to keep them rolling for a day or two, but actually degraded performance over time.

The next day, we appeared at 130 Ops in mid-afternoon after lunch at the officers' club and were airborne at 4:45 P.M. Our first stop was Ban Me Thout. Ban Me Thout is about halfway between Saigon and Pleiku. The airfield at Ban Me Thout was manned primarily by Vietnamese, with only an occasional U.S. Army forklift driver or officer appearing in the cargo area. The military base there was some distance from the airfield. On previous stops at Ban Me Thout, which we didn't often go to, there was usually at least one U.S. person there to supervise the loading or accept the cargo. But on this day, we landed after the normal duty hours; and when we taxied into the cargo area there was no U.S. personnel present. In addition to several passengers, our load was 3 pallets of U.S. food, including boxes of frozen meat and fresh eggs stacked 3 feet high on the pallets. The Vietnamese offloaded the pallets and placed them side by side just off the cargo area. We then closed up our aircraft and departed back to Tan Son Nhut.

We flew one more mission, to Nha Trang and then back to Tan Son Nhut, where our crew day ended at five minutes after midnight. We had now worked our way back on the day shift for the shuttle and got one day off to adjust our sleeping patterns. That day was spent investigating the area around the Globe Hotel, which was bustling but not very interesting.

In a discussion with the desk clerk who spoke some English, we discovered that the South Vietnamese government had recently, at U.S. urging, stepped up its military draft provisions and was taking an increased number of young Vietnamese into their armed forces to participate in the war. Evidently, this did not include the hotel owner's son who, although of prime draft age, still spent his days riding around town on his motorbike. In what must obviously have been some kind of tradeoff or substitute maneuver, the old Pakistani, who was in his mid–40s and used to be the porter in the hotel, was taken into the ARVN and no longer worked at the Globe. In such mysterious ways did democracy and the war effort progress in South Vietnam.

On 2 November, we got up in the dark, caught a shuttle cab and appeared on base at 3:00. Two hours and forty-five minutes later, we were airborne and spent the day flying to Da Nang and then flying three flights out of Da Nang to the marine base at Dong Ha, close to the DMZ. Our day ended at 3:35 in the afternoon at Tan Son Nhut, just in time to eat on base and have a drink or two in the officers' club. We logged five hours of flying time in a fourteen hour day.

The next day we arrived at 130 Ops at eight in the morning, but our aircraft was being worked on and was not ready to fly until mid-afternoon. We packed in an early lunch at the O club and finally got airborne at 2:20 in the afternoon on a clockwise passenger run. It just so happened that our first stop was at Ban Me Thout. It was only a twenty-minute stop; but while people were deplaning in the cargo area, we happened to notice that the three pallets of U.S. frozen food and eggs which we had left four days earlier were still sitting in the sun where we had left them. We then flew on and made stops at six other bases before returning to Tan Son Nhut at 10:00 in the evening.

By now the new pilot we had been shepherding proved to be quite all right as far as knowing the procedures and doing all the right things. On November 7, we got a late afternoon takeoff and flew the counterclockwise passenger run to four air force bases on the east coast. The passenger runs were usually flown in the daylight, but this one was evidently delayed due to maintenance.

We were airborne at 5:45 P.M. and rapidly flew through stops at Phan Rang and Cam Ranh Bay. The next stop was to be Da Nang. As we approached Da Nang from the south, we were told that the weather was a thin overcast with a ceiling of 700 feet and good visibility on the ground. The approach control asked if we would like a radar approach. Hal and I voted to tell them no. We both recalled being shot at on a similar radar approach in the past. The low ceiling would dictate an instrument approach in the States, but here it would be better to just go out over the sea and let down to go in visually. The pilot refused our well intentioned advice and told Hal to agree to the radar approach. Shortly thereafter, we were given a heading to fly and told to descend to 3,000 feet. Within a minute or two of taking up the new directions, up through the clouds in the black night came tracers just ahead of the nose of the aircraft. No one said, "I told you so," but the feeling was certainly there. We rapidly got the pilot to cancel the instrument approach, turn right to fly out over the ocean and let down. This was the second time, in almost totally similar circumstances, when we were fired on going into Da Nang at night under instrument conditions.

We had no further problems in Da Nang. We offloaded passengers and took new ones on. We were airborne again 40 minutes after landing and proceeded to our last en route stop, Nha Trang. We finished just at midnight. As we pulled into our parking space at Tan Son Nhut, we saw a well intended larceny. A C-130 loaded with lettuce, tomatoes and other fresh produce from the Philippines had just landed. The vegetables were meant for the clubs and dining halls in the Saigon area. However, the desk officers in C-130 Ops knew that there had been no fresh vegetables in Mactan for over a week. The vegetable loaded aircraft was sent to the bomb dump across the field where there was less lighting and at least one pallet managed to be loaded on our Wing's rotational aircraft, which was being readied for takeoff at dawn.

Due to yet another aircraft maintenance problem, we were never called to report for the rotation aircraft until two days later. Then, due to a large weather system, or typhoon, we flew direct from Tan Son Nhut to Mactan without the usual stop in Clark. We again got our two days in the Magellan hotel and then returned to the base to wait for our next shuttle.

On our return, we found that Mactan Air Base was getting some urban renewal. Instead of the heavy tent material top with which we had lived since arrival in February, our six to eight man wood and chicken wire homes were now getting a metal roof. It would seem that the metal might be hotter than the heavy cloth that was the previous roof, but the metal reflected the hot sun rather than baking it in.

On our first morning back after staying in the hotel in Cebu, I woke up about seven in the morning and looked across the narrow aisle to Major Kahn's bed, which was directly opposite mine. Kahn was sleeping straight up on his back with a pillow behind his back and head. Just as I was looking at him, the contract workers who were replacing the roofs tore ours back and the sunlight hit the good major right in the face and eyes, waking him from a sound sleep. Kahn, who had been in the officers' club the night before, opened one eye and looked straight up to see two or three grinning Filipino faces looking down at him. "Beautiful, just fucking beautiful," he said as I broke out laughing at the situation and his heartfelt comment. The place actually was cooler later in the day when they got the metal roof in place, but not all that much. It was still 90 degrees plus in there for most of the day, especially in late afternoon.

Both Kahn and John Dunn had been looking forward to being promoted to the next higher rank, lieutenant colonel. Promotions for higher rank were done annually when a list was released denoting everyone who was promoted out of all those eligible. Both men were eligible for promotion, but neither appeared on the list. It was a shock and embarrassment to both that they were not promoted. It was also very hard to think that the air force was looking after its own in the proper manner. They were first class officers and flyers and here they were in a war zone getting combat experience. Their non-promotion didn't make a lot of sense. Kahn remained in service and several years later was promoted. John Dunn left the air force shortly after this tour and spent the remainder of his career in the National Guard. One would think that in the midst of a war the military would alter their normal procedures and promotion rates to ensure that good men, especially those actually in the

1966 — Mactan tents get metal roofs.

war, would be promoted and kept in service. Unfortunately, due to budgets, procedures and mistiming, that never seemed to happen.

Christmas was now coming and the base exchange (BX) had a special deal for the holidays. You could bring in your own pictures and have them made into Christmas cards, which you could then send off to the States. I provided a picture that I had taken of myself on the Mactan beach, lying on the beach in a bathing suit, straw hat, flying sunglasses and with a San Miguel beer raised in my hand in a toast. I had several dozen of this pose made into cards and sent them to all my friends and relatives back in the States. After the holiday, my mother wrote to let me know that she was shocked I had sent a card to all our kith and kin that showed me drinking.

13 November: We went back on the shuttle, stopping at Clark and Cam Ranh Bay on the way to Saigon. Our first mission was the next day, when we took off at 8:30 in the morning and flew 15 minutes over to Bien Hoa. We picked up several passengers at Bien Hoa and were taking them to Da Nang when one engine began to act up. We then turned around and headed back to Tan Son Nhut for repairs. Tan Son Nhut tower told us that there was firing around Saigon directly in our path, so we diverted back into Bien Hoa as an alternate. Just as we touched down at Bien Hoa, the firing advisory was canceled and we were cleared for a direct flight to Saigon, where we landed five minutes later. Once on the ground, the passengers were put on another flight and we waited in 130 Ops for our airplane to be fixed. Three hours later, the fix still hadn't been made and we were dismissed for the day: Dinner and drinks in the officers' club and then into crew rest.

The following morning was an army counter-clockwise passenger run. We were up at 4:00 A.M., airborne at 6:20, and we stopped in Nha Trang, Qui Nhon, An Khe, Kontum, Pleiku and then back to Tan Son Nhut. All stops were less than 30 minutes ground time and we were done for the day at 12:40, just in time for dinner and drinks in the O club. It was almost getting to be as convenient as life on a commercial airline.

One day later, we were cargo hauling loads consisting of troops and vehicle mounted equipment. We went from Tan Son Nhut to Pleiku, then to Da Nang, from Da Nang to Hue, Hue back to Da Nang, Da Nang back to Pleiku and then Cam Ranh Bay prior to final landing at Tan Son Nhut at 4:00 P.M. All off and onloads were accomplished in less than 40 minutes since the passengers walked on and off and the vehicles rolled on and off. We got five hours of flying time for an 11 hour crew day.

17 November: Took off in mid afternoon and dropped cargo off in Ban Me Thout and Pleiku. When we got back to Tan Son Nhut, there was a heavy rainstorm over the field and all kinds of aircraft holding in orbit waiting for landing clearance. The storm continued for some time and the normal one hour flight time from Pleiku to Saigon turned into three and a half hour hours before we got back on the ground. Tan Son Nhut was now the busiest airport in the world and a second runway was being built (and paid for by Yankee dollars) to make it even busier. The schedule for the day and all loading activity was so disrupted by the rain that we were sent into crew rest at 8:00 P.M. The next evening we took off at 7:35 P.M. and hauled cargo to Binh Thuy and Cam Ranh Bay. We were finished at 11:45.

The following day, we reported at six in the evening; but there were no flights going out. Enemy rockets had been fired into Tan Son Nhut during the morning hours and one had hit the left wing of a C-130 parked directly

Mid-1966 — The author on Mactan beach.

in front of the C-130 Operations building. Since the C-130 carried fuel in its wings (known as a wet wing), a fire resulted. The fire was extinguished, and the metal revetments which surrounded each aircraft parking area ensured that no other aircraft were damaged. However, for the remainder of the day, all returning aircraft were sent to the bomb dump for parking; and no further flights were loaded or sent on missions while the parking areas around 130 Ops were cleared of debris.

Next day was another early reporting hour. We caught the shuttle bus into the base at 5:00 A.M. and spent the day on an army combat assault support mission. We flew six 30 minute flights between Tan Son Nhut and Phan

Thiet hauling army troops and vehicles with drive on and run off loads. Our final flight was from Phan Thiet to Tay Ninh almost on the Cambodian border and then back to Tan Son Nhut. We were finished at 3:50 in the afternoon, having logged four hours and 15 minutes of flying time in an 11 hour crew day. The loadmaster was virtually exhausted from tying down and unchaining vehicles all day in the high heat and humidity. We officers retired to the officers' club for dinner and drinks, while the loadmaster and flight engineer hurried back to quarters to clean themselves up and rest.

23 November: We started our day at nine in the morning and took off for Bien Hoa at 11:30. But that was the only flying we did all day long. After picking up cargo at Bien Hoa and taking it back to Tan Son Nhut, our air-

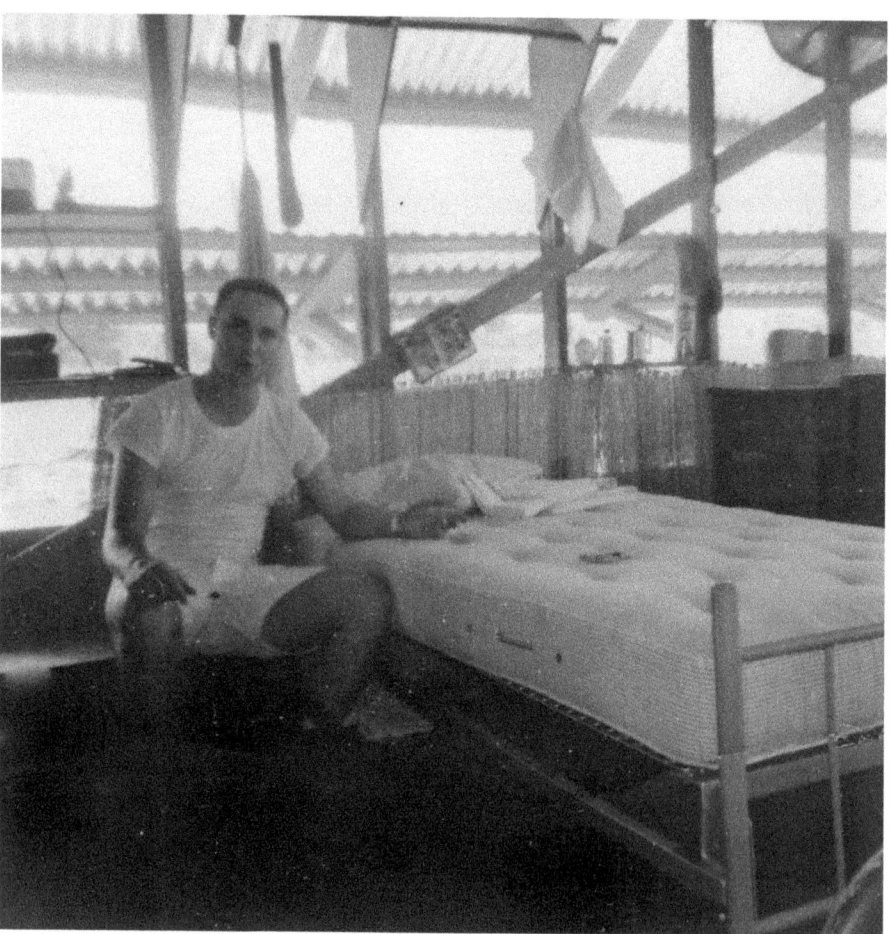

1966 — The author in his metal-roofed residence.

craft went into maintenance and we went into crew rest in mid-afternoon. The following day we were scheduled to return to Mactan. When the rotational aircraft arrived in early morning, we left and flew through Nha Trang and Clark. We arrived back in Mactan at five in the afternoon.

We remained in Mactan for twelve days after that shuttle, and were fortunate, or unfortunate, enough to be there for Thanksgiving. While we had been away on our last shuttle, the Mactan dining hall had upgraded its service so that now each table had a tablecloth on it and food was served on real plates by recently hired Filipino waitresses. No more World War II style eating off of mess tins and washing them in boiling water barrels. As a further upgrade, it was announced that there would be a full U.S. style Thanksgiving meal of turkey and the trimmings.

In addition, Arthur Godfrey, a U.S. television show host and his USO show would be at Mactan on Turkey Day, participate in the meal and put on a show. The great day came, Godfrey and company ate with us, and at the end of the meal the base commander got up and thanked the USO troupe and also called for a great hand for the dining hall staff for an excellent holiday feast. Huge applause followed. The next day everyone on base had diarrhea.

One of the members of the USO troupe was Frances Langford, a singer who had previously entertained troops during World War II as part of USO shows. In the 1940s she was a gorgeous young starlet (see the James Cagney movie *Yankee Doodle Dandy*). By the mid–1960s she was what might be called a Hollywood has-been. Big Stoop's second in command, a leather-faced lieutenant colonel, had been assigned to escort Miss Langford while she was on base and was asked if there had been any romantic interaction during the duty. "Are you kidding?" he replied. "She has more wrinkles than I do."

We did not fly again until December 6. There was now a short period of time in which the Wing had more crews than it needed. Many new crews had just arrived and were in various stages of local and theater training. Some of them were already fully qualified and taking their places in the shuttle. The first crews to have arrived at Mactan for a 13 month tour back in November of 1965 were still on base, getting ready to leave but not yet gone and still flying shuttles as well.

John Dunn was now an instructor pilot and on this shuttle he had a student, Major Lou Malloy, who was going to take over our crew once he got qualified. Malloy, like Dunn, was an ex-fighter pilot. He was 40 years old or so and had been assigned in nonflying logistic jobs for some time before this assignment. This was evidence of the impact of the war on air force procedures. In order to meet the requirement to rotate people from the Vietnam related flying jobs in a year or two years, they had to reach back and return ex-flyers to cockpits in order to make the assignment process work. Some of these old flyers should never have been returned to flying duty. Malloy handled the transition well, though, and he was a good pilot.

The return of elder officers to cockpits also caused some trouble with regard to who got which senior supervisory positions and who just went back to flying. Many of the seniors had seniority over people who held Wing jobs and had held them since the Wing first moved to Mactan. One full colonel was put in the cockpit with his own crew because he was junior in seniority as a colonel. His copilot later told me that on their first shuttle and visit to Saigon he led them into a massage parlor on a day off. Shortly thereafter, the U.S. Military Police (MP's) raided the establishment looking for some AWOL personnel. The colonel, who was elderly and corpulent, appeared at the front desk of the parlor with only a towel on and his .38 revolver, belt, and holster worn over the towel.

At any rate, we landed at Clark on the 6th at 9:35 in the morning. By three in the afternoon we did not have a load onboard and our aircraft had a slow leak problem in the hydraulic system. Rather than take the same aircraft in-country, we flew it back to Mactan. The following morning, with a new aircraft and that day's rotation crew deadheading in the back, we again flew through Clark for a cargo pickup. Then we went on to Phan Rang and Tan Son Nhut, landing there just after five in the evening.

On our first shuttle mission the next day, we started on the night shift with a 7:00 P.M. cargo haul to Da Nang and then back through Pleiku to Tan Son Nhut. When we got back at 1:15 A.M., they put us in crew rest so they could get the airplane ready for the next day's army field support missions. Since we had landed after midnight, we got the rest of that day off and rotated onto the early morning shift in the shuttle. On the off day, we gave Malloy the cook's tour of Saigon, with a beer on the main street in one of the old French hotels and a steak dinner in the Rex that evening.

The next morning we were up at 3:00, caught the bus to C-130 Ops and were airborne at ten minutes after five. We spent the day flying three sorties between Bien Hoa and Tuy Hoa hauling army cargo. We were back in Saigon at three in the afternoon after a twelve hour day and four hours and forty-five minutes of flying time. Naturally we retired to the officers' club for dinner and drinks and to introduce Major Malloy to that environment. The next day was more of the same, another twelve hour day. We took off at 8:40 A.M. and hauled cargo to Phan Thiet, Dalat, An Khe, and Pleiku before returning to Tan Son Nhut.

The following evening we took off at 6:30 P.M., flew to Pleiku and picked up army passengers and vehicles to take to Bung Bung and Quan Loi. Again, it was after midnight (1:25) when we got back to Saigon, so we got another day off to rotate fully to the early morning shift.

15 December: We began our day with a flight test of an airplane which had just gotten out of maintenance. Just as we took off it was plain that maintenance had not fixed the problem (engine fluctuations) and we flew to the end of the runway we had just taken off from and returned. Two and a half hours later, the plane was fixed again and we did three cargo runs to Kontum, Kham Duc and Qui Nhon before returning to Saigon. We were done at 4:30 P.M., so there was time for yet another meal in the club and a few drinks. We started the next day late in the afternoon and it was a repeat of the day before, with three cargo runs to Qui Nhon, Da Nang and Chu Lai. Our day, or night, was over at 2:30 A.M.

The following day we got up at 3:00 A.M. and were airborne at 5:45 hauling army cargo between Bien Hoa, Qui Nhon and An Khe. That day was over just after noon. On December 19 we flew a passenger haul between Bung Bung, Bien Hoa (twice), An Khe, Pleiku and Phan Rang. We were done at 5:05 P.M. and adjourned to the club for drinks and dinner.

After a day off, we flew the rotational plane out just after noon on the 21st and got into Clark at 9:05 that night, where we remained overnight so that we could take a load out in the morning. It was too late to go to the club at Clark, so we retired to one of the downtown Angeles City motels. The next morning, a shuttle bus took us into Clark and we departed without incident, arriving back in Mactan at three in the afternoon.

On the 24th of December, with Lou Malloy now serving as the aircraft commander, we flew from Mactan to Clark with a load of passengers, mail and cargo. We left at 7:45 in the morning and, due to loading problems at Clark, didn't get back until 5:00 P.M.—a twelve hour day with three hours and five minutes worth of flying time.

While we were in Clark and refilling for the return trip to Mactan, we stopped to get the mandatory weather briefing from the Filipino who manned the weather station there. He had probably been doing that job since the end of World War II. As it was a clear late afternoon throughout the Philippines, he had the entire briefing memorized, from takeoff temperature to winds and visibility. It was a great comic performance and very well done.

That evening, John Dunn and I went over to Cebu for what would pass as a Christmas midnight mass ceremony in the U.S. Actually, it was a sunrise service, the only time I've ever been to one of those on Christmas. But I neither have known many Christmases where the temperature was in the '80s either. We then returned to the base for Christmas dinner with all the fixings, but without the violent aftermath of the Arthur Godfrey Thanksgiving turkey dinner. The next day we again flew a one day mission back and forth to Clark.

One New Year's Eve, we left Mactan at 6:50 in the morning, went through Clark and arrived at Tan Son Nhut at 2:40 in the afternoon. Lou Malloy had come down with an illness over the holidays, and John Dunn was back flying one more shuttle with our crew. Hal Thorson and the enlisted men went to the Globe Hotel in the air crew taxi, while Dunn and I retired to the officers' club at Tan Son Nhut to celebrate the New Year. Tan Son Nhut has been growing and growing in terms of how many U.S. individuals worked there as opposed to the early 1965 days when it was only an airfield. The U.S. Theater Command Headquarters and a host of subordinate commands and communications and hospitals were now also on base. As a result, the officers' club was largely filled by early afternoon and the crowding continued on after we had dinner.

We knew that we had a six o'clock show-up time the next day for an 8:00 A.M. launch, so Dunn left soon after dinner and repaired to the hotel in a cab. Since the holiday was also my birthday, I stayed in the club and enjoyed a few more drinks. About 11:00 P.M., champagne appeared in the club, at $1 a bottle. Soon everyone was shooting corks at each other. A glorious night was had by all, or at least as glorious as it can get in a war zone without women. Shortly before midnight, I retired to C-130 Ops and went to sleep on one of the couches in the waiting room. There weren't many flights that night and I was still on the couch when our crew arrived at six the next morning.

Later in the week, I found out that I was not the only one celebrating (perhaps too much) that night. Just outside Tan Son Nhut, some of the crews staying in one of the villas had their own New Year's Eve party on the flat roof of the place. Late in the evening, two of the enlisted men, who had more than they should have to drink, got in an argument. Shortly thereafter, the two of them appeared on the roof wearing their service revolvers, which we all carried in Vietnam, and were going to have an Old West-style duel right there on the roof. The classic gunfight never happened, as more sober partiers tackled both shootout artists before a shot was fired.

January 1967

U.S. Troops in Vietnam	U.S. War Fatalities
400,000	5,800

We began the new year with a quadruple legged cargo run to Qui Nhon, Ban Me Thout, back to Tan Son Nhut and then Pleiku and back. The following day we started in mid-afternoon and flew to Tuy Hoa, then Qui Nhon, where we picked up damaged communications equipment and flew it across the South China Sea to Clark. We got into Clark at 10:30 at night and went into crew rest. The next day, we left Clark at 2:45 in the afternoon and flew cargo to Cam Ranh Bay and then on to Tan Son Nhut where we landed at 8:40 P.M. We then retired to the Globe.

On January 4, we flew what was now the late afternoon counterclockwise air force passenger run to Phan Rang, Cam Ranh Bay, Da Nang, Nha Trang and then back to Tan Son Nhut. We then got a day off to transition from the night to the day shift. Beginning at six in the morning on 6 January, we flew the early morning counterclockwise army passenger run to Nha Trang, Qui Nhon, An Khe, Kontum and Pleiku. We finished flying just after noon, as passenger unload and load times at most bases were now down to less than 30 minutes each. For the next two days, we didn't change our mission time within the shuttle and flew the counterclockwise army shuttle three days in a row. Our landing time back at Tan Son Nhut didn't vary more than 25 minutes for all three days.

11 January: After the third day of passenger hauling we got another day off and rotated to the very early morning shift with a 3:00 A.M. appearance in C-130 Ops. We took off at five, but were back on the ground within twenty-five minutes to have maintenance look at one of the engines. Four hours after that, we took off and flew to Cam Ranh Bay and then flew two round-trip sorties out of there to Ban Me Thout hauling cargo. We flew back to Tan Son Nhut and called it a day at 4:00 P.M.

The day after that, we flew a late-afternoon, four-stop, air force counterclockwise passenger mission and got done in just over three hours. Our reward for being so efficient was to be sent to Da Nang with an additional load of passengers. Every day that we flew, we were given a new "call sign" to identify the aircraft without openly declaring over the radio that we were a C-130. Our call sign for this day was Bunny 815 (last numbers in the aircraft's tail number). It just so happened that a troupe of Playboy bunnies was touring the U.S. military bases at this time as part of USO entertainment and morale building activities.

On our way north, the highest ranking passenger was a full , who was the head of security at Da Nang. He sat up in the cockpit with us on the flight. During the hour and a half that it took us to get to Da Nang, we told him that we could use some boxes of C-rations so that we would have an emergency food supply for those missions when we flew all day and couldn't stop at a base and eat. He let us know that he was in a hurry to get somewhere on base right after we landed and would appreciate it if we asked the

ALCE in Da Nang to send a staff car for him. A deal of sorts was thus agreed to. We would ask Da Nang to send a staff car to meet our plane on landing and also tell them to put several cases of C-rations in the car.

This request, together with our Bunny call sign, was all that the people at Da Nang needed to immediately start a false rumor that we were landing with the Playboy USO show on board. When we landed in Da Nang and taxied to the parking area, which was usually deserted except for loading personnel, a large crowd had gathered. There was much disappointment and gnashing of teeth when no bunnies hopped off our aircraft and all they got back was the head of base security.

We got another day off and on January 14 flew the rotator aircraft through Phan Rang and then on to Clark. We had a deadhead crew in the back of the aircraft, including Lou Malloy and the full colonel who had earlier appeared in a Saigon hotsi bath place wearing a towel and his .38 revolver. He was in Saigon on some paperwork assignment and was now riding back on our airplane.

When we left Phan Rang we climbed out slowly after takeoff. Near the coast we hit a downdraft. The air was perfectly clear and there was no vibration at all. We just suddenly dropped 500 feet or so in clear air. The colonel riding with us was standing on the cockpit steps pouring himself a coffee when this happened. He ended up lying on the floor near the cockpit door with one foot twisted up under him. He sat on the bunk for the rest of the flight and moaned about the foot all the way to the Philippines. We landed in Clark in mid-afternoon with no further problems or incidents.

Once on the ground, we were told to go into crew rest, as a load for Mactan wouldn't be ready until the following morning. All of the crew trailers on Clark were full, so we were checked into a motel in Angeles City. Malloy and the full colonel opted to stay with us. We all caught a bus to the motel and the colonel went off to the hospital to have his foot looked at.

We cleaned up and changed into civilian clothes and then set off in a taxi to the Clark Officers' Club, knowing that we had a mid-morning takeoff the next day. We enjoyed the bar in the club for happy hour and then went in the dining room and ate together. We then retired back to the bar for one or two nightcaps.

The full colonel joined us at the bar with his foot in a cast and using a cane to get around. The downdraft had fractured his ankle. We were now quite mellow and listening to the colonel describe his injury when Malloy broke through the crowd in the bar and told us he had just run into a real treat in the stag bar downstairs — a red hot, round-eyed stewardess. With no further ado we all swallowed our drinks and followed Lou into the basement.

It was equally crowded there between the drinkers, the slot machine players and the snack bar munchers. Finally, deep in the dimly lit bar we found Malloy and the lady. Wow! She was indeed a stewardess. In fact, she was the head stewardess for one of the airlines which now had the contract for ferrying GIs in and out of Vietnam. This was part of her farewell tour with the airline. She was retiring and they were giving her a world tour as a retirement bonus, concealed as a stewardess inspection tour. She was older than blazes, had more wrinkles on her face than we had on the soles of our feet, and she was drunk out of her mind. After the initial disappointment went away, we all got a good laugh out of Lou finding a spare stewardess.

When we finally took a taxi back to the motel, both the stewardess and the limping colonel went with us. When we awoke the next morning to start our day, the two of them were still sleeping fully clothed in the sitting room of the building which all of our rooms were in. Still feeling good and laughing about the previous evening, we flew on to Mactan, arriving just before noon.

Mactan was now still crowded with air crews, but the jam was slowly receding. Almost every night there was a party in some tent or other for one of the original crews leaving the next day on the shuttle aircraft to Clark. Such parties were composed of loud music, much beer and champagne drinking, singing and card playing.

While we were gone, one of the best known young pilots in our squadron had his crew's party a few doors up from our tent. The pilot was known for drinking a pretty good bit up to his limit, at which time he would immediately pass out. Since this event happened somewhat regularly while home at Mactan, he was engaged in card playing at his good-bye party and was deliberately fed numerous drinks while so engaged. Then, as expected, he passed out.

The next morning, he awoke lying in a stretcher in the rear of the rotational aircraft on his way to Clark. His right foot was in a heavy cast and a crutch was situated next to the stretcher. He was told that he had broken his leg the previous night, but would be all right to go back to the States in his present condition so long as he did not try to walk too much on the broken leg. Sometime between his waking up and when he was due to get on the contracted airliner taking him back to the U.S., he learned, or figured out, that the foot was not actually broken and that the cast was a large joke that had gone exactly as planned. He was last seen standing in the Clark passenger terminal which abutted the operations building and snack bar, banging the cast against the side of the building and unraveling it.

We also learned that our tent mate, Capt. Civil, whom we had rarely seen, since he was usually gone on shuttle when we were home or vice versa, had now left Mactan at the end of his 13 months. That left one empty bed and considerable space in the tent. Civil was a budding artist, in addition to other things, and he left behind some 20 paintings and draft paintings on canvas. A quick review of the efforts revealed little talent above that displayed by Adolph Hitler as a house painter. Accordingly, Jaime Montez and I arranged a display of paintings on the sidewalk outside the tent which led to the community shower room. Each one was labeled an Early, Middle, or Late Civil period piece, and prices were accordingly graduated from $2 to $5 to $10. After a week on display, only one Early Civil was ever sold. The remainder of the art collection was put in the trash.

Our crew pulled a week of duty crew and then, on January 26, we left Mactan after almost two weeks and flew through Clark and Phan Rang to Saigon, where we landed and went into crew rest at 3:10 in the afternoon. John Dunn was no longer with us and Lou Malloy was now our aircraft commander.

During my one year tour, I always kept two wallets and interchanged them depending on whether I was in the Philippines or elsewhere. The only thing that was common to the two was that I always put my identification card in whichever wallet I was going to carry. Unfortunately, for this shuttle I had stayed too long at the Mactan Officers' Club the night before leaving and had taken the wrong wallet with me to Saigon. Now, instead of U.S. dollars and Vietnamese script, I had a wallet full of Philippine money and no ID card. I begged, borrowed and stole enough U.S. cash to get me through, but the lack of an ID card made it hard to function without being with someone else, and always in uniform. There was no place I could go on base, like the movie theater or the Base Exchange, where they would ask for an ID card in order to enter. Accordingly, for the length of the shuttle, I rode the crew busses everywhere, ate only in the officers' club or the Shit Creek Snack Bar.

We began shuttle duty on the mid-afternoon shift with a 4:15 takeoff. We hauled two loads of cargo and passengers to the marine base at Dong Ha. On our last flight, it was just before midnight when we were approaching Dong Ha. Hal called in to the approach control there and told them that we were bringing in cargo, passengers and mail and that we needed a radar approach because the weather consisted of low clouds and rain. The marine control gave us a "Roger," on the request and then commented that they had received no mail at Dong Ha for over a week. The control tower called back and said we were cleared to land in conditions consisting of light rain, a cloud ceiling of 400 feet and 2 miles visibility.

Hal reminded the marine controller that air force weather minimums required at least 500 feet for Dong Ha as opposed to USMC aircraft minimums of 400 feet. In other words, the weather was just on the margin for not shooting an approach, despite how badly the marines wanted their mail. "Oh, wait a minute," said the Marine controller. "We've just had a new weather report and we now have light rain, a ceiling of 500 feet and 2 miles visibility." Malloy made an easy landing as we broke out of the low ceiling well above five hundred feet with good visibility. We all laughed about the "coincidence" of the sudden marine weather report and the fact that we were carrying mail. We landed in Saigon at 2:40 in the morning and went into crew rest.

We got our usual off day the next day to transition to the early morning shift and reported at 4:00 A.M. on the 29th for flights, but our airplane was not mission worthy. After sitting half the morning waiting for it to come out of maintenance, we returned to crew rest and appeared the next day at the same time. We ended up with the early morning counterclockwise army passenger run. Six stops and back to Tan Son Nhut and we were done for the day at 11:15 A.M.: Three hours and five minutes of flying time in a six and a half hour day, with no stop more than twenty-five minutes. Boy, we were really getting efficient at hustling people on and off airplanes. The next day we did it all over again, almost exactly but not quite as well. Now it was three hours and twenty minutes' flight time in a seven hour total crew day.

The following day our aircraft was again broken and, after sitting for five hours in 130 Ops we were dismissed and sent into crew rest. On 2 February, we stumbled into operations at 2:00 A.M. and were airborne on a combined army and air force counterclockwise passenger run with six intermediate stops: Five hours and ten minutes of flying time for an eleven hour and forty minute crew day.

We were done just after 1:40 in the afternoon and Malloy and I retired to the officers' club for drinks while everyone else went back to the BOQ. Malloy was as charming a companion as Dunn. Plenty of good old fighter pilot stories and he keeps running into old friends of his. One of our passengers today was a black air force colonel named Chappy James, who was an acquaintance of Malloy's from fighter pilot days. Nice guy. He later went on to be a four star general and vice chief of staff of the air force.

3 February: We left at 8:20 in the morning, hauling cargo to Pleiku, Da Nang, Hue, Da Nang, Cam Ranh Bay and then back to Tan Son Nhut. On the leg between Da Nang and Cam Ranh Bay we experienced fluctuations on one of the engines. The load taken on at Da Nang consisted of 15 manifested army passengers, a large army truck and a small trailer which the truck towed behind. Both the truck and the trailer were filled with duffel bags and assorted other cargo.

The army had filled out the cargo sheet for the flight, and that included the weight of the load and the names and weight of all the passengers. Because we were going home to Saigon from Cam Ranh we took the maximum gasoline load out of Da Nang so we would not have to fill up again. The flight from Da Nang to Cam Ranh usually ran about 70 minutes from takeoff to landing and the route was almost entirely over water.

The day was bright and sunny and we were 30 minutes or so into the flight when we lost an engine. Accordingly, we lost some altitude and airspeed after shutting the engine down and feathering the propeller to reduce its wind drag. Almost as soon as that was done, another engine on the opposite side began to act up and looked as if it too would have to be shut down. That was when the engineer calculated that with the remainder of our fuel load and the weight of the truck and trailer in the rear, we could not stay airborne on two engines if we did shut the second one down.

The plan immediately became to jettison the truck and trailer as soon as possible in the event the second engine was lost. By regulation, all of the manifested passengers sat forward of the truck. That is, they were seated right behind the crew cabin and fire wall in the rear of the cargo hold. The truck and its rear end full of cargo came next and then the trailer, which was chained down on the ramp. Together with the rear cargo door, this formed the sealed rear of the aircraft. The truck had been driven onto the aircraft and would exit backward out the rear end in the event of jettisoning. Both the truck and the trailer were chained down to the floor and ramp.

Now the loadmaster undid any excess chains not likely to be needed in flight. This was in anticipation of jettisoning the load and would reduce the time necessary for undoing all of the remaining chains and then jettisoning first the trailer and then the truck. For 10 or 15 minutes, we monitored the sputtering engine, and then, as suddenly as it had begun acting up, it stopped and everything was normal. By that time, we were much closer to final landing at Cam Ranh. Before long the loadmaster reconnected the chains to ensure both vehicles were secured prior to landing. Suddenly, over the interphone, Gross said, "Hey, guess what just showed up in the back of that truck we were ready to jettison?" We couldn't imagine, so the reply was a simple, "What?" "There are six guys we didn't know about sleeping in it," he said.

I sometimes wonder what it would be like to be awakened from a sound sleep by a sudden flash of light and the rush of wind, and to look up into a clear blue sky to see the open tail end of a C-130 disappearing from view and then to remember that you were sleeping in a truck which had very recently been parked in the hold of the very same aircraft. Luckily, in this situation, no one had experienced that sensation, but some had come closer to it than they might ever know. We landed back in Tan Son Nhut at 5:25 in the evening and had dinner and a few drinks.

The next day we took off at 9:00 A.M. for a modified passenger run. First we were in and out of Phan Thiet and then did two round-trip shuttles between Cam Ranh Bay and Tuy Hoa. We were back in Saigon at eight in the evening. The following day, we reverted to the late afternoon shift. We ate lunch at the officers' club on base and then went to 130 Ops and picked up our schedule, then went on to Base Ops to file. We were off the ground at 4:15 carrying cargo to the army at An Khe, then back to Saigon for a load to take to Pleiku.

At Saigon, there were problems in the cargo storage area; and it took four hours before we got a load onboard. While we were waiting, I walked up the taxiway which extended from the end of the C-130 loading area. I was walking due east parallel to the runway, just out to get a breath of fresh air after waiting for several hours in the lounge adjoining C-130 Ops. It had just rained in Saigon and the ground was still wet. Just off to the side of the taxiway was a ditch full of about 6 inches of mud and water.

I was just about to turn around and walk back to our airplane when suddenly, out of the dark night, came a large flash of light straight ahead of me. It was a large, very bright red weapons round soaring into the air and headed straight at me from outside the base perimeter. *Uh-oh*, I thought, *here comes a rocket or mortar attack and it's headed right at me.* I was just ready to jump face down into the ditch. Something, however, held me back.

The round was large, bright and headed my way, but it was also the wrong color. Weapons rounds at night are usually orange-red. This was pure red. I paused one minute. A large red fireworks round exploded and filled the night air. The Vietnamese holiday of Tet was going on or just about to start. I almost dunked myself in the foul creek as the result of a fireworks rocket. Shortly thereafter, we did get a load of pallets on the aircraft and took them to Pleiku. We were back in Tan Son Nhut and called it a day at three in the morning.

We got the rest of that day off and were back on the morning shift on 7 February. It was a long day of cargo hauling, with six stops after leaving Tan Son Nhut at 4:20 A.M. In order, we saw Nha Trang, Pleiku, Cam Ranh Bay, Ban Me Thout, and Nha Trang again, Pleiku again, and then back to Saigon at 3:40 P.M.

The following day, the eighth, should have been a lark. It wasn't. We started the clockwise passenger run with a 7:10 A.M. takeoff, stopped at Pleiku, and then got to Da Nang at 9:15. In Da Nang we got a mission change and discontinued the normal passenger run. Instead, we took on cargo for Hue but had to wait for the proper load to be found and on-loaded. It was five minutes after two before we took off for Hue. From Hue we went back to Da Nang, where we picked up two pallets and some passengers for Pleiku. Then it was back to Pleiku for a quick drop off. We then went on to land in Saigon at five minutes before 6:00 P.M.

The next day, 9 February, was historic. It was the day of our last shuttle flight, marking the end of a 13 month tour in Southeast Asia. I bid Tan Son Nhut a hearty farewell at 9:15 in the morning. After a short stop to offload cargo at Phan Rang, we flew direct to Mactan, getting in there at 2:10 in the afternoon. A week later the tour was over. I boarded the daily shuttle airplane as a passenger and flew to Clark. I spent the night in the Clark Club eating dinner and having a drink or two and the next morning, together with 100 or so other passengers, I left on a chartered aircraft to return to the U.S.

By regulation and contract, there were no drinks served or allowed on the airliner flight home. Miraculously, after a few hours in the air, several whiskey bottles appeared out of passengers' luggage and toasted farewells to Asia were consumed numerous times. By the time we got to Travis Air Force Base in California, there were several drunks among the passengers. Just before we landed, a fellow traveler from Mactan told me he was now sorry that he had left. He suddenly realized that he loved the Filipino girl he had been dating. His Mactan honey provided oral sex, whereas his stateside wife never would. Once in Travis, it was up to each and every one of us to find our way to our next destination.

Between Tours Yet Again

On returning to the States, my next assignment was to return to Langley AFB, again flying C-130s. There was a new wing, the 316th Tactical Airlift Wing, established at Langley when my original wing, the 463rd, had left thirteen months earlier. The 316th was equipped with C-130Es. They differed from the C-130B in that they had an external fuel tank mounted under each wing which gave them a longer range with a full fuel load. The E model also had some different equipment and electronic upgrades in comparison with the B, but otherwise it was largely the same airplane.

I arrived back at Langley in March of 1967 and spent the next eleven months getting checked out in the new airplane. Missions at Langley were much like the local training missions of the 463rd: many local airdrop missions at low altitude and short trips to other bases to conduct the same type training at varied locales. There were a few cargo hauling missions to Europe and around the U.S., but not many.

In the 463rd on my first tour at Langley, that wing was full of veteran C-130 types. This wing was brand new. Now I was one of the veteran C-130 types. There was a heavy load of training new crew members, and accordingly, most of the others who had just returned from a Southeast Asia tour and I were made instructors and became the cadre to train others. In addition to returnees like me, the Wing had a large number of people just out of flight school and older officers who had been put back in a cockpit from desk jobs. Lacking people with lots of Tactical Airlift experience, the command of the Wing and their procedures were somewhat shaky. The Wing was really one large training and schooling exercise. Due to the heavy training load, the Wing had no requirement to send squadrons on rotation.

In accordance with established policy, in addition to being an instructor navigator I was also a member of a formed crew. My aircraft commander was Captain Joe Daly. Daly was a senior captain and a returnee to a cockpit, since much of his recent experience had been in desk jobs in logistics and training.

The copilot was First Lieutenant Ron Hardy. He was my age and with equivalent experience. While I was flying out of Mactan, he was experiencing an equivalent Southeast Asia tour flying C-130s from Taiwan into Vietnam and Thailand. Ron was a very good pilot who was a bit frustrated at still being a copilot to someone who had less experience in C-130s than he did. But the matchup between him and Daly was a good blend of young capability and elder maturity. They got along very well and each learned something from the other in the course of our flying together. Ron was from New Orleans and spoke with a deep Cajun accent.

The remainder of the crew was Technical Sgt (TSG) Weiss as the flight engineer and Airman Benson as our loadmaster. Weiss was a veteran air crew maintenance man, but this was his first flying assignment. He was very good for a new trainee. Benson was just out of basic loadmaster training. Weiss was from one of the western states and he frequently told tales of his fistfights with Indian children as he was growing up. He became known to us as "the Indian fighter."

In January 1968, after eleven months of training, we were sent to Pope AFB, North Carolina, to take part in a large army/air force exercise. We arrived in Pope on the morning of 23 January and were told to go into crew rest and "sleep fast," as the exercise would begin early the next morning. By the time we got to our motel, we were right on the border of not meeting enough crew rest to take part the next day. Once again the air force had gotten its rules confused with man's physical makeup. If you are not tired, and few are before noon, trying to "sleep fast" so you'll feel better the next morning doesn't work.

At the same time that we were learning to "sleep fast," in another part of the world the North Koreans had seized the USS *Pueblo*, a U.S. Navy intelligence gathering ship. It was then unclear what actions the U.S. was going to take with regard to the seizure of the *Pueblo*. At the same time, the North Vietnamese and the Viet Cong had launched the Tet Offensive, a major surprise attack against the cities of Vietnam.

We returned to Langley at 5:00 A.M. on 26 January, after a hectic exercise with the army in Florida. We were immediately told to go into crew rest and be ready for an extended deployment mission in support of the seizure of the *Pueblo*. For the next nine days, all the other crew members and I at Langley sat at home and waited for the phone to ring. When and if it did, we were expected to arrive on base within two hours with all of our bags for an extended many-month deployment. Such procedures were known whimsically as a "Two Martini" alert. The longer the alert went on, the greater the number of martinis added to the title. By the end of the first week of alert, crew members were no longer sitting alone waiting for the call; many were gathered together at "alert parties," where they assisted each other in counting the number of martinis consumed and unofficially allowed.

Our alert ended in the early morning of 5 February. As I left my apartment to report to base, the phone rang. It was the operations officer of another of the Wing's squadrons looking for my roommate, who could not be found. I told them to call the home phone of the host of the last alert party I knew he had attended.

We left Langley at 12:30 P.M., heading west through California and Hawaii for Pacific points unknown.

FIVE MONTHS IN JAPAN AND VIETNAM

February 1968

U.S. Troops in Vietnam	U.S. War Casualties (KIA)
540,000	16,000

We arrived in Tachikawa, Japan, at 6:55 A.M. on February 5, 1968. In three days (sixteen hours each, which were shrunk to two calendar days because of crossing the international date line), we had exited Langley and gone through Hawaii and Wake Island on the way to Japan.

Tachikawa was a U.S. air base located northwest of Tokyo. It was home to a C-130A wing and also a stopping point and logistics center for strategic airlifters (C-141, C-135, C-124) flying the North Pacific. As we approached Tokyo from the southwest, we called into the Tokyo approach control and reported our position. The last reporting point before Tokyo was Yokosuka, which was identified on the flight charts by the letters YKS. I gave Ron Hardy the time that we were over the over-water reporting point (coordinates) before YKS and then our estimated times for both YKS and Tokyo. He came back in his Cajun drawl and asked, "How do yaw pronounce that next point?" "No problem," I replied. "It's Yocko Suka." "Got it," said Ron. "Yocko Suka."

He called in the customary location and timing message, "over yadda, yadda, yadda at 0530, estimate Yocko Suka at 0610, Tokyo next; request clearance to Tachikawa." There was a pause and then Tokyo control replied in English, "Roger, over [coordinates], at 0530, Yakuska next. Take up heading 290 for approach to Tachikawa. Contact Tachikawa approach control at frequency 121.3." Hardy turned in the copilot's seat, looked back at me and said, "Yocko Suka, eh?" while Daly and Weiss laughed.

Tachikawa was a very large base with a small runway. The runway was about 5,000 feet, whereas most of our home bases were on the order of eight to ten thousand. The base itself, however, was sprawling with depots and hangars all over and well dispersed. Our quarters were old abandoned visiting crew quarters that were about to be demolished. When you opened the front door, there was a central lounge with five bedrooms opening individually off of it. We each got our own ten by ten foot room with a bed and dresser. The central lounge had a TV which got two or three American black and white stations. There was no kitchen as such. We had a refrigerator and there were electrical outlets in the rooms if someone wanted to buy a hot plate or heater to eat on. Mostly we lived off bags of snacks, cold soda, and beer. Meals were eaten in the officers' club or one of the seven or eight other clubs which were on the base. A telephone just outside of the front door was our connection to squadron operations and base facilities.

To get around the base, there was a regular bus line which ran every 20 minutes. It was supplemented by on-base taxi service which arrived some 10 minutes after they were called for. There were several movie theaters on base, each of which had a different English language feature film nightly. The officers' club was large, had a great round bar, a dance floor with a nightly band, and a restaurant with a broad regular menu and Kobi beef specials. Closer to our quarters was a combined civilian/military club which offered many of the same features.

Tachikawa was home to a large number of U.S. military, civilians, and their families. There were a number of U.S. facilities near Tokyo which did not have their own housing areas and Tachikawa, or Tachi as it quickly became known, was home to them as well. Where there are families there is a need for family support and that was present as well. There was quite a large population of nurses and teachers on the base, which made our temporary stay there that much more enjoyable. Some of them were young and enjoyed the clubs as much as we did. The quarters right behind ours were inhabited by single teachers. Joint parties and visits soon became the norm.

Tachikawa was also well served by nearby trains which could whisk you to Tokyo in just about an hour. All of the Japanese who worked on Tachi spoke English to some degree or other and were a big help in getting us acquainted with the base and its facilities. Once off base, it was a different matter. Not many Japanese in Tokyo or elsewhere spoke English, or if they did they did not volunteer it. Those with whom we could communicate were less than fully conversant in the language, and conversations resulted in a lot of "pidgin" talk and hand signs accompanied by confusion and consternation.

Shortly after we first arrived, I walked around to some of the other people's quarters just to become familiar with who was where in the area. I walked in on one old captain navigator who was just getting dressed to go out on a night on the town off the base. He was stuffing oranges into a paper bag he intended to take with him.

"What's with the oranges?" I asked. He told me he had been stationed in Japan about ten years ago, right after the end of the Korean War. Oranges and imported fruit were worth more than money in those days. A good orange, or a couple of them, could buy you a night's companionship, according to him. Somehow I got the impression that he wasn't aware of how much the Japanese economy had changed in the meantime. He went off for his fruity night on the town and I went back to my own room for the night.

We got our bags unloaded into our quarters and settled in. We were briefed on the situation with the *Pueblo* and also regarding the ongoing Tet offensive in Vietnam. Within a day or two, the squadron began flying missions into Korea. Some were single day out and backs and others were multiple-day shuttles, usually operating out of Osan Air Base, which was just outside of Seoul. One of the first crews to fly into Korea ended up spending several days operating out of Osan. They said the biggest event of their stay was the night they had all the spaghetti you could eat in the officers' club for a dollar. Despite the great price, one of them said that all you could eat, regardless of the price, was one mouthful.

10 February 1968: Four days after arriving, we got our first mission. We took off from Tachikawa at 10:15 in the morning and flew to the U.S. marine base at Itazuki in western Japan, where we picked up cargo and a few marines. From Itazuki we flew an hour and twenty minutes to Kunsan Air Base in Korea.

As it was February, it was winter when we arrived in theater and the temperatures in Japan were daily in the range of 30 to 40 degrees. When we got off the airplane in Kunsan, it was freezing. Snow was everywhere and there was a great deal of humidity in the air, which made the cold seem even worse. We had been forewarned about the cold, of course, and we all had long underwear on under our flight clothes; but even then we were still cold. While the loadmaster struggled with the cargo, Daly, Hardy, and I went into base operations to recheck the weather forecast and any notices they might have regarding our next stop or Korean procedures in general. There was nothing of any importance in the base operations center; but there were two incidents of note.

There was another C-130 crew in the building when we got inside. They were C-130A flyers from the wing permanently based at Tachi. The navigator on that crew had been an instructor when I went through flight training in Texas four years earlier. He was known there as kind of a queer duck with no personality.

Now he was standing in the operations center checking his fight plan times and routes. This navigator was wearing the standard air force severe winter flight suit we were all issued. The suits were designed to keep you warm should you crash land in the Arctic or similar terrains. He was the only one that I ever saw actually wear the thing. It was so heavy and padded that it was difficult to walk while wearing it, and working in it in an airplane that had heat in the cockpit must have been unbearable. The only thing I could figure was that he must take it off and fly in his underwear; but we didn't ask.

While we checked the weather and read the notices, the Korean colonel who commanded the base came in, awaiting a visitor who was flying in on the next aircraft. This guy was about six feet tall and well built, not at all like the Japanese, Vietnamese or Filipinos with whom I was acquainted. He had a totally Asian face, slanted eyes and slightly yellowish skin. The amazing thing was that he spoke perfect English with a British accent. He told us that he had been assigned to Britain as a liaison officer and had learned the language from the Brits. Accordingly, he had picked up all their terminology and accents. The combination of his deeply Asian face with the unexpected British speech was totally unreal.

From Kunsan, we flew thirty minutes to Kwangju, where we offloaded the remainder of our cargo and then flew back to Tachi, landing at 9:25 P.M. Flying from Tachi to bases in Korea and back on a daily basis was much like flying from the Philippines to Vietnam and back as we had done on my first tour three years earlier. From Japan to Korea was a two hour flight, whereas from Clark to Saigon had been more like three and a half hours. South Korea was a much more compact country than Vietnam, but the terrain was very rough and mountainous. That, combined with the freezing weather, quickly convinced me I would not like to be stationed there.

During the following five days, which we spent back at Tachi, our mission was further defined and changed. We had rushed across the Pacific to play a role in saving the *Pueblo*, but now we were being sent back into Vietnam. A squadron shuttle mission was set up with Cam Ranh Bay as our in-country base. On a daily basis the squadron would send an airplane into Cam Ranh and another would return to Tachi. It was exactly the same flight arrangement that we had had flying from Clark and Mactan into Saigon.

16 February: We got our chance to depart on the shuttle out of Cam Ranh Bay. Our airplane was broken for most of the day, so we sat around the quarters waiting for our official notification call. We sure hadn't been sleeping the whole time, but that is how the game was played. We were alerted by the weekly schedule that today was our day to begin the shuttle. Usually the call came early in the morning for the shuttle crew, but due to the broken airplane, our call didn't come till mid-afternoon. That began the clock for our official crew day of 16 hours.

We got off the ground at 5:35 P.M. and passed through Naha Air Base, on Okinawa, where we picked up a pallet of cargo and a few passengers. By six in the morning (thanks to different time zones) we were in good old Da Nang, South Vietnam. It was still just as hot as ever at Da Nang, especially so since we had come from wintertime in Japan. After an hour on the ground in Da Nang, we were again airborne and landed at Cam Ranh Bay just after 8:00 A.M.

The C-130 operation at Cam Ranh was run much as the one was in Saigon. Crews rotated through a day/night operation, with the first crew done with its mission each day moving into the next later slot in the following day's schedule. The administration and duty desk assignments were handled by the wing out of Tachikawa so that all our crews did was fly missions or provide people to ground operations if someone on the crew went sick. If one or more people got sick on multiple crews, then the crews were combined to provide one full flying crew, and the remainder pulled ground duty.

I'd been flying into Cam Ranh since the base was activated in my first 1965 tour; but other than being on the airstrip, I had never set foot on the rest of the base. It was a real sand castle. I don't think there was a tree anywhere near the whole place. And hot! Even in Saigon or Nha Trang, once the sun went down the heat would dissipate and the nights would be some 20 degrees cooler. That also happened at Cam Ranh, but not as rapidly. The sand and lack of trees or shade would keep the temperature up until several hours after dark, even with a sea breeze.

Cam Ranh had been a virtual sand wilderness before the U.S. came and started to turn its natural harbor into a logistics center. The buildings were all standard U.S. construction consisting of two-story wooden barracks. Bedrooms were laid out on both stories and the lower floor held a shower room for all inhabitants. There were some air conditioners in the buildings, but most of them didn't work. The heat and the sand were our constant companions about 18 hours a day; after that it was just sand that was in the rooms and on everything. It was something like a beach vacation without piers or amusement rides.

There was a USAF F-4 fighter wing stationed at Cam Ranh, in addition to the C-130 shuttle crews and many, many navy and air force strategic airlifters and specialty aircraft like sub-hunters and reconnaissance types. Our quarters were in buildings which had previously been inhabited by the fighter guys. They left behind graffiti scrawled on the walls and in the bathrooms, and hordes of girly magazines. The magazines came in handy because, unlike

Saigon, there was precious little to do in Cam Ranh on days when you weren't flying or were transitioning from day to night shift.

We got our first full day at Cam Ranh off, since we had landed so late on arrival. Meals were taken in the officers' club, which was pretty sparse: Concrete floor, tables with red and white cloths and that was about it. Go through the line and get the daily special, or take a hamburger or sandwich if you didn't like the special. Late in the afternoon, the bar that adjoined the dining room opened. The bar was mostly a beer joint. Ice cold beer, all of the same brand, depending on what had just come in on a ship or airplane. Besides, hard liquor and wine could do terrible things to your head in the heat and the sunshine that abounded.

One other aspect of the atmosphere in the Cam Ranh Club was the fact that there was a contingent of air force nurses on base who maintained the hospital that was part of the complex. They were small in numbers and I can't recall any of them who would have won a stateside beauty contest. Since we were there for only short periods and then gone again, it was like we were visitors and not residents and therefore did not qualify to seek their hand or pursue them.

But the nurses and the fighter jocks were both full time residents on one year tours. Virtually every other night, there would be a fight in the bar, with two fighter types engaging each other. Airlifters were basically peaceable types and refrained from outright brawling when possible, but fighter guys thought it was part of their image and seemed to immediately respond to slights or invitations of any kind. Over time, the combatants were sometimes the same, but the damsel they were fighting for was different. None of the fights were ever marathons; each combatant's supporters would break up the brawl after a punch or two with little or no blood spilled. But the fisticuffs did make the place entertaining.

In this, my fourth tour in Vietnam, there was a group of veteran crew members among us, primarily fighter pilots, who had not been there before. They had been put in the Wing at Langley to transition to Tac Airlift after careers in desk jobs. They were all good and reliable men who had served in the Korean War. Now, late in their careers and flying talents, they had been summoned to another American conflict and meant to do it right. Initially their reaction had been to seize each opportunity for creative energy and to volunteer for the most risky or hazardous of missions. Lacking these, they were willing to put in more time or return later in their crew day than were other aircraft commanders.

All of this was met with a sense of restrained antagonism by the Vietnam veteran crew members who served under them. It was only over a period of time, lasting individually weeks to months, that these genuinely dedicated warriors transitioned to pessimistic Vietnam veterans like us. Afterward they could be seen enjoying an early end-of-the-day beer at the officers' club, bar rather than being off on another day-extending flight to haul a load of God knows what to some remote airstrip or worse while volunteering themselves and their crew for the next day's most hazardous mission.

Momentum, borrowed incorrectly from the already overstated connection between pro football and real combat, is a terrible thing to witness dying. In this case, however, the negligent impact of the mighty U.S. of A committing team after team of willing and skilled airmen to a task with no quick or respondent payoff had a slightly humorous but inwardly poisonous impact.

The next day, we picked up our first shuttle mission. It was a Cam Ranh based version of the old army clockwise passenger run. Taking off at 10:30 A.M., we hit five army/marine bases with very short ground times and ended up in Da Nang in late afternoon. At Da Nang we refueled and then flew marines into Hue, where they were still fighting to take control of the city the Viet Cong had seized some two weeks earlier at the start of the Tet offensive. From Hue it was back to Da Nang and then on to Cam Ranh. We got six and a half hours of flying time in a thirteen hour day, just like old times.

The day after that, we had a sick aircraft and sat around for several hours while it was being repaired. We got off at 5:25 P.M. and flew an hour to Saigon with a cargo load. The operations at Saigon were pretty much just as they had been when I had left a year earlier: Same ramp, same buses, same Shit Creek Snack Bar, etc. After an hour and fifteen minutes on the ground, we turned around and flew back to Cam Ranh; but the airplane was again broken on landing and that was the end of our day: Two hours of total flying time for a ten hour crew day, most of it spent on the ground in the heat.

20 February: Airborne at 4:00 P.M. We spent the night hauling cargo from Bien Hoa to Hue and then from Hue to Da Nang. We did a rapid offload at Hue, rolling the cargo off the ramp while still taxiing through the loading area. It is now a very busy place. The Tet offensive was ongoing and the Marines were fighting to retake the city.

The following day we took off at 6:15 in the evening. First stop was again Hue. We spent an hour and ten minutes on the ground. It was a rainy, cold, overcast night in the makeshift maintenance, loading and operations center they had created in a tent just off the runway. Someone once wrote that in war, retreat or losing has a sour smell to it which is not present at other, better times. In that tent, in the rain, that's how Hue smelled. Even the coffee was bad.

From Hue we went to Da Nang and picked up more cargo, which was then taken and offloaded at Cam Ranh. The finale of our night was a cargo drop-off at Qui Nhon. Then we took off from Qui Nhon and headed south for Cam Ranh. On the way, we flew abeam of Nha Trang. Hardy pointed out to Daly where Nha Trang was and how close it was to Cam Ranh Bay (roughly half the distance between Qui Nhon and Cam Ranh). You could see the lights at Cam Ranh as we came abeam of Nha Trang.

This was of interest to us because our squadron operations officer had been sitting in Cam Ranh for five days now trying to get to Nha Trang to set up a shuttle operation there. This operations officer just happened to be Big Stoop, from my days in Mactan. When his tour there was over he also was transferred to Langley into the same wing we were in. He was now also part of the Tachikawa deployment. "Holy mackerel," said Daly when he realized the relationship between the two bases, "Big Stoop could have walked up there." The cockpit filled with laughter. We were done and back at Cam Ranh at 4:25 in the morning.

For the next five days, we sat at Cam Ranh Bay, in the heat, reading virtually every girly magazine in sight; but we didn't fly. Some of our aircraft were not mechanically ready and there had been a breakdown in the daily shuttle from Tachikawa. One night in the officers' club I ran into a pilot in the F-4 outfit who had been an underclassman in my squadron at the air force academy. We had dinner together and spent the night discussing old times, with little emphasis on the present. He was TDY into Cam Ranh out of one of the bases in Thailand. I didn't see him again during his stay in Cam Ranh. I found out much later that two months after this he and his backseater were shot down and killed by antiaircraft fire over North Vietnam.

Finally, on 26 February, we got airborne again, taking cargo from Cam Ranh to the army at An Khe and then doing the same to Da Nang and from there back up to Hue. From Hue, we returned to Cam Ranh and crew rest at seven in the evening. While we were parked at Da Nang waiting an onload, a C-130B out of Saigon pulled in beside us.

They called into the Da Nang ALCE and said, "How about a rapid onload. This is our last stop and we're going back to Tan Son Nhut and calling it a day." ALCE replied, "Candy 13 [their call sign], come in and talk to us." Back came the B model pilot laughingly, "No, we don't want to talk. Get a load on us so we can get out of here. We have just barely enough time to get to Saigon in our crew day." A slight pause followed and then ALCE said sternly, "Your crew day has been extended. Your next mission will be to Khe Sanh and then Saigon." Now a longer pause ensued. Suddenly, in an agitated voice, the B model pilot said, "Are you shitting me?" At that time Khe Sanh was under siege, each transport attempting to deliver cargo was sure to get shot at, and the only loads being delivered were by parachute. We watched the crew exit their airplane and walk towards ALCE, but by then we had a load and were on our way out.

The next day we were told to pack our bags and get ready to move to Nha Trang. Big Stoop had gone home without ever getting to Nha Trang, but his assistant arrived after he left and he did get there and established our new home for shuttle operations. We left Cam Ranh at 4:00 in the afternoon and flew a four-stop counterclockwise passenger mission ending up in Da Nang at 8:20 in the evening. At Da Nang we refueled and reverted to hauling cargo and passengers to Hue and An Khe. From An Khe we flew direct to Nha Trang, where we landed at 1:35 in the morning.

Nha Trang was the new home of our shuttle operations. A lot had changed since 1965, when Nha Trang was a relatively small operational base (with primarily army activity) and we lived downtown in a medical villa while operating out of there. Now it was jam-packed with army and air force troops, including many Special Operations types. For quarters we each got a cot in a large tent set up immediately behind the officers' club in what had been an open plot. With the tent flaps tied up and the air blowing through, it was actually cool in the tent at night; and as long as no one snored, we slept pretty well. It was rather like sleeping in an outdoor wedding tent once the reception was over; and had it been colored red and white instead of army green we might have pretended we had joined Ringling Brothers for a road tour. We showered and shaved in barracks which adjoined the area but were already filled with other inhabitants. The closeness to the club meant that we could access the dining room and bar at all hours, as long as it was open and we weren't flying.

We were up at six the following morning, and when we were filing our flight plan for the day we also got an intelligence briefing. The captain, intelligence honcho for the base, told us that the Tet offensive was still going on full blast in many places around the country, most notably in Saigon and Hue. I asked if our side was reluctant to use maximum force in Hue due to its history as the capital of the country and the buildings and whatever which preserved that heritage. The answer was that this was true initially, when the city fell to the Viet Cong, but that now there were no restrictions on the firepower or weapons being used to take it back. We filed out and walked to the aircraft, which we got off the ground at fifty minutes after eight. Our first stop was Pleiku, then Tan Son Nhut, Cam Ranh Bay, Phu Cat, Cam Ranh again and then back into Nha Trang, exactly 12 hours after we left.

We sat for two hours during the stop in Saigon while we were waiting for a load to be put on. The battle for downtown and Cholon was still going on. The crews flying out of Tan Son Nhut had some good stories to tell about recent events. Some aircrews had been staying at quarters in Cholon when the initial battles broke out. One of the quarters (possibly one I had stayed in a year or so earlier), which was right on the city's edge, had been broken into by the Viet Cong. One aircrew member hid under his bed and just barely survived a quick search and bullet spray by the intruders. Also, there was a firefight on Tan Son Nhut itself when a guerrilla squad broke through the base perimeter and fought it out against the fence. Someone said this proved that the U.S. services had their roles reversed, as the air force was fighting a ground war against the intruders while the army provided air support through the use of helicopters. It also turned out that several base employees were actually Viet Cong undercover agents and joined in the fighting once it started. One of them was a barber in the base exchange shop. That must have given some residents second thoughts about close shaves they had had recently.

We were supposed to fly back to Tachikawa on March 1; but our airplane was taken for a higher priority flight, so we sat around all day waiting for it to return. It got back in the late afternoon but needed maintenance before it was ready to fly us back. We finally took off from Nha Trang at 1:10 on the morning of the second. We landed in Tachi at 9:15 A.M.

We spent a week on the ground in Tachikawa. During this time it became clear that the officers' club and its bar and dining room were just as busy, if not more so, than the similar facility at Clark had ever been. In addition to all the residents and aircrews living on base, there were many, many visitors, transiting crews and their passengers, and American workers from around the area. Oddly enough, one of the busiest nights in the bar was Monday, which is usually a dead night elsewhere in the world. That fact alone was enough to mark the place and those times as strangely out of synch with normality.

I was in the bar early one evening when my drinking companion noticed that all the single girls in the place had been already taken by transiting aircrews who belonged to the Military Airlift Command (MAC). Being an enterprising sort, he went to the telephone in the lobby and called the club office. Shortly thereafter, an announcement came over the club's audio system: "All MAC personnel should immediately report to their operations center." The announcement was then repeated. Within an hour, all the MAC personnel reappeared in the club only to find that my drinking companion and other members of our squadron had moved in on all their deserted women. On another occasion, the same drinking companion was heavily attracted to an unaccompanied young lady sitting at one of the tables near the bar. There was a band in the club that night and he asked the lady to dance. When she stood up, she said to him, "Are you sure you want to dance with us?" She was eight months pregnant.

We left Tachi on Saturday, March 9, for another shuttle out of Nha Trang. The previous night, Friday, had been a big night in the club, as more young teachers than usual came out of the woodwork and appeared at the club. Again, there was a band. Early in the next day's flight, Ron Hardy mentioned that he had seen me chatting with a certain long haired redhead and inquired if the conversation had led to anything further. I told him that I hoped not, because if it had I couldn't remember it. Sgt. Weiss then chimed in to say what a terrible thing it would be to make such a conquest and not be able to remember it.

After stopping at Naha on Okinawa, we proceeded to Nha Trang and arrived there just after six at night. The officers' club was open for dinner; the bar was open and we checked back into our cots in the tent behind the club. We got the next day off, and we spent the day after that waiting some six hours in Base Operations for our airplane to be fixed. It never was, so we went into crew rest just after noon. The following day, we finally got into the air and flew army cargo missions out of Bien Hoa to bases at Song Be and Tay Ninh, both north of Saigon near the Cambodian border. We made two stops in Song Be before returning to Nha Trang in late afternoon.

As Song Be was within 40 miles or so of Saigon, I had always thought of it as a safe haven among many wartime stops, even though it was close to the Cambodian border. It was almost totally manned and protected by ARVN troops and had been a field we had stopped at since 1965. Little did I then know that a C-130E had been shot down by ground fire there only ten days earlier. The war was again changing context.

After dinner that evening, we decided to take in the movie at Nha Trang. The theater was something like a U.S. drive-in combined with a baseball stadium. It was set up in the middle of the base with a large screen surrounded by a big flat area in front and wooden bleacher seats in the rear. Movies were shown nightly; they were mostly old U.S. Hollywood productions with an occasional new release. Or rather, they were shown nightly as long as the base intelligence officer didn't interfere with the schedule. This guy was known as "Captain Doom." The word was out that every day in the base staff meeting he would foretell a Communist assault on Nha Trang begun by a mortar attack. Some days, his indications of this mass assault were so strong that the movie was canceled in advance so as not to present Charlie with a large human audience. Captain Doom was to interfere with several more of our evenings, but the mass attack never materialized.

The following day was spent hauling single pallets, vehicles and many

U.S. Army personnel to five locations between Saigon and the Cambodian border. The locations included Song Be (twice), Tay Ninh again, Quan Loi, Phuoc Vinh and Bien Hoa. Once again we were back to Nha Trang in mid-afternoon. On arrival, we overflew the base at 5,000 feet while asking for a visual approach and landing over the opposite end of the field. The tower approved that and, as we turned over the base and descended, we could look down and see that some 20 camouflaged C-47s had arrived since we left that morning. They were all parked wingtip to wingtip along the runway. It looked just like a scene out of World War II, since that was how old the planes were. "I wonder if they brought back all the old pilots to fly those crates," I muttered. We landed and retired to the club bar for drinks and dinner.

Just after midnight, an hour or two after we had gone to bed, alarm sirens sounded. We had been briefed on this possibility and quickly jumped into our pants and boots and ran into the concrete bunker adjoining our quarters. The foundation of the bunker had been dug about four feet into the ground and the domed ceiling was reinforced concrete, which we were assured would stop a mortar shell.

There was a good crowd in there, about 50 people. While the siren sounded, the inhabitants began lighting cigarettes and pointing flashlight beams around to see if their buddies or crew members were all accounted for. After ten or twenty minutes, someone got the bright idea that everyone should be looked at carefully and vouched for by buddies to ensure that Charlie wasn't in the bunker with us and ready to set off a charge. The light went around on each face and from somewhere else in the bunker would come that identification, "Yeah, that's Joe," or "OK, he's on our crew."

Just as the light reached the last corner of the building and was extinguished an Asian face appeared stuck near the door and behind someone else. "Hold it," I shouted, recognizing a potential, threatening enemy when I saw one. "Who's that guy?" Back came the answer: "For Christ's sake that's Joe, our Navigator." So much for knowing thine enemy. The light went out, while Daly and Hardy chuckled over my astuteness and concern. After an hour and a half in the bunker with no rounds landing on the base and no outposts being attacked, we went back to bed in our tent. Captain Doom had struck again. Thank God he hadn't been around Nha Trang in '65 when we lived downtown in the hospital and there was firing on the hills at night, every night.

14 March: We stumbled out of bed the next morning, having gotten no credit with regard to crew rest for the two hours we spent in the bunker, and got off the ground at 8:00 A.M. on the dot. We spent the morning again hauling a few pallets and vehicles, plus people, to army bases around Saigon and the Cambodian border: Bien Hoa, Soc Trang, Dau Tieng and Bao Loc. We spent the afternoon hauling U.S. Marine equipment and personnel in and out of Hue and the aircraft base at Chu Lai. After a twelve hour day, we landed at 6:05 P.M.

The next day was more of the same, with all of the same bases taken in except Bien Hoa. We added a last day's stop at Ban Me Thuot, where we let people off and then returned to Nha Trang. We started and stopped the whole day within five minutes of the previous day's times.

16 March: We had now rotated to the night shift. Originally there was no night shift at Nha Trang, but the pace of the war with the Tet offensive still going on had changed all that. We were keeping eight aircraft at Nha Trang and only one or two flew nights. We took off just as night was falling, at 7:40. We carried cargo into Hue and Da Nang and then flew to Bien Hoa to take another load up to Hue. We spent an hour on the ground at Hue each time. The place was very busy, with extra loading crews working 24 hours a day. We didn't see any sign of combat activity either on base or in the vicinity on the way in and out.

We got back into Nha Trang at 5:10 in the morning. As it was St. Patrick's Day, we took a nap and then cleaned up and spent most of the day in the club and bar. It was virtually impossible to sleep in the tent during the daytime due to sunlight, heat, and noise. We were ready for bedtime when the sun went down and, luckily, Captain Doom didn't sound the attack alarm during the night.

18 March: We took off at seven in the morning and continued hauling cargo to some of our favorite places: Ban Me Thuot, Tan Son Nhut, Song Be, Bien Hoa, Hue and then back again. We finished the day at fifteen minutes to five in the afternoon. At one stop, Daly noticed I was working the crossword puzzle in the daily *Stars and Stripes* newspaper, which we either bought or picked up at the club each day. The puzzle wasn't too hard and I could usually solve it inside of 30 minutes. We established a daily bet: each day that I solved the puzzle he would owe me $1. But the next day I would get one minute less to solve it, and I would owe him $1 for each failure to solve it. The cumulative debt was to be paid upon our return to Tachi, and Hardy was the bookkeeper of who owed how much.

The next day was more of the same, except that all the flights were to army bases in the area around Saigon and Bien Hoa. We hit Bao Loc and then used Bien Hoa as a central point to take loads out of and put them into Song Be, Dong Xoai and Phan Thiet. We got back into Nha Trang at 5:45 in the evening.

The following day, it was off at 8:00 A.M., then to Ban Me Thuot, Bien Hoa, Hue, Da Nang, the marines at Quang Tri and then back to Nha Trang, which we didn't get into until 7:00 in the evening. Now we seemed to be on a two day routine of flying to the same two parts of the country every other day. One day we hauled army equipment, vehicles and personnel around Saigon and Bien Hoa; the next day it was Da Nang, Hue and the northernmost I Corps, hauling marine cargoes and people. On the 21st of March, we split the difference, doing two stops in Saigon to take one load to Song Be and another to Hue. We got back to Nha Trang by 5:50 P.M.

22 March: Back on the night shift, we were off the ground at eight in the evening. Our first destination was Da Nang, with a cargo load of five pallets. We flew up the coast at 20 thousand feet. The weather was clear at altitude and out over the ocean, but inland there was a deep undercast. As we approached Da Nang, we came back overland headed almost due north and straight for the runway, which ran in the same north/south direction. Ron called Da Nang approach and they told us to descend to six thousand feet and prepare for a radar approach. *Uh-oh*, I thought, *here we go again*.

I immediately said, "Hey, why don't we go out over water and do a visual approach? This radar approach could get us shot up." I was remembering two past experiences. Daly was surprised by the request. Hardy agreed with me. As Joe was making up his mind, we saw a burst of orange/yellow tracers erupt through the undercast just in front of us. Daly needed no further explanation. We held altitude and turned sharp right and went out over the coast, let down to approach altitude and airspeed, and landed visually. In three years, I'd been shot at three times on the same approach to the same destination. I wonder how many artillery shells or bombs had been vectored to take care of that gun right on the approach course. I also wondered how many planes had been hit by it in the interim. The continual reeducation of pilots and crews was part of the cost of one year combat tours.

We spent the night flying two trips with cargo and passengers from Da Nang to the marines at Quang Tri. The Quang Tri radar approach was out and the weather in the north was spotty clouds and rain. We flew an Airborne Radar Approach (ARA) into Quang Tri both times with no problems.

Along with the Tet offensive throughout the country, the marines were engaged in heavy fighting throughout Northern I Corps and in the area along the DMZ stretching west to the Laotian border and Khe Sanh. We left Quang Tri at 2:25 in the morning and landed back in Nha Trang at 3:50. It was 5:00 A.M. before we got to settle into our cots in the tent. Dawn came soon thereafter, with everyone else in the place waking up, taking their bags and stumbling out to meet the day. I slept till about noon, when the heat, noise and light became too much to bear. I had lunch in the officers' club and then packed up.

At four in the afternoon on March 24, we reported to the ops counter, which was one desk in a second story office along the flight line. We were going home, or at least back to Tachikawa. We had been in-country for 16 days. We took off at 6:05 in the evening and went back to Japan, landing in Tachi at 6:05 A.M. after a one hour and forty minute stop in Naha, Okinawa, to take some people onboard.

It was just turning to dawn when we flew into Tachi. The weather was clear. We had heard about Japanese Communist Party protests on the west end of the base, and as we flew in, we could plainly see them. There was a ten foot chain link fence about two hundred feet off the approach end of the runway. Right up against the fence were hundreds of bamboo poles with red flags and stars on them. Some were 20 or 30 feet tall, although all were well below approach height at that point. This belt of poles and flags was the scene of frequent demonstrations, marches and speeches against the U.S. presence in Japan and against the Vietnam War. On our days off in Japan, we always used the gates on the opposite end of the base to enter and depart whenever we wanted to visit the natives.

This time, we got three days off. Daly and I took two of them and went to Tokyo. We stayed at the U.S. military hotel in downtown Tokyo and went sightseeing on a bus tour. There were three Swedish SAS stewardesses on the bus, but only the fat one spoke English, so we broke no ground there.

Getting around Tokyo was not easy, as there were virtually no English signs or directions on the streets. Few of the natives appeared to speak English, and none volunteered if they noticed we were having trouble getting around. The first night, we told the taxi driver, who spoke pidgin English, to take us to the red-light district since we heard that was the best place to get a genuine Japanese hotsi bath. We got out of the cab and paid him before discovering that he had dropped us at the U.S. Embassy, which was nowhere near the red-light district. Another cab delivered us safely to that destination.

When we got back to Tachikawa, there was a sprinkling of new crew members there who had just arrived from Langley. The increase in flight activity on the shuttle, plus more trips in and out of Korea, had led our deployed squadron to request reinforcement. Most of the new guys had all been in Southeast Asia before and accepted their posting with good spirits. They said that the Wing back home was forming up a list of replacements for us, but no one had any idea when that changeover would take place.

Having returned from our Tokyo tour, we were scheduled to go back on the shuttle the next day, March 28. The night before our departure, Daly paid me $10 for winning the crossword puzzle-solving bet on the last shuttle. Then Ron told him that I had cheated by putting in any letter when there were gaps left as my daily time ran out. Since Joe never checked my entries but only looked to see if all the blocks were filled, he would have never caught on. At his request, we set up a new bet for the next shuttle. Whoever lost the most weight on the shuttle starting the next day would win a dollar for each pound in excess of what the other bettor lost.

We flew out the next day at 1:40 in the afternoon, after a delay in getting the load on in the morning. Instead of going to Naha and then on to Nha Trang, this time we flew six hours and forty minutes and went to Clark. It turned out that we weren't on another shuttle at all. On March 29th we carried Air Force cargo and passengers from Clark to Cam Ranh Bay and then flew back to Tachikawa with some empty pallets and more passengers. We got 10 hours and twenty-five minutes of flying time in a fifteen hour day, getting into Tachikawa at 11:05 in the evening.

While we had been gone, it snowed at Tachi. There was about two feet of snow everywhere, which made getting about a little more difficult. One afternoon, with nothing else to do, I stepped outside of our shared quarters and called the closest movie theater on the phone that sat just outside our common room door. A Japanese voice answered my request to know what was playing that night. "Arrr ... tonight feature is Bwanny and Cryde!" I hung up laughing; besides I'd already seen it back in the states.

On the 31st of March, we set off again from Tachikawa on what was going to be the most ill-fated of all my adventures in C-130-land. We left Tachi at 8:30 in the morning and flew to the U.S. fighter base at Misawa in northern Japan. We then went into crew rest while several pallets of air force equipment were loaded on the airplane.

The next day, we flew out of Misawa for a four-hour flight to Osan in Korea. Osan is adjacent to Seoul, but it is also quite close to the Korean DMZ. The weather in Korea was cold with broken clouds. We took a radar approach to Osan and at one point the controller, who was American, put us on a course straight for the DMZ and then apparently lost us or forgot about us as he vectored other aircraft. After what seemed like a very long time, but was probably only a minute or two, I told Ron to make a comment on our status just to make sure the controller wasn't going to let us fly right into North Korea. Ron said, "Flabby 315 (our call sign) holding on course 320 at 4,000 feet." Back came the controller: "Oh, yeah, turn right take-up course 130 and descend to 2,000 feet." We were back in the picture and landed without further incident. We spent two and a half hours at Osan loading palletized cargo for a U.S. radar site on Chejudo Island.

Chejudo is a large island which sits off the southern coast of the Korean peninsula. The U.S. maintained a radar site there that featured a grass airstrip for its resupply. We were carrying in a full load of pallets with food, fuel, radar parts, movies and assorted other cargo for the U.S. contingent which ran the radar site. The C-130 was equipped for landings on grass strips. In our training flights, we would frequently land on dirt strips as part of assault landing practice; and in Vietnam many of our landings were on packed dirt or laterite runways rather than concrete.

But the Chejudo field was just that: A large, wide, not quite flat, rolling grass covered pasture. The edges of the field were marked by colored panels which lay on the ground. As we approached after an 85 minute flight from Osan, Ron called in and got us landing clearance. Joe put the plane down and we rumbled and bounced a bit to a final stop and then taxied to the offload area where a truck and six people waited for us with a forklift.

It was 6:30 in the evening when we landed, and the Korean forklift operator had our pallets off very quickly. Seeing that we were going to be leaving Chejudo with no cargo on board other than one of his people, the U.S. major who was the site commander asked if we could take a 2½ ton truck which was having engine trouble and needed to be worked on.

"No problem," Daly said. We regularly hauled such trucks, and in about a half hour Benson had it onboard and chained down for departure. As we boarded the airplane to get ready for takeoff, Ron asked the major if we could taxi all the way down the field to give us the maximum distance for takeoff, since the truck had added a large number of pounds to our takeoff weight and we would need more length to get airborne, especially on the rolling grass field. "Sure, no problem," was the reply.

We closed up the airplane, strapped in, started engines and began the taxi to the far end of the meadow. It was now twilight and getting darker every minute. The far end was bordered by a small rocky beach and then the ocean. As we got within about 50 yards of the ocean, Joe began a 180 degree turn for takeoff.

That's when the trouble started. We had gone through roughly 90 degrees of the turn when the airplane slowed down in its taxi and turn and then began to lean to the right. In actuality, our C-130 had begun to sink. The grass surface this close to the beach was of a different composition than the area we had just taxied through. The ground was wet from a recent rain or snow melt, and it was muddier and a little lower than the rest of the field. The weight of the plane plus the truck plus the turning activity was more than the soil on that end could support.

"Shut down three and four," Hardy shouted over the radio. "The props are about to hit the ground on the right." Weiss pulled the emergency handles on the two engines on the right side and we lurched to a stop. The plane lurched because it was now noticeably listing to the right. The other engines were shut down and we all bailed out to see what kind of a predicament we were in.

All five of us clambered out the forward crew door and were met by the major and his Korean forklift driver. In the deepening gloom, we could see that the plane had broken the surface of the grass field and was stuck in the mud about three feet deep, stuck so much that the doors which closed around the wheels on takeoff and usually sat two feet off the ground when open were in contact with the ground and bulging out a little. The tip of the outboard propeller on the right side was about a foot off the ground. We had come very close to allowing it to hit while still turning, which might have caused it to snap out of the mounting or break and fly into the side of the aircraft. So now we were stuck in the mud in Chejudo with night falling around us.

We all went back to the radar site, where beds were prepared for us. It turned out that in addition to the radar, Chejudo is one of the great pheasant hunting sites in the world. Accordingly, there was a set of quarters set aside for high brass visitors who frequently hold conferences and meetings on Chejudo and then went pheasant hunting on the side.

We ate in the dining hall on site, which was a room set aside for that purpose inside what passed for the command post. A Korean cook and waitress were provided out of dues levied on all the Americans on post. It was nice, but not overly elegant, almost like a hunting lodge. There were movies and a small library in the same facility.

Later that night, we were informed that an engineering team was coming tomorrow to get the airplane out of the mud. There was a civilian airport on the other side of the island, some 40 miles away by a dirt road. The team would land there and then make their way over to us. We went off to bed with great hopes of recovery in our minds for the morrow.

2 April: We were up around six in the morning and had a good American ham and egg breakfast. Then we sat around the club waiting for the engineering team to arrive from the other side of the island. In my mind, I imagined some 20 or 30 men with a small crane or lifting device, a steam shovel or digger, and a tractor with a tow bar to get the plane out. The weather was clear and sunny, thank God, with a temperature in the high fifties. If it had rained or snowed last night we would really have had a time getting the plane out and might have started second careers on the island.

At 10:30, up the road and into the compound came a jeep with a trailer. It must be the advance party of the engineering team! Well, guess what. They *were* the engineering team, all of it. It consisted of a lieutenant colonel and two

Above and following page: 1968 — A C-130 stuck in the mud at Chejudo.

master sergeants. In the trailer they had a gas driven motor and six or eight large, heavy, rubber balloons.

We all drove out to the airplane. While the engineers looked it over, we managed to get the onboard auxiliary power unit (APU) going to put power on the airplane. We opened the rear ramp and door. Next, after an inspection to make sure that it wouldn't hang-up on exiting, the truck we had loaded last night was driven off. Even with it gone out of the cargo compartment, there was no lifting of the plane body. It was still stuck just as far down by the wheels as it was yesterday.

The lieutenant colonel who headed the engineering team was really a maintenance officer at Osan. His plan for freeing the aircraft was to dig out

the right side of the plane and put the air bladders under it. The bags would then be inflated using the gas motor until the plane lifted enough to raise the right side wheels into the air. We would then shovel dirt and rocks into the gap until the plane was level and back on solid ground. Then perforated steel planking (PSP) would be laid under the wheels and on top of the ground so that the plane could complete its turn for takeoff. A search of the radar site turned up about 60 feet of PSP.

We spent the rest of the day making this plan work. Everyone, including us, the engineering team, radar site personnel not on duty, and a few Koreans took turns digging the plane out. Amazingly, the bags actually lifted the plane so that the wheels were off the ground enough for soil and PSP to be put under them.

Two additional problems then surfaced. The plane's batteries went dead. They were needed to start the APU, which was necessary for engine start. This problem was fixed by jump-starting the batteries off of the batteries from the truck that we previously had as cargo. The next problem was that the 60 feet of PSP amounted to only 30 feet when put under the plane's wheels on both sides. To complete the turn, we had to lay out a 30 foot path, taxi the plane to the end of it and then, with the engines running and the props turning, pull up the PSP and relay the PSP forward to cover the next 30 feet. In this instance, the C-130 was like working on an old car; if the established procedure didn't work, we could always jury-rig something else.

By six in the evening, we were finished. It took about seven separate 30 foot digs and PSP laying exercises to get the plane turned around and far enough forward in the meadow to be sure it was on firm ground. The weather was forecast to be clear all night and the next morning. No one wanted to attempt another dusk takeoff. We retired to the club for dinner, drinks, and an evening of fellowship.

Since we were leaving the next day, the radar site crew decided to let us know that they had several female Korean employees at the base that we had not seen. Not knowing exactly who we were or how long we'd be staying, they decided to keep the girls' presence a secret. Now that we were leaving and could no longer be a threat, they decided to let us know. It appeared also that some of their weekends in camp could turn into drunken binges, but we only suspected that.

3 April: We soared out of Chejudo at 11:25 A.M. We flew back to Osan and dropped off the engineering team and their jeep/trailer with much fanfare and well wishes. While we were in Osan they put on a load for Japan. We arrived back in Tachikawa at 5:20 P.M. When Daly appeared in squadron ops, the duty officer handed him a shovel.

6 April: After two days off, we were back on the Vietnam shuttle. We took off at 7:20 A.M., passed through Naha with an hour and a half ground time and arrived in Nha Trang at 5:10 P.M. The large tent behind the officers' club was still there, but we were assigned rooms and cots on the second floor in one of the wooden, two story barracks which sat next to the tent.

We began to shuttle the next evening, and took off at 6:50 to fly cargo to Qui Nhon and back and then from Nha Trang to Cam Ranh Bay. We were on the ground for five hours at Cam Ranh due to loading delays and lack of working forklifts. We landed back in Nha Trang at 3:05 the following morning.

That evening, after a minimum of 14 hours of crew rest and trying to sleep in the hot barracks, we took off at 7:35 and carried a load to Tan Son

Nhut, then went back to Nha Trang and from there on to Hue and back. Khe Sanh had been relieved, but there was a lot of airlift activity now around the country, with most of it continuing to go to I Corps. It was cooler flying the night shift, but ground time was also somewhat longer, since the night loading crews aren't as well manned as the day shifts.

April 9 found us still on the night shift hauling cargo. We took off at 9:10 and flew to Tan Son Nhut, then Da Nang, then back to Nha Trang. We landed at 3:35 in the morning after an 8½ hour day. We got the rest of that day off and reverted to the day shift on 11 April. We took off at six in the morning and hauled small mixed loads of people and cargo/vehicles from Can Ranh, Saigon, Song Be, Bien Hoa and then made one more shuttle between Cam Ranh and Nha Trang: Three hours and forty minutes of flying time in a 13½ hour day.

When we checked through squadron operations after landing, we were told that the next day, our entire contingent was going back to Tachikawa and our operations in Nha Trang were terminated. No one knew why, but a lieutenant colonel and his crew used the occasion to begin drinking up all the 2 ounce bottles of "mission whiskey" kept behind the counter for crews returning from a flight each day. Later, the colonel and his flight engineer were seen staggering out of a van and packing their bags. They were so drunk Daly called them the "missing links."

The next day, we left Nha Trang at 11:40 A.M. and flew directly back to Tachi, arriving there at 8:10 in the evening. On the flight, the lieutenant colonel and flight engineer who emptied the mission whiskey the day before were each strapped to a pallet and slept all the way back.

Since it was Friday night, we did a quick cleanup and made it to the officers' club, where drinks were flowing freely and the band was playing loudly. In the Second World War, U.S. bomber crews based in England used to fly missions against Germany in the daytime and then take their off days in London, with its pubs and blacked out dance halls. Now we were doing the same thing between Vietnam and Japan. It was truly a "crazy Asian War," as a later country song would call it. In addition to the usual people that lived on base, the teachers and all the aircrews and passengers that were transiting Tachi, there were people around for Easter weekend.

By the time we got to the club, it was nearing midnight and our squadron mates had a great lead on us in the consumption of alcohol. One squadron member tipped over backward from his stool at the bar. As he lay on the floor, he looked up at one of those who were trying to pick him up and muttered, "Harry, what are you doing lying up there?" We had no hope of catching up with them this night.

13 April: Easter Saturday. The squadron scheduled a party at the officers' club for eight that evening. The evening came and the squadron party turned into nothing more than a cocktail hour with hors d'oeuvres. It was announced that five flyers who were not regular officers were being offered a regular commission. Each of the five was named and asked to say whether he would accept the regular commission or not. Four of the five declined, meaning they would soon be exiting the service rather than seeking to be promoted at the next promotion opportunity. It was a sign of the times and the impact of the Vietnam War that such a high percentage of regular commission opportunities were declined. I think the squadron command staff was quite surprised by the result, especially since it was all done openly and in front of the rest of the officers. Once the cocktail party was over, everyone broke into individual groups and went to dinner and the bar.

As the evening drew to a close, several squadron members remained at the bar. The next day was Easter. Tachikawa was still covered with about two feet of snow. There was a large rock just outside of the main entrance to the officers' club. One of the squadron members, who had gone home to bed by this time, was known by his first two initials, J. C., rather than by a first name. The much liquefied group still at the bar decided that it would be a fitting Easter event to take the large rock in the front of the club and deposit it in front of J.C.'s bedroom door. The squadron maintenance officer's pickup truck was borrowed for the occasion. With the help of six or eight men, the rock was moved and placed. J.C. slept through the rock delivery and was said to have taken 20 or 30 minutes to get out of his room on Easter morning.

On Easter Monday we were assigned to fly a one day mission to Korea carrying equipment to Kimpo Airfield and Osan. Our mission was to take an aircraft to Kimpo and leave it. The aircraft would be used for loading training and later in a forthcoming exercise. We flew to Osan and then came back to Tachikawa as passengers in an Air America plane. Air America was well known as a CIA operated airline in the Far East.

Two days later, we took off as part of a four ship exercise to move Korean troops and equipment between Osan and Kimpo. We flew two shuttles between the bases and then returned to Tachi at 6:35 in the evening.

20 April: We left Tachi at 2:15 in the afternoon and flew to the U.S. base at Iwakuni to pick up a full load of palletized cargo, which we then flew to Clark. We arrived in Clark at 10:15 in the evening and went into crew rest in an air-conditioned trailer. We were to fly out of Clark for a few days, so our bags were unpacked and left in the trailer when we reported the following evening at 6:30. We took a full load of palletized cargo from Clark to the marine base at Chu Lai. We landed there at five minutes to midnight and got a quick offload.

As we were taxiing out to the runway to take off, we passed some 10 or 12 navy A-6 Intruders that were parked wingtip to wingtip on a taxiway. The Chu Lai runway was some 10,000 feet long and we were stopped just short of it and awaiting takeoff clearance when back along the taxiway there was a very large explosion among the A-6s. A mass of flames lit the night. Chu Lai tower immediately directed, "Chubby 31 [our call sign], you're cleared for immediate takeoff." "Roger. We're rolling," said Daly, who had already started our takeoff roll at the first sight of the flames. As we lifted into the sky and turned over the China Sea heading East to Clark, the fire spread quickly to successive planes in the A-6 lineup. We landed back in Clark at 3:15 believing we had just escaped a rocket attack on Chu Lai.

We got the rest of April 22 off to eat and drink at the Clark Club. The next morning we were up at 3:30 and airborne at 5:40. We flew again to Chu Lai and dropped off equipment, then quickly turned around and flew back to Clark, landing at 12:10 in the afternoon. The next day was a repeat of the same mission, with a 1:30 afternoon takeoff and a return to Clark at 8:20 in the evening. During our 40 minute stop in Chu Lai, we asked one of the loading crew about the rocket attack two evenings before. It turned out that there was no rocket attack. One of the ground crew was filling the A-6s with gas and spilled some of it on a hot surface. The blaze from the first A-6 that caught fire spread to the airplane next to it and the action/reaction cycle continued until some six aircraft had been destroyed. When we got back to Clark, there was still time to grab a quick shower and make it to the club from our trailer. We did this and had dinner and a drink or two.

Thursday, 25 April: We took off from Clark at 11:30 in the morning and arrived back in Tachi exactly six hours later. Anticipating a weekend off, I decided to go to Tokyo on my own (no one else wanted to go) rather than spend another few days in the Tachikawa clubs. I checked into the U.S. Forces hotel downtown again and did some sightseeing, including the zoo. On Saturday night, I walked around the corner from the hotel and spent the evening drinking with an American engineer at the revolving bar on the top of Tokyo's newest hotel. The engineer convinced me that, right after we won the Vietnam War, Vietnam would be turned into a hydroelectric generation site and tourist paradise.

At about midnight I stumbled out of the bar and got on the elevator where a room service waiter tried to convince me, in Japanese, to join a large party in one of the rooms. I made it to the front lobby and decided to have one for the road in the small lounge that sat just off the front door. Well, guess what? It was filled with Russians who couldn't wait to engage me on world affairs. Since there was still snow on the Tokyo streets and I was dressed in a thin seersucker suit and sporting a deep suntan, I think they had me down cold as a visiting Vietnam visitor. I denied all that and claimed I was a candy salesman. After about an hour, we parted company joyfully, having solved all the Cold War world's problems.

29 April: The next morning at exactly 8:00 A.M., my feet swung out of bed and intended to take me to the bathroom in my room. Just at the same moment, the phone rang. I knew immediately I was in for a long and troublesome day. It was the squadron calling. I was scheduled to leave for the Cam Ranh Bay shuttle as soon as I could get back to Tachi.

My head hurt badly from the previous evening's gaiety as I slammed my clothes into a travel bag. In the next few hours, I managed to get lost on the Tokyo subway before finally getting back to Tachi and stumbling aboard the waiting aircraft, which was now several hours overdue for its takeoff. We were actually supposed to be on the shuttle plane leaving the next day, but a full colonel from Cam Ranh who had been in Tachi for the weekend decided he had to be back a day early and our spot in the rotation moved up a day.

When I got to the airplane, I scrambled in the front door and saw all the rest of the crew sitting in the cockpit. "Hiya, kiddies!" I shouted. Just then, the full colonel hooked his head around the cockpit wall and gave me a thorough scowl. For the rest of this shuttle, Daly and Hardy greeted me every day with the refrain "Hiya, kiddies."

We left Tachi and flew direct to Cam Ranh Bay to begin another shuttle operation. We were immediately put on the night shift, with quarters back in an old fighter squadron building with old and new girly magazines. It was just as hot, sandy and boring at Cam Ranh as it had been the last time we were there. The first evening we arrived for duty at 10:00 P.M., but our airplane was broken and undergoing maintenance. Six hours later, at 3:50 in the morning, we soared into the stratosphere to carry cargo to the marines at Chu Lai. Then it was back to Cam Ranh to take cargo to Bien Hoa and from there back to Chu Lai.

Our load out of Chu Lai was a group of about 80 Vietnamese marines. In order to get them and all their combat gear aboard in one lift, we had to combat load (seat them not on seats, but on pallets locked into the floor with loading straps stretched across the pallets for them to hold onto). While Benson was locking the pallets into the floor locks, we were all standing outside along the fuselage of the aircraft. Suddenly we heard twangs and whizzes going by us in the trees along the taxiway. We were being shot at from somewhere off the base. One round hit the tail of the aircraft and left a small visible hole in the skin. Evidently, whoever was firing was a long way off and couldn't bring his weapon to bear any lower than 10 or 15 feet above ground. We immediately called the tower and reported the shots while Benson rapidly completed the pallet lockdowns so we could get out of there before the shots got lower or the shooter got luckier.

The captain in charge of the Vietnamese marines intervened and asked us to delay takeoff so he and his men could go get the shooter. We had to tell him that we didn't have time to do that and that our mutual best course of action was to exit quickly. Reluctantly, he agreed and we packed the marines aboard and flew to Da Nang where we let them out. It was refreshing to see a Vietnamese unit show some anger and aggressive behavior toward the enemy. Maybe Vietnamization was going to work after all. From Da Nang we flew back to Cam Ranh and landed at 1:55 in the afternoon. We were then told that we were on the schedule 14 hours later for a multi-ship airdrop the next day.

We trudged back to our quarters and went to the officers' club for dinner. That's where we found out that the airdrop the next day was scheduled to be in the A Shau Valley, west of Da Nang/Hue and south of Khe Sanh. The A Shau Valley was an old supply route and arms depot for the Viet Cong and the North Vietnamese Army which the U.S. had gone into and cleared out several times before. A week earlier, a C-130B from Tan Son Nhut had been shot down there on an airdrop and seven others had been damaged by ground fire. This day, one of our shuttle aircrews had flown there as part of an airdrop mission and had been hit and badly shot up. That aircraft had recovered at Da Nang. Supposedly, the VC in the valley were dug into spider holes on the approach to the runway/drop zone. The spider holes had hatched camouflaged covers so that they could not be seen from the air beforehand. The VC opened the holes up and emerged to fire at a plane as it came in for the drop at slow speed and low altitude.

We were up bright and early at 4:00 the next morning for the mission. In the briefing, we and seven other crews were told that we would be dropping CDS loads and heavy equipment in the morning and then return in the afternoon and drop again after C-123s had airlanded other equipment. As a result of the damage done to the drop force the previous day, we would be escorted by fighters who were to provide ground attack capability to support us.

There would be a radar beacon on the drop zone to help us locate it and drop. The air force had an all-weather drop capability using such a beacon, in which the drop was made with a combination of a distance check mark at two miles as indicated on our airborne radar and a forward and cross-check countdown using the airborne Doppler. The other crews in the formation, which were all Pacific Air Force (PACAF) units, were told to use the all-weather system if necessary to complete their drop. Because we were a TAC crew and not PACAF, we were told that we could only drop visually, even though we were also checked out in the all-weather procedures. We just hadn't been checked out in them by PACAF.

As we were preflighting the aircraft and getting ready to take off, I paused to consider that I was now, after 4 years in this war, going to be involved in a combat airdrop in the face of hostile fire that in the past week had shot down one C-130 and damaged over ten. How in the hell did I get myself in this predicament?

Fortunately, there was not a long time within which one could contemplate such sentiments. We took off for the mission at 6:25 A.M. and were the number two aircraft in a flight of eight. Each plane took off at fifteen minute increments from the one preceding it and flew north toward the drop zone. When we got close to the A Shau Valley, we made contact with the ALCE at Da Nang. They told us that the valley was weathered in and that the radar beacon on the drop zone was not yet operational. All eight aircraft went into a holding pattern at 500-foot altitude intervals using a bearing and distance off the Da Nang Tactical Air Navigation (TACAN) station.

After an hour in the holding pattern, Da Nang informed us that weather in the valley was a broken undercast at drop altitude but that the beacon was now working and the formation was cleared for drops at five minute intervals. The first airplane called back that it was leaving its drop altitude and proceeding to air drop. Five minutes later, we did the same. As we descended toward the valley and the much lower drop altitude, I could see the escorting F-4 fighters far above us and off to the side. They had problems staying with us and providing any kind of covering fire due to our slow (130K) drop airspeed. It was the only view of them that any of us had for the rest of the day.

When we departed the orbit and began descending to airdrop altitude, we lost contact with Da Nang; but we switched to another frequency and immediately got contact with the drop zone. My radar was in good condition and I shortly picked up the beacon, which we then used to establish our distance from the drop zone and heading into it. We had descended toward our 400-foot drop altitude above the terrain when the drop zone notified the first aircraft that its drop was ½ mile beyond the DZ. Something was evidently wrong, as a CDS drop should be much closer to the desired point of impact than that.

At 400 feet above ground level (AGL), we were in and out of sparse, wispy clouds. It was now after 8:00 A.M.; but due to the mountains surrounding the A Shau, dawn was just breaking. The clouds were thicker below drop altitude and we had only intermittent views of the ground as we approached the drop zone. At two minutes out from drop time, we were level and at drop altitude. We were also on centerline of the radar beacon and moving toward the two mile marker. The CDS load in the back had been unlocked for airdrop and the rear ramp and door were open. So far, we hadn't seen any visual signs that might assist us in finding or identifying the DZ. We were in the clear at drop altitude, but below us there were still dense, scattered clouds. A dirt road appeared on the ground; but it was gone again, obscured by the clouds.

The marker beacon return appeared at the two mile distance on the radar. I turned the Doppler to the preset course and distance module for the airdrop and returned to looking out the window for the DZ. We were one minute from airdrop. I couldn't see anything on the ground but broken clouds. No DZ. No panel marked impact point. Nothing.

The Doppler and the radar indicated that we had reached the desired drop position. I hacked my watch. We could still see nothing as the watch counted down in seconds. Just as the watch reached the point where I must call "Red Light" to terminate the airdrop at the far end of the DZ, Ron Hardy called, "Do you see that smoke?" I looked down and to the right of where he pointed. There was one wisp of colored smoke among the broken wisps of cloud. "Green Light," I called. Out goes the load. The airplane, relieved of the several thousand pounds of cargo, surged upward as Daly began to gain altitude and turn to the escape heading.

I went back to my desk to record the values I had used to estimate the drop and looked in the radar to see where we were, generally. Except for a small hole and a few returns in the center of the scope, everything else was black. We were on a collision course with something.

I threw the radar range out from the 5 miles it had been set on for the drop to 20. I turned the elevation of the radar up a degree or two. Normally, the elevation is set a degree or two below the nose of the aircraft. We were in a 100 degree turn from the drop heading, which was near 360 degrees north, to the planned escape heading of 260 degrees. When I reconfigured the radar, the first clear space that I saw on it was near 230 degrees. Everything else remained black, even though we were climbing as best we could. I immediately hit the interphone and said, "Joe, climb as quick as you can and turn to a heading of 210 degrees." It was evident from my voice tone that we were in deep kimshy, as the Koreans say.

Slowly, as if every second were an eternity, we climbed and turned. At last, after what seemed like a millennium, the clear space on the radar began to expand. Now I called for a heading of 200. The clear area was growing greater by the minute as we turned toward it. Relieved, I pulled my head out of the rubber cover that surrounded the radar scope and looked up into the cockpit. Weiss was sitting, turned 90 degrees in his engineer's seat, and looking at me with eyes as wide and white as giant sized dollars. Following his eyes, I looked out the cockpit window behind Ron Hardy's seat. The cloud layer was now below us and straight ahead and on all sides just below was nothing but dense treetops and forest. The right wing looked as if it was 50 feet or so above the top of the jungle and the lateral distance to the jungle also appeared to be 50 feet. Individual leaves and branches of trees could be seen as we turned away from and above a mountainside. We had just missed becoming a permanent navigation aid on the mountain.

We flew back to Cam Ranh and landed at 10:35. They had questions about our drop and indicated that it landed long, or far beyond, the drop zone. Joe and I testified to the weather conditions and what had happened from our point of view. Ron Hardy swore to everything that we said. Nothing was said as to what happened to the drops of the planes behind us. There had been no reports of aircraft damage or firing from the morning drops. Either Charley had moved out of his spider holes on the approach, or the morning weather had kept him from seeing us as much as it kept us from seeing the DZ.

We got new information (weight and chutes) about the load that we were going to drop in the afternoon. Again it was a CDS load, but the weather forecast for the second drop was different from that expected for the morning. We went back to the airplane and got ready for our next sortie. For the afternoon drop, we were again number two in a drop formation of eight C-130s. But ahead of us in use of the A Shau DZ and runway were ten C-123s which were to land and offload palletized cargo. Once the runway was cleared of the C-123s and their loads, we would be cleared to airdrop our CDS.

We left Cam Ranh at 25 minutes after noon and proceeded to the orbit point off Da Nang. When we got there, we were directed by the Da Nang ALCE to once again get into orbit with the remainder of the C-130 force and hold with 500-foot separation until cleared to begin dropping. The weather in the valley had deteriorated, even from the broken conditions which had existed in the morning. The C-123s had not been able to land at the scheduled times. When they did begin to land, the third aircraft landed and blew a tire on the runway. That put a stop to all further landing attempts while a ground crew tried to locate and put a new tire on the damaged aircraft.

We stayed in orbit for an hour. The damaged C-123 was still on the runway down in the valley. Whether they were having trouble getting the load off the aircraft and then changing the tire or just changing the tire, we had no idea. We could talk to the Da Nang ALCE, but not to the army in the A Shau. The ALCE could relay anything we had to say to the army and vice-versa, but we could not all communicate with each other. The weather in orbit was broken. We were in and out of clouds 50 percent of the time. The other 50 percent, it was clear at our altitude and for a thousand or so feet below; but below that it was completely undercast.

Suddenly, as we turned one corner of the orbit, out of the clouds came an army Flying Crane (CH-54) helicopter. He was exactly at our altitude and turned broadside to us. He was there five seconds and probably never saw us; then he disappeared into the clouds and was gone. Ron Hardy immediately contacted Da Nang to tell them that our orbit had been penetrated by a giant helicopter. "Roger," came the reply. "Be advised we have no contact with them." "Roger," Hardy shot back. "Hope we don't either."

As our second hour in orbit arrived, several of the other C-130s began to call Da Nang and we all could listen in on the conversations. Some of them had heavy equipment loads rather than CDS, and thus had different weights and fuel loads than we did. One said that if we didn't get drop clearance soon he would have to return to Cam Ranh or Da Nang to refuel. The remainder of the C-123s vacated their orbit and returned home due to low fuel. Their part of the mission was over. The ALCE listened to all the comments and said little except that they would pass them on; they weren't in charge of the airdrop, they were merely its message relay. Although some officer in the C-130s may have outranked anyone else in the formation, neither he nor anyone else was designated in command of the formation.

My radar was still working well, and from our orbit I had a very good radar picture of the A Shau Valley below. The north and west of the valley were bounded by steep and relatively high karst mountains that rose steeply from the valley floor. As the afternoon wore on, I could see clouds form behind those mountains and slowly build over them. By the third hour in orbit, it was becoming clear that the cloud formations were building and merging and slowly moving over the mountains and into the valley itself. Da Nang ALCE was told of this impending weather, but again it could do nothing more than pass on the message.

Shortly thereafter, ALCE called and said that the airdrop was cancelled and we should return to Cam Ranh. It had begun to rain in the valley. Nothing further was said of the C-123. As one C-130 left orbit for the return, he called into ALCE and let them know that the entire effort with regard to A Shau had been "a God damned disaster."

"Roger. Copy," was the reply. We landed at Cam Ranh at 4:25 and went to dinner and back to our rooms. We hadn't been shot at or hit, but the day had been a long and unrewarding experience nonetheless.

The next day, May 3, we flew out of Cam Ranh at 9:30 in the morning and went to Da Nang. From Da Nang we flew three round-trips of palletized cargo and passengers into the marines at Dong Ha. There was still a lot of combat activity in I Corps. We landed back at Cam Ranh at 6:20 P.M.

We got the next day off and on 6 May rotated to the night shift. We spent the day in the special night shift rest quarters at Cam Ranh. This was a barracks with window shades on the windows of the wooden rooms and signs all over saying don't make noise. It was impossible to sleep there in the daytime, and by now we had read virtually every girly magazine on base.

We showed up for night duty at 5:30 P.M., not being particularly rested, and took off at 7:50. Somewhat similar to a nighttime repeat of our previous workday, we hauled three loads of pallets and passengers between Da Nang and Hue before returning to Cam Ranh at 4:40 in the morning. On our way home, flying down the coast in the dark of night, we had witnessed a navy ship trading fire with an enemy force about halfway between Da Nang and Qui Nhon. We altered course to get a better look at the fight but, as we drew near, enemy tracer rounds began to come up at us. So we backed off, called the local area control and told them there was a fight going on and then continued on south. A fighter pilot passenger, whom we had allowed to sit in the cockpit, saw all this and wanted us to sit over the firefight and let him direct the action over the radio. We finally convinced him that we were not a gunship and that his brainstorm was not a good idea.

The following day, we took off two hours later feeling not a whole lot more refreshed, since we couldn't get anymore sleep in Cam Ranh after about noon. We pulled another night of three loads of cargo and passengers between Da Nang, Dong Ha and Phu Cat, again all in I Corps. We landed back in Cam Ranh at 5:15 in the morning.

On our return to Cam Ranh, Benson, our loadmaster, went on sick call due to a strain in his back. Without a loadmaster, we weren't a full crew, so we went off flying status. We sat around for three days waiting for Benson to be put back on status. Finding something to do 24 hours a day in Cam Ranh was not an easy task. Other than lunch and dinner and drinks in the officers' club, together with being a spectator at an occasional fighter pilot boxing match, every day was boredom. There was a library, but there was nothing in it worth reading.

Finally, on May 12, a navigator on another crew was put on sick call and I became their navigator in the interim. Daly, Hardy, and Weiss became the duty crew at Cam Ranh. It turned out my new partners were the same crew that had dropped just in front of us on the morning mission to A Shau.

The pilot was a Daly type: older, relatively new to the theater, and calm. The copilot was Asian-American and about my age. We all got along well. They were staging out of the base at Ching Chang-Kuan (CCK) on Taiwan, which now had a permanent shuttle out of Cam Ranh.

We took off from Cam Ranh and carried palletized cargo to Da Nang. Once on the ground in Da Nang, we spent two hours waiting for directions as to where to go next. The North Vietnamese had attacked the U.S. Special Forces camp at Kham Duc. At first Gen. Westmoreland had decided to reinforce and hold Kham Duc. Later in the day, it was decided to abandon the base and use tactical transport planes to land and take the forces there to safety. In the confusion caused by the surprise attack on the base and the complete change in the U.S. Air Force mission to save and then evacuate the place, there was much confusion.

One crew from our deployed squadron at Tachikawa was new to the theater and was tasked to take a combat control team (CCT) into Kham Duc to coordinate the original reinforcement order. Their airplane required maintenance after they were tasked, and it wasn't until later that they finally took off with the CCT aboard. By this time, the camp had been ordered to evacuate, but the C-130 crew did not know it. They landed at Kham Duc and the CCT drove off the ramp of their plane in a jeep. For all intents and purposes, the CCT were now trapped on a base that everyone else thought had been evacuated. Once the situation became clear to aircraft in the area, a C-123 (flown by Col. Joe Jackson, who won a Medal of Honor for the act) landed in the face of intense enemy fire and took the CCT out again.

All of these activities were taking place as we sat at Da Nang waiting for a mission and our next load of cargo. Finally, at 11:20 in the morning, we were told to return to Cam Ranh and await further orders. We landed at Cam Ranh an hour and ten minutes later and were informed that we were now the number two alert crew for dispatch to Kham Duc in support of the evacuation mission. We sat for about two hours and then were told to go into crew rest. The evacuation of Kham Duc was complete and no more crews were needed for that action.

Kham Duc was a cardinal example of the "fog of war" principle. It began with a surprise enemy action, went through two exactly opposite command decisions as to how to respond, and, with messed up communications, resulted in both heroism and tragedy. By the time it was over, Kham Duc cost losses of two C-130s, an A-1 Skyraider, and five helicopters. One of the 130s crashed and killed 150 to 200 Vietnamese onboard that it was trying to evacuate.

I was not especially looking forward to flying into Kham Duc in the face of NVA troops, who clearly surrounded the place and would have been firing directly on us in any further evacuation flights at that point in the afternoon. After a day spent sitting in the cockpit in the heat of Da Nang and Cam Ranh, once we were released from alert I literally skipped off the plane and made for the officers' club, an early dinner and a goodly number of drinks. Once there, I shortly ran into Daly and Hardy, who informed me that the following day we were going back to Tachi.

The next day, May 13, we all heard that we were being recalled to Tachi and that some of us would soon be going back to the States. Malcontents in the squadron, who had complained loudly that they were back in Southeast Asia illegally and against their wishes, had caused a congressional investigation of our whole deployment. It appeared that our dispatch to save the *Pueblo* and subsequent assignment to Vietnam had violated a congressional directive limiting the size of the U.S. military force engaged in the Vietnam War.

When the investigating team arrived at Tachikawa, they found that the deployment squadron commander and some of his staff were on a cargo carrying mission to Hong Kong. Several of the passengers on the trip were nurses from the Tachi hospital. That flight appeared as a "boondoggle" of the highest order and did nothing to impress the inspection team as to the validity of our mission as a wartime deployment shuttle. All of the aircraft which we had at Cam Ranh left the base on the thirteenth. Ours had been in maintenance much of the day and we did not take off with all of our bags until 10:35 in the evening. We passed through Naha to let off pallets and passengers. Then we went on to Tachi, where we landed at ten minutes to nine in the morning.

Five days later, I left Tachikawa as the navigator on a rapidly configured crew, all of whom had previously spent a 13 month tour in Southeast Asia. We proceeded across the Pacific in a somewhat random manner. We flew as a deadhead crew to Mactan, where we picked up a C-130B that was going back to the U.S. for major maintenance and inspection. Our route home was from Mactan to Clark to CCK in Taiwan, and then to Midway Island and McClellan AFB in California. From McClellan, I flew home on a commercial jet. My last tour in support of the Vietnam War was over.

Ron Hardy, who also had served a previous tour in Southeast Asia, returned to the States on a similar flight. Our places in the deployment squadron at Tachikawa were taken by new arrivals from Langley who now faced an indeterminate tour of several months. Joe Daly, Weiss and Benson all got to stay a few months longer at Tachi since none of them had done a previous tour.

On my last night at Tachi, I had to pay Daly for our weight bet. He had deliberately overeaten the night we made the bet and weighed to establish the base weights. On the night we settled the bet, he ate next to nothing at dinner, which was just before the final weigh-in. He had lost 12 pounds, while I was down five. Once again, I had been taken in Asia as part of the Vietnam War.

Aftermath

...they had learned nothing and had forgotten nothing.
Talleyrand, speaking of the return
of the Bourbons to the throne of France

Those who do not know history are doomed to repeat it.
George Santayana, Spanish-born American philosopher

In 1972, at the height of a North Vietnamese offensive against the South, I was sitting in a bar in my hometown of Scranton, Pennsylvania. Next to me was my older brother and on the other side of me was the anchorman for the local CBS television station, whom I did not know personally. The television in the bar was showing pictures of the South Vietnamese retreat in the area south of the DMZ. The dialogue of the television commentary was that the ARVN were hopelessly defeated in the combat and running in chaos from the battlefield. The pictures shown depicted ARVN in formation, with no evidence of chaos, pulling back from the DMZ and taking up new positions south of it. I turned to the newsman next to me and pointed out the dichotomy. He agreed with my assessment but offered no rationale for why it might have been so.

The South Vietnamese, with U.S. air support, eventually halted the spring 1972 North Vietnamese offensive. The U.S. public, however, got a somewhat warped view of what really happened at that time in the conflict. Like so much of the rest of the Vietnam War, the reports in the media and what really happened were often and widely at odds.

I thought of the Vietnamese marines on the day we had picked them up at Chu Lai who had wanted to delay our flight while they would have willingly deployed to go into combat with enemy elements that were firing at the airplane while it was on the ground. In actuality, many of the Vietnamese units fought with courage, conviction and professionalism; they rarely got credit for it in the U.S. media.

In early May of 1975, I was a staff officer for Air Intelligence at NATO's Central Region Headquarters in Holland. My office was a small cubicle in the headquarters' basement. My U.S. counterpart in the army section of intelligence came in and closed the door so no one could hear our conversation. "We have just lost our ass," he said in reference to the fall of South Vietnam. I could do nothing but agree. The U.S. was the senior partner in NATO, facing the Soviet led Warsaw Pact across a Europe-wide border stacked with all the instruments of modern warfare, including nuclear weapons.

We, the U.S., held more than a fair share of the highest level command positions in NATO and were the dominant military force in the Alliance pledged to save Western Europe from the communist, Russian led hordes. Our most recent ally, South Vietnam, had just lost its freedom to a relatively poorly equipped military force which had grown from guerrilla ranks. The position we had held in NATO since its inception was now very much tainted, if not totally in doubt. The myth of our military invincibility had been destroyed. So, too, was our image as the principled, truth speaking leader of the democracies of the Western World. To a large degree, this remains true today, and especially so in the context of our ongoing disengagement from the misguided attempt to spread democracy by military means into the Middle East through Iraq.

Casualties

When U.S. military involvement in the Vietnam War ended in 1972, our armed forces had suffered over 55,000 killed in action (KIA). Perhaps another 300,000 had been wounded. Additionally, the United States lost over 3,300 aircraft and four thousand helicopters during its 13 year (1960–72) involvement. American forces committed to the war and their losses resemble two large bell curves when plotted graphically. Both graphs peaked in 1968, when there were 540,000 American troops in Vietnam and they suffered 14,400 KIA.

In the text, I have mentioned the casualties that I knew of during the war. I did not mention the additional losses which accrued from those casualties, or of the casualties of which I was not then aware. Many of the men who were lost had families and children they left behind. The children and the widows had to grow up or change their lives missing the husband or father figure from a war the American public wanted to hear no more of.

There were also numerous other losses which were never attributed to the war but were certainly of its making. I know of at least two suicides, the seeds of which were planted in the period I have just written about. They were mirror images of each other, with common patterns of separation, infidelity, guilt, remorse and ever deepening depression. I also know of countless divorces, unhappy marriages and mentally and physically deprived adults that grew out of Vietnam-era childhood. The total costs of the war involve much more than the list of casualties within its time period.

Insults

On my return to the States in early 1967, after my one year tour, I took a civilian airliner from San Francisco to San Antonio on my way home. It was winter stateside. I was tanned and had a military short haircut (in a time of long male hair and pony tails). It was evident I had just come from the war. No one commented, asked or said a word regarding the war or my part in it as I transited the airports and the streets. My seat partner on the flight asked if I had been in Vietnam. He then asked if it was really bad, as he had read. The man then commenced to tell me about the divorce he had upcoming and his ongoing problems with his wife in dividing up kids and property. Okay, he had other things on his mind but at least he had asked. He was the only one.

Of those presidents in my lifetime who served overseas or in combat, only Truman, Eisenhower, Kennedy, Nixon, and the first Bush were later rewarded with the nation's highest office. Truman served in World War I. Eisenhower was the European Theater commander. Kennedy was a true hero as a PT boat skipper; the same was true of George H. Bush, who was a navy fighter pilot. Nixon may have been the best card playing supply man in the Pacific. But they all served and shared the dangers, monotony and experiences of their generation.

When the first President Bush searched for a vice president after winning his party's nomination in 1988, he came upon Dan Quayle, a young congressman from Indiana who was a darling of the Republican's strong right wing. Bush introduced a wide-eyed ("deer in the headlights"), surprised, and clearly out of his element Quayle to the media, who quickly asked about his Vietnam service. Quayle had no Vietnam service. He had defended Indiana as a member of the National Guard. Quayle had entered the Guard through the use of political influence as a means of avoiding the draft. Bush was asked if Quayle's actions during the Vietnam War had entered into considerations of his selection to be a vice-presidential candidate. "No," Bush replied, "we never thought of it."

Fifteen to thirty years after the U.S. participation in World Wars I and

II, veterans (Truman, Eisenhower, Kennedy, Nixon, and the first Bush) of those wars moved into the presidency and other high offices in Washington. Following them, no veterans of Korea or Vietnam have reached similar political levels. As far as Vietnam is concerned, rather than those who fought the war, we have instead gotten those who dodged it (Quayle, Clinton, George W. Bush, and Cheney) as our leaders.

The Greatest Generation

In the late 1990s, NBC news anchor Tom Brokaw wrote a book titled *The Greatest Generation*, in which he recounted events relating to World War II and some of the men who were young soldiers in that war. A generation can be a time period, or a group of people who were born into and grew up in a given time period. Brokaw put the title "greatest" on the latter definition regarding those who fought World War II. We won World War II with a total national effort against enemies who attacked or declared war on us. There was no shortage of courage, effort, enthusiasm, professionalism or intelligence among the young men who went and fought World War II, and the same can be said of those who fought in Korea or the Vietnam War.

That the Vietnam effort led nowhere was not our fault, but rather that of the politicians and bureaucrats who sent and kept us there. Great leaders led the young men who won World War II. Our entrance into Vietnam was a mistake perhaps explainable within the context of the then ongoing Cold War. By the time our then leaders figured out that it was a mistake, we were in too deeply (in costs, casualties and prestige) to exit rapidly.

I'm glad I went to Vietnam and served. The experience has taught me many lessons that I have benefited from in my later life. The experience, however, was not worth the cost to the nation of too many years of war and casualties. Nor was it worth twenty years of war and casualties and the loss of freedom for the people of South Vietnam, whom we had promised repeatedly to make free.

Author's Military History

William A. (Bill) Barry is a native of Scranton, Pennsylvania. He graduated from the U.S. Air Force Academy in June of 1963 with a bachelor of science degree in basic sciences. He graduated from navigation training at James Connally Air Force Base, Waco, Texas, in December 1964.

As a first lieutenant, he was assigned to the 774th Tactical Airlift Squadron of the 463rd Tactical Airlift Wing at Langley AFB, Hampton, Virginia, in early 1965. Through local training, Lt. Barry was qualified as a Tactical Airlift navigator in the C-130B. The 463rd Wing was a unit of the Tactical Air Command (TAC) and had a mission of carrying cargo nationally and internationally as well as supporting the U.S. Army through the airdropping of paratroopers and equipment.

Qualified in over-water navigation, Barry accompanied elements of the Wing in a deployment to Clark Air Base in the Philippines in the spring of 1965. During this deployment, he first flew as an active crew member in navigating the Pacific Ocean via Hawaii, Wake Island, Guam, and Okinawa to the Philippines. From Clark, daily cargo hauling missions were made to Da Nang, Nha Trang, Tan Son Nhut and a variety of other bases in South Vietnam. Returning to Langley, he finished his C-130 navigator training by becoming qualified in low-level (300–500 foot) flight routes and personnel and equipment paradrops.

In October 1965, Barry again deployed to Clark AB, this time as a member of a regular crew on a scheduled 60 day rotation. Again, the mission was flying cargo support from Clark to Vietnam. However, rather than one-day, daylight only flights, the mission included week long stays in Vietnam carrying cargo and personnel from Saigon and Nha Trang to smaller bases all around the country.

Following a two month return to the States to finalize personal affairs, he returned to the Philippines in February 1966 and spent a 13 month tour flying 10 to 14 day deployments in Vietnam from a remote home base at Mactan Island in the southern Philippines. Barry's primary base of operations in Vietnam during this period was at Tan Son Nhut Airport in Saigon. He completed this tour in February of 1967, and he was promoted to captain a month later.

Captain Barry returned to Langley AFB and became an instructor navigator in the newly formed 38th Squadron of the 316th Tactical Airlift Wing, flying C-130E models. In February 1968 he deployed with members of the Wing to Tachikawa Air

Base, Japan, as part of a show of force opposing the North Korean seizure of the USS *Pueblo*. This deployment lasted until May of the same year, with the deployed aircraft and crews flying cargo and airdrop missions primarily in Vietnam and Korea.

On returning to Langley, Captain Barry upgraded to a position as Wing standardization evaluation navigator in the 316th and took part in two rotations to Europe, operating out of Mildenhall AB in England and flying missions to Germany, Italy, Turkey, Greece, and various African locations. In 1969, he transferred, on base, to headquarters TAC and spent two years as a nuclear war plans officer and logistic support planner.

In 1972–1973, he attended the University of Notre Dame and attained a master's degree in government, Soviet area studies. He next spent one year as a student in the Defense Intelligence School (DIS) in Anacostia, Virginia, where he was promoted to the rank of major. Following graduation from DIS, he served three years as the assistant chief of the Air Intelligence Division at NATO's Allied Forces Central Europe (AFCENT) headquarters.

From 1977 to 1980, Major Barry returned to the 463rd Tactical Airlift Wing to fly in the C-130H and serve as an instructor navigator, squadron navigator and squadron resource manager of the 772nd Tactical Airlift Squadron, where he was promoted to lieutenant colonel. In his next assignment, he spent one year at the Hoover Institution at Stanford University, California, as a National Fellow conducting research on the Soviet Union, the Warsaw Pact, and the rise of the Solidarity Movement in Poland. He retired from his military career in 1983 as chief of the Political-Economic Division within the Intelligence Directorate at headquarters, Strategic Air Command (SAC), Omaha, Nebraska.

Lt. Col. Barry had over 4,100 hours of flying time (715 of which were Southeast Asia combat hours) and was a master navigator. His military awards and decorations include the United States Air Force Meritorious Service Medal with one cluster, the Air Medal (six clusters), the Joint Service Commendation Medal, the Air Force Commendation Medal, Presidential Unit Citation, Air Force Outstanding Unit Award (5 clusters), Combat Readiness Medal, National Defense Service Medal, Vietnam Service Medal (5 clusters), Air Force Longevity Service Award (3 clusters), Small Arms Expert Marksmanship Ribbon, and the Republic of Vietnam Campaign Medal.

Now retired from 20 additional years as a defense contractor to Army Theater Missile Defense development efforts, he lives in Huntsville, Alabama.

INDEX

A Shau Valley, SVn 189–93, 195–96
Agent Orange 25
Air America (airline) 186
Air Force Academy 3
Aircraft: **A-1** 195; **A-6** 187; **B-52** 82; **C-7** 68; **C-47** 8, 84; **C-119** 84; **C-123** 25, 30, 189–93, 195; **C-130A** 7; **C-130B** 5–8, 25, 32, 55, 74, 100, 123, 141–42, 147; **C-130E** 161; **C-141** 82; F-4 34, 168; **F-100** 25, 86; **F-101** 86, 101–2; **F-105** 34; **KC-97** 5; crashes 13, 35, 60–61, 137, 195
Airlift Control Element (ALCE) 10–12, 26, 51, 117, 193
Airlift operations 83, 110–11, 176, 180, 189–93, 195; airdrop requirements 5, 21, 23, 87, 113, 189–92; assumptions 1; cargo 12–13, 37, 51–52, 93, 99, 103, 105, 111, 122–26, 129, 135–36, 158
An Khe 41, 49, 88, 102, 107, 116, 119, 132, 151, 159, 171
Angeles City, Philippines 16,
Australians 42, 46, 68

Ban Me Thout, SVn 30, 39, 82, 91, 142–43, 146, 152–53, 176
Bangkok, Thailand 9, 22, 34, 37–39, 46–48, 130, 140
Bao Loc, SVn 175–76
Barner, Col. Harry 41, 45
Bataan, Philippines 10
Benson (airman) 162, 194, 196
Bien Hoa AB, SVn 25, 53–56, 91, 96, 102, 107, 120, 126, 128–29, 133–34, 146, 148, 150–51, 170, 174–77, 185, 188
Big Mac hamburger 89
Biggs AFB, TX 7–8,
Binh Thuy, SVn 101
Bohol, Philippines 113
Buddhists 10, 33
Bung Bung, SVn 95, 151
Byrd Field, VA 21

Cam Ranh Bay AB, SVn 29–30, 36–37, 39, 49, 57, 67, 71, 89, 93, 102, 111–12, 117, 120, 126–28, 132, 140, 146, 153, 157, 159, 167–72, 179, 184–85, 188–95
Can Tho, SVn 50
Catecka, SVn 41–42, 45
Cebu City, Philippines 22, 66, 76–78, 98–99, 151
Chejudo Island, Korea 179–84
China 57, 109
Ching Chang-Kuan AB (CCK), Taiwan 195–96
Chu Lai, SVn 108, 111, 119, 127, 129, 132, 135, 176, 187–89, 198
Civil, Capt. Curt 63, 100, 155–56
Clark AFB, Philippines 9, 13–15, 18–19, 22, 25, 36, 39, 44, 48, 57, 67, 74, 78, 89–90, 98, 100, 105, 109, 112–14, 116, 131, 133–34, 138, 140, 146, 150–56, 160, 179, 186–87, 196; Officers Club 5–19, 25, 44–46, 58–59, 140–41, 154–55, 160
Combat Control Team (CCT) 195
Corregidor, Philippines 10, 48

Dak To, SVn 133
Dalat, SVn 120, 126, 150
Daly, Capt. Joe 161, 164, 166, 178, 180, 184, 188, 191, 194, 196; bets 176, 178–79, 197
Danang AB, SVn 10, 13–14, 19, 36, 49–51, 57, 72–73, 75, 78, 82, 86, 90, 92, 102, 108, 111, 114, 116, 119, 127, 129, 132, 135–36, 142, 146, 150, 153, 157, 160, 168, 170–71, 177, 185, 189–90, 192, 194–95; fired at on approach 93, 143, 177; protocol office 103
Dau Tieng, SVn 175
Doctor Zhivago (movie) 114
Dominican Republic 6
Don Muang AB, Bangkok 37, 74
Dong Ha, SVn 57, 73, 142, 156–57, 194
Dong Xoai, SVn 176

205

Index

Dunn, John 23, 28, 32–34, 39, 41, 51, 56, 58, 63, 69, 75, 86, 88, 91, 93, 101, 111, 116, 131–32, 135–36, 139, 144, 149, 151–52

Fighter pilots 168
Filipinos 16, 139
Flight attendants 46, 154–55, 178
Fort Lee, VA 21
Frame, Ed 23,
French Onion soup 91–92
French priest 95

German bombs 90
Globe Hotel, Saigon 79–80, 86, 101, 105, 108, 110–11, 116, 128, 141–42, 152
Godfrey, Arthur 149
Gross, Carl 23, 51, 90–91, 105, 108
Guam 25, 62

Habu (snake) 130–31
Hardy, 1Lt. Ron 161, 164, 166, 174, 179–80, 188, 191–92, 194, 196
Helicopter, CH-54 193
Hickham AFB, Hi 25, 58, 62
Ho Chi Minh Trail 84–86
Hong Kong 196
Hue, SVn 36, 127, 146, 157, 160, 170, 176, 194

Ia Drang Valley, SVn 50
Iwakuni AB, Japan 186

Jackson, Col. Joe 195
James, Col./Gen. Chappy 157

Kadena AB, Okinawa 109
Kahn, Maj. Ned 63, 126, 129, 144
Kennedy, John F. 3
Kham Duc, SVn 72, 151, 195
Khe Sanh, SVn 69–71, 171, 177
Kimpo, Korea 186
Kontum, SVn 81, 120, 151
Korat AB, Thailand 34, 46, 74, 130, 140
Korea 166–67; casualties 43–44
Korean War 4
Kunsan AB, Korea 166
Kwangju, Korea 167

Langford, Francis 149
Langley AFB, VA 5, 21, 25, 58, 138, 161–63, 169
Lapu Lapu, Philippines 66, 76
Lewis, Col. David 69–71
Loc Ninh, SVn 104, 122
Luc Thinh, SVn 110
Luzon, Philippines 9

Mactan AB, Philippines 19, 22, 58, 62–66, 74, 76, 89–90, 98, 105, 109, 112, 114–16, 126–27, 130, 140–41, 143–45, 150–51, 196
Magellan Hotel, Cebu City 98–99, 109, 112, 126–27, 133, 138, 144
Malloy, Maj. Lou 149, 154, 157
Manila, Philippines 9, 19
Mao Tse Tung 3, 54
McClellan AFB, CA 25, 196
McNamara, Robert S. 4
Medals 119–20
Mekong Delta 12
Michelin tires 102
Midway Island 58
Military Airlift Command (MAC) 7, 173
Misawa AB, Japan 179
Montez, Capt. Jaime 112

Naha AB, Okinawa 168, 174, 179, 184, 196
NATO 198
News film 95
Nha Trang, SVn 11, 13, 32, 34, 39–41, 43, 45, 49, 57, 71, 132, 140, 142, 159, 168, 171–74, 179, 184; mortar attacks/alert 174–78
Nhakom Phenom AB (NKP), Thailand 34
Nui Bara 95, 102, 136

Operational Readiness Inspection (ORI) 21, 58
Osan AB, Korea 166, 179, 186

Phan Rang AB, SVn 78, 108, 127, 132, 136, 150–51, 154, 156, 160
Phan Thiet, SVn 148, 150, 159, 176
Phu Cat, SVn 172, 194
Playboy bunnies 153–54
Plei Mei, SVn 50
Pleiku, SVn 30–31, 35, 41–42, 49–50, 73, 102, 127, 132, 138, 146, 150–52, 157, 159–60
Pope AFB, NC 6, 21, 162
USS *Pueblo* 162, 166–67

Quan Loi, SVn 151, 175
Quang Nai, SVn 135
Quang Tri, SVn 176–77
Qui Nhon, SVn 11, 13, 32, 36, 41, 43, 49, 71, 86, 89, 90, 93, 97, 105, 115, 130, 133, 135–36, 151–53, 171, 184

Rex Hotel, Saigon 84, 105, 127–28, 132–33
Russians 188

Saigon, SVn 10–11, 19, 22, 27–28, 84, 127–28, 137, 150, 168, 172
San Miguel beer 109, 145
Scranton, PA 198
Seward AFB, TN 5
Soc Trang, SVn 175

Song Be, SVn 122, 174–77, 185
South China Sea 12, 67, 131
Stars and Stripes (newspaper) 51, 121, 135
Strategic Air Command (SAC) 7, 75, 112
Surface to Air Missile site 131
Surigao Strait (WWII) 113

Tachikawa (Tachi) AB, Japan 100, 164–66, 173–74, 178–79, 185, 187–88, 196–97; Officers Club 185–86
Tactical Airlift 5–6; 21, 58, 75, 91, 99, 139–40, 161, 171
Taiwan 25
Takhli AB, Thailand 34, 39, 75
Tan Son Nhut AB, SVn 11–12, 26, 30–32, 49–50, 53, 71–72, 73, 79, 81–89, 91–98, 101–12, 116–30, 132–38, 140, 146–50, 152–54, 156–60, 170, 172, 176, 185; Officer's Club 26, 86, 94–95, 103, 108, 121, 152; Shit Creek Snack Bar 80, 87, 100, 106, 110, 136, 170
Tay Ninh, SVn 107, 174–75
Tet Offensive 162, 172, 195
Thanksgiving 1966 149

Thorson, Hal 23, 32, 58, 63, 75, 77, 88, 105, 111, 116, 131, 141, 143, 157
Tiger picture 133–34
Tokyo, Japan 178, 187–88
Travis AFB, CA 58
Tuy Hoa, SVn 86, 116–20, 141, 150, 153, 159

Ubon AB, Thailand 34, 57, 127, 140
Udorn AB, Thailand 34, 39, 75, 105–6, 109, 140

Vietnam passenger runs 92, 103, 106, 111, 116, 135, 143, 146, 153, 157, 159
Vietnam War 198–201; casualties 9, 62, 152, 164, 199; personnel limits 27, 196
Vietnamese train 100
Vo Dat, SVn 54–56
Vung Tau, SVn 50, 67, 95
VVLE, SVN 128–29

Wake Island 25,
Weiss, TSgt. 161–62, 164, 192, 194, 196

Yokosuka, Japan 164

www.ingramcontent.com/pod-product-compliance
Ingram Content Group UK Ltd.
Pitfield, Milton Keynes, MK11 3LW, UK
UKHW042001140426
5217IPUK00015B/927